POLITICS OTHERWISE

VIBS

Volume 242

Robert Ginsberg
Founding Editor

Leonidas Donskis
Executive Editor

Associate Editors

G. John M. Abbarno
George Allan
Gerhold K. Becker
Raymond Angelo Belliotti
Kenneth A. Bryson
C. Stephen Byrum
Robert A. Delfino
Rem B. Edwards
Malcolm D. Evans
Roland Faber
Andrew Fitz-Gibbon
Francesc Forn i Argimon
Daniel B. Gallagher
William C. Gay
Dane R. Gordon
J. Everet Green
Heta Aleksandra Gylling
Matti Häyry
Brian G. Henning

Steven V. Hicks
Richard T. Hull
Michael Krausz
Olli Loukola
Mark Letteri
Vincent L. Luizzi
Adrianne McEvoy
J.D. Mininger
Peter A. Redpath
Arleen L. F. Salles
John R. Shook
Eddy Souffrant
Tuija Takala
Emil Višňovský
Anne Waters
James R. Watson
John R. Welch
Thomas Woods

a volume in
Philosophy, Literature, and Politics
PLP
Leonidas Donskis and J.D. Mininger, Editors

POLITICS OTHERWISE

Shakespeare as Social and Political Critique

Edited by Leonidas Donskis and J. D. Mininger

Amsterdam - New York, NY 2012

Cover illustration: "Hamlet", Marco van Ieperen, pen drawing, 2010

Cover Design: Studio Pollmann

The paper on which this book is printed meets the requirements of "ISO 9706:1994, Information and documentation - Paper for documents - Requirements for permanence".

ISBN: 978-90-420-3464-8
E-Book ISBN: 978-94-012-0746-1
© Editions Rodopi B.V., Amsterdam - New York, NY 2012
Printed in the Netherlands

CONTENTS

Part One

The Politics of History / The History of Politics: Shakespeare and Machiavelli

Part Two

Circumscribing the Political

Part Three

Governance, Law, Public Politics

Part Four

Shakespeare and the Politics of Translation

PREFACE

Classical literature often does a better job of revealing the organized world's forms of power and authority structures than do works of political philosophy. At this point, the classics of European literature, including those of François Villon, François Rabelais, Niccolò Machiavelli, Sir Thomas More, William Shakespeare, Christopher Marlowe, Miguel de Cervantes, Jonathan Swift, and Voltaire, deserve honorable mention, even if we put aside their purely literary fame.

Most importantly, classical literature allows us to study the modern moral imagination and to grasp the nature of the tension between value and truth better than anything else. The same applies to modern literature that may well be defined as the battleground of opposed visions of the world and humanity. This allows us to assume safely that the ideas and moral concerns of great writers will never become out of date, as far the ability of literature to critically question, to shed more light on, or else affect disconnected politics is concerned.

An enormously rich scholarly literature exists on Shakespeare and his age, from the English-speaking world to Russian literary scholarship with its time-honored interest in Shakespeare. My humble opinion on Shakespeare has been formed by several educational systems and schools of literary scholarship, first by Lithuanian and Russian, and then by British and American. In addition to them, Armenian and Georgian schools of literary and theater scholarship on Shakespeare deserve honorable mention. The same applies to Lithuanian theater productions of Shakespeare's plays, especially those by Eimuntas Nekrošius and Oskaras Koršunovas.

I developed an infatuation for Shakespeare's *Romeo and Juliet* when I first saw Franco Zeffirelli's film version of *Romeo and Juliet* (1968), a superb classical production that has yet to be surpassed in the myriad of Shakespearean adaptations. Yet my mental map of the world of Shakespeare would be incomplete without recalling magnificent Shakespearean adaptations by the Russian film director, script writer, and playwright, Grigory Kozintsev (1905–1973), such as *Hamlet* (1964) and *King Lear* (1970). These films immortalized the name of Kozintsev, urging the great master to search for a new language of cinematography, and allowing him to escape from Soviet censorship.

Happily, one thing radically separated the former Soviet Union from George Orwell's Oceania, namely, that translations, studies, and staging of Shakespeare were if not encouraged, then, at least, allowed and tolerated without replacing Shakespeare's language with the New Speak. In the end, the great traditions of Russian culture prevailed over Soviet ideological barbarity, preventing the fulfillment of this Orwellian prophecy. In addition, Kozintsev calls for the title of a cinematographic bridge between Shakespeare and Cervantes, for his adaptation of *Don Quixote* (1957) was, and continues to, be a landmark in the history of cinematography.

To cut a long story short, in the 1960s and 1970s, Kozintsev ably filmed two Shakespeare tragedies, *Hamlet* and *King Lear*. Both great Shakespeare tragedies were photographed by the brilliant Lithuanian cameraman Jonas Gricius, who has filmed all the greatest Lithuanian feature films.

Obviously, in those days the creators of the film could not just decide to go to Denmark and shoot Elsinore Castle in Helsingør. Elsinore was filmed in Türisalu, Estonia. The film was first shot in this lovely Estonian sea-side location, famous for its cliff, and was completed in Alushta, Crimea. The castle's ever longer shadow falling on the sea and fanning out in its dark waters is *Hamlet's* very beginning and at the same time one of the film's most memorable episodes. It settled in my memory for as long as I'll live, I think, and is firmly bound up with *maestro* Gricius's name (as are the storm episodes in *King Lear*).

The great Russian cinema master, unabashadedly partial to Baltic actors, marshaled them for both of these films. The immortal Innokenty Smoktunovsky (in my eyes, the greatest Hamlet of all times) is paired with the Latvian actress Elza Radzinia (Gertrude). The music for *Hamlet* and *King Lear* is by Dmitry Shostakovich, and the text is based on Boris Pasternak's translations: such is the unbelievably august (for Soviet times!) tapestry of Russian high culture into which Baltic actors were woven.

In *King Lear* Kozintsev unfolded a whole constellation of them: the Estonian Juri Jarvet (Lear), Elza Radzinia (Goneril), and the Lithuanians Regimantas Adomaitis (Edmund), Donatas Banionis (Albany), and Juozas Budraitis (King of France). I believe that as long as this film is being shown no one will forget the prematurely deceased Russian actor Oleg Dahl playing the part of the Fool. And Estonia is where *King Lear* was filmed.

American film critics have often pointed to *Hamlet's* musical score and called Dmitry Shostakovich Shakespeare's biggest ally in this film. The English director Peter Brook evaluated Grigory Kozintsev favorably by observing that he consciously subordinated the cinema to the theater and its language but he also judged Kozintsev's "post-Eisentsteinian" realism to be a romantic interpretation of Shakespeare allegedly doing away with his epic character, his mixture of barbarity and nobility, his closeness to life.

No academic textbook in political theory or political science in general will ever be able to replace Shakespeare's plays and sonnets, Machiavelli's comedies, Swift and Daniel Defoe's travel accounts, Voltaire's historical chronicles, plays, and philosophical tales, or George Orwell's fables. Their political and moral lessons are crucial now when politics in the classical sense is almost annihilated by modern bureaucracy and its countless technical policies, when technocracy proudly assumes the role of democracy, and when brutal power politics, fanaticism, bigotry, and cowardice walk in the guise of the struggle for peace and human dignity playing a sinister role in the contemporary world.

Eastern European perspectives on Shakespeare and the epoch of the Renaissance have long been quite helpful and unique in the world of literary scholarship, cultural history, and social and political philosophy. Some of the crucial Eastern European and characteristically Russian foci may best reveal the modern political dramas and sensibilities, as revealed by Shakespeare, his fellow Elizabethan dramatists, and great European humanists, such as Erasmus of Rotterdam. For instance, we greatly benefit from revealing the intellectual and political dramas behind Hamlet's grim and pessimistic reflection on Denmark as a huge prison and on the world as a prison in general, and also from Hamlet's exchanges with Horatio, who is suspected to have been Erasmus of Rotterdam (according to the Ukrainian-Russian writer Yuri Olesha's observation) disguised as Hamlet's friend. Or suffice it to recall the insights of the Russian philosopher and political émigré Alexander Herzen, who thought of Shakespeare's *Hamlet* as a specific creation of the epoch of Protestantism with its craving for liberty and modernity.

Russian literary criticism, literary theory, and cultural history have always been a landmark field of modern Russian intellectual culture. Just think of Mikhail Bakhtin without whom we could not imagine the studies of François Rabelais, his carnival of language, and other masks of being and becoming. Or how could we imagine modern literary theory without the eminent Russian-Estonian literary theorist and semiotician Yuri Lotman? The same applies to the Russian cultural historian Leonid Batkin regarding his magnificent works on the Italian Renaissance and the great legacy of Florentine humanists. Or consider Aron Gurevich, a great Russian medievalist who was among the most original exponents of the history of mentalities and historical anthropology oriented to the study of the Middle Ages.

Russian humanists have always had a strong sense of the uniqueness of early modernity in Europe with its Renaissance legacy and impact on at least several major national versions of modern European culture, including, without a shadow of a doubt, enormously rich and sophisticated Russian culture—not only in its manifestly literary and artistic manifestations, but also in such faculties of Russian modernity as the art of translation, hermeneutical codes and interpretation of the major texts of European literature and philosophy, and application of innovative research methods and comparative perspective. It suffices to recall the Russian Formalists with their groundbreaking theories of art and deeply original interpretations of European literature.

This book, which allows a comparison of North American and European sensibilities and sensitivities informed by culturally diverse approaches to Shakespeare, his wisdom, philosophy, and politics, includes, among other things, an interview with Tomas Venclova, a noted Lithuanian poet, literary scholar, and translator, who translated *The Tempest* into Lithuanian, and who may best be described as a humanist bridging literature and politics.

A wonderful undertaking by my colleague Dr. J. D. Mininger, with whom I have had the privilege and pleasure to co-edit this volume, it also reveals the nuances of North American, continental European, and specifically Lithuanian scholarship on politics and literature.

Prof. Leonidas Donskis,
Member of the European Parliament
(MEP ALDE 2009–2014), and
Visiting Professor of Social and Political
Theory at Vytautas Magnus University
in Kaunas, Lithuania

INTRODUCTION

Directing his caustic wit against the erosion of wisdom in philosophy and the poverty of academic integrity in his mid-nineteenth-century contemporaries, the intellectual and spiritual provocateur Søren Kierkegaard opens his magisterial *Frygt og Bæven* [*Fear and Trembling*] with the following assessment of his era: "Ikke blot i Handelens, men ogsaa i Ideernes Verden foranstalter vor Tid ein wirklicher Ausverkauf. Alt faaes for en saadan Spot-Priis, at det bliver et Spørgsmaal, om der tilsidst er Nogen, der vil byde [Not merely in the business world, but also in the world of ideas our age is staging *ein wirklicher Ausverkauf*. Everything is to be had for such an absurdly low price that the question remains whether in the end there is anyone who wants to bid]" (101). Of particular note in the original Danish is the mid-sentence code-switch in which Kierkegaard momentarily abandons his beloved native language of Danish in favor of the German phrase "ein wirklicher Ausverkauf." Kierkegaard clearly intends this as a dig at Danish Hegelians, who in Kierkegaard's opinion have *sold out* to this German system of philosophy that subsumes all that exists, whether ideational, material, or spiritual, within its own immanent order of historical and logical movement and method (i.e. *Geist* and the dialectic). The thinker who borrows the Hegelian system and method thus absolves himself of performing the act upon which his praxis is supposedly founded, namely, independent thinking.

This rather simplistic interpretation of Hegel as a philosophical pac-man who munches down the entirety of the world, its empirical details, and its orderings, should not be misunderstood in this context as a serious explication of Kierkegaard's understanding and critique of Hegel's philosophy of Spirit [*Geist*], let alone an independent reading of the enormous complexity of Hegel's work itself. While Kierkegaard certainly reserves plenty of space in other places in his oeuvre for a direct critique of Hegel, we must carefully note that Kierkegaard here concerns himself with a critique of his immediate context, including even and especially the social and political implications of his contemporaries' intellectual object-choices and methods.

Just as Søren Kierkegaard targeted the lack of creativity in his Danish contemporaries' intellectual objects and methods, masked as it was behind the veil of systematic rigor and assumed objectivity, so too does the 'spirit' of this volume establish a critical distance in relation to its own intellectual climate. This volume of essays offers vastly differing modes of social and political critique; but, along with the commonality of using Shakespeare in admittedly varying ways, these essays dovetail on the plane of remaining faithful to the historical conditions of the present which call for such critical perspectives. Perhaps also not unlike Kierkegaard's own strategy(s) in *Fear and Trembling*, this volume looks to stories written in and about the past for inspiration in rethinking the future of the study of politics and political thinking more generally.

Today universities are ruled by bureaucracy, disciplines are guided by re-gressively conservative and internal territorial border patrols, and the politics of intellectual life remains tethered to a technocratic understanding of the very field of the political. The stakes of taking on this Leviathan of intellectual pro-tection and production (which in this climate amount to the same thing) are really nothing less than the Enlightenment-esque modes of independent think-ing that Kant famously referred to as the politically motivated breaking of the intellectual bonds of our self-incurred immaturity. As Heidegger asked of this same sort of intellectual *Ausverkauf*: not only what *is* authentic thinking today, but what *calls for* thinking in our contemporary marketplace of ideas?

By using Shakespeare as a productive window into topics of contemporary social and political relevance, *Politics Otherwise* challenges the business of pol-itics, political science, and political thinking as usual. Because of its interdisci-plinary qualities the book is equally relevant for students of European Studies, political theory, literature, philosophy, cultural studies, history, and film. In the current normative order of political science research and publication, which relies so often and heavily on pseudo-objectivity and truth-claims devoid of the content of socially relevant (and therefore politically integral) praxis, *Politics Otherwise* intervenes as an exception to this order. But these essays, taken both individually and as a collected singular volume, do not impair, mutilate, let alone fully negate the contemporary order of the study of politics as usual. If anything, its sheer exceptionality as a work meant to teach and challenge po-litical ideas via recourse to Shakespeare likely intensifies and exaggerates the elsewhere typical reliance on the supposed objectivity of crunched numbers, opinion polls, and the master-signifier of this discourse: collected data. How-ever, because this volume's intervention in the field of political science and the study of politics is essentially more negative (i.e. *ex negativo*) than positive, its potential for creating new and imaginative forms of political thinking and social critique is so much the greater for its almost *ex nihilo* status within the field of typical academic forms of political study.

These comments expose an assumption made at the heart of the genesis of this volume, namely, that despite relevance for readers across many current disciplines, *Politics Otherwise* is intended to serve teachers, scholars, and stu-dents of politics and political thinking. But this is not to suggest that the book turns away entirely from the vast body of secondary literature we might simply refer to as the Shakespeare industry, housed largely in English departments of universities around the world, though hardly limited to just those lovers and critics of the Bard. Of course on the one hand, because Shakespeare fig-ures prominently in so many of these essays, this volume contributes yet other product to the output of that industry. Yet, on the other hand, at least in terms of intended audience, this volume turns away from the Shakespeare industry, working along its limits and thresholds like a paradox functions in a logical system. But, as Shakespeare's creations demonstrate a thousand times over, it is so often the very process of intention to undermine itself; and so this work remains a kind of negative space in both disciplinary discourses. Its lack of conformity to traditional disciplinary organization is part and parcel of its very political commentary and posture.

The vast majority of social and political critique offered in the volume crystallizes around the shared focal point of Shakespearean plots, characters, language, and historical context. What makes Shakespeare lasting and relevant for such a project of contemporary social and political intellectual intervention is not the timeless nature of the content of Shakespeare's ideas, stories, characters, or language; such claims are naïve, if not comprised of downright drivel. If anything, the "eternal" quality to be found in squeezing out a "message" from Shakespeare's work(s) is the very transience of those ever-shifting interpretations. This is not relativism, of course; far from it. It is simply a historicist claim insisting that truth content flashes up out of the ground of the given demands of the present situation. This claim therefore implicates social and political critique as praxis: eternally transient in terms of its truth content; political praxis insofar as Shakespeare both forms and informs the present conditions of social and political understanding.

Often the social and political critique available to read into and out of the Shakespearean text involves a negative projection of political praxis. In his *Aesthetic Theory*, Theodor W. Adorno admirably summarizes this point with an example from Shakespeare: "In *Romeo and Juliet* Shakespeare was not promoting love without familial guardianship; but without the longing for a situation in which love would no longer be mutilated and condemned by patriarchal or any other powers, the presence of the two lost in one another would not have the sweetness—the wordless, imageless utopia—over which, to this day, the centuries have been powerless" (247). Adorno suggests that Shakespeare's work continues to have social and political relevance precisely because it refuses to positively suggest or represent political utopias. The importance of Romeo and Juliet's tragic dedication to one another is not the love we see enacted in the play, but precisely the love we do not—cannot—see staged. Because the concrete reality of love outside the bounds and laws of suffering and injustice does not appear to us positively, its political truth is all the more poignant and pertinent for its imaginative and innovative potential.

For this volume of essays, Shakespearean politics is a politics seen and practiced against the grain: always present as the hope and promise of what lies, transformed and transformable, beyond the material suffering and injustice of the present. Just as Shakespeare's works continue to astound, challenge, and delight us with renewed contexts and points of political and social relevance, so too does this volume aspire to a condition of academic exceptionality, as a negative space of political praxis rooted in the hope that social and political thinking and acting can be *otherwise*.

* * * * *

As with most intellectual operations, the wisdom, patience, and efforts of many others have contributed to the genesis of this book, and I wish to acknowledge at least some of that enormous debt here. For both the inspiration and opportunity to work on this book project, I would like to extend my deepest gratitude to my friend, colleague, and mentor Prof. Leonidas Donskis, with whom I have had the honor of co-editing this book. I would also like to thank Prof. Egidijus Aleksandravičius, my colleague at Vytautas Magnus University, who has graciously granted me work space in Kaunas on the top floor of the Lithuanian Emigration Institute for the past few years. Though they likely do not know the extraordinary extent to which they have taught me, I wish to acknowledge the importance my graduate students at Vytautas Magnus University have played in the development of this volume. And just as my students have taught me much, so too of course did my former Shakespeare instructors inspire me. While one cannot teach the love of literature as such, one can certainly model it: and this is precisely what Dr. Ervin Beck, emeritus professor of English and Shakespeare teacher (and performance director) extraordinaire, demonstrated in his undergraduate course on Shakespeare at Goshen College that I had the privilege of attending. His mentorship plays no small role in the fact that I so often find myself returning to Shakespeare's plays as a spectator, an actor, a teacher, and a smitten reader. Finally, I wish to thank my family: Vilma, Elijus, and Nojus—I wear you all three in my heart's core, ay, in my heart of heart.

Dr. J. D. Mininger
Associate Professor of Social and Political Theory
Vytautas Magnus University, Kaunas, Lithuania

Works Cited

Adorno, Theodor W., *Aesthetic Theory*, trans. Robert Hullot-Kentor, Minneapolis: University of Minnesota Press 1997.

Kierkegaard, Søren, *Frygt og Bœven*, *Søren Kierkegaards Skrifter* 4, København: Gads Forlag 1997. English: my translation.

Part One

THE POLITICS OF HISTORY / THE HISTORY OF POLITICS: SHAKESPEARE AND MACHIAVELLI

One

MACHIAVELLI VS. SHAKESPEARE: LOVE, HATRED, AND THE EMERGENCE OF THE MODERN INDIVIDUAL

Leonidas Donskis

1. The Sociogenesis of Modern Feelings

What are the origins of political consciousness? How does our understanding of political power and its exercise originate in literature? Why do the early manifestations of political and religious tolerance appear in utopian literature rather than in philosophical treatises? Is it possible to do fictionally what others prefer to do academically and theoretically? These are the main foci that allow us to analyze the relationship between power and imagination, politics and literature, the principle of reality and that of imagination.

In William Shakespeare's tragedy, *Romeo and Juliet* (1597), the character of Escalus, the Prince of Verona, appears infrequently but is nevertheless an extremely important figure. He represents a new type of authority and power structure, profoundly different from the Montague and Capulet clans' essentially traditional kinship-tribal structure of authority and power that is based on family and blood relations. The Montague and Capulet clans divide Verona and all of the social reality that it represents into two warring clans, two completely separate zones, and two spheres of loyalty, but Escalus chooses a radically opposing model of symbolic authority and order. In Verona, Escalus creates and embodies a modern structure of authority and power, at the same time laying the foundation for the supremacy of law.

Escalus compels himself to forget his tribesman, relative, and family member in order to be fair to Verona and to the law. Tybalt kills Romeo's friend Mercutio, and at the end of the play Romeo kills Paris in the crypt of the Capulets. Yet both Mercutio and Paris are relatives of Escalus. While the death of Tybalt creates an irresistible urge on the part of the Capulet family to seek lethal vengeance (Juliet's mother speaks of the poison that she herself will find to murder Romeo), the murder of Escalus's beloved cousin Mercutio only strengthens Escalus's determination to learn the truth and to restore the order and authority of law in Verona. Consequently, when Romeo kills Tybalt in a duel and not only avenges Mercutio's death but also puts to death Mercutio's murderer, Escalus experiences no gratitude toward Romeo, but feels the obligation to punish Romeo and banish him from Verona.

In this work by Shakespeare, the elder Capulet's restless and bellicose nephew Tybalt, who even hates yet unborn Montagues, accurately represents traditional morality, the vendetta, the metaphysics of family and kinship, and the clannish-tribal structure of authority. Escalus, in contrast, creates and supports a modern structure of power and authority by seeking truth and justice. After the deaths of Mercutio and Tybalt, Escalus, arriving on the scene, asks Benvolio, as an honorable young man of untarnished reputation, to tell him the whole truth—exactly what had transpired.

In a premodern, hierarchical society, family, blood relations, tribe, relatives, and clan are the sole social building blocks, also the sole space for the construction of social ties, loyalty, and solidarity. In a modern society, where initial equality is increasingly clear, the main elements of social ties, loyalty, and solidarity become love, friendship, and patriotism. Here we consider modern patriotism in a wider sense and not only as a tie to our native town, language, or country, but also as love and respect for the place where it is possible to seek truth, justice, and a reliable social and moral order, together with authentic authority.

In falling in love with Romeo, Juliet chooses someone distant; she understands that her family and friends hate the Montague name and have long forced her to hate it also. She chooses an unknown person, but not this person's name and her family's hatred for that name. She chooses a person, not words. The friendship between Romeo and Mercutio also transcends the boundaries of clannishness; each is ready to sacrifice his life for the other, even though they are not related by blood.

Finally, Escalus chooses not revenge and the unconditional defense of his relatives, but justice and the rule of law. If we consider love and friendship to be the primary forms and expressions of a modern society, that is, modern social ties, loyalty, fidelity, sacrifice, and consciousness embodied by action, then we will have to acknowledge that Shakespeare reveals the birth of the modern person and the structure of modern authority.

What else does Shakespeare's *Romeo and Juliet* reveal? First, this work reveals modern feelings—love and friendship—and their sociogenesis. Love and friendship emerge here as the feelings of a modern person. We could simply call them modern feelings. When thinking sociologically, we are always drawn to oppose law with family. These two principles have battled each other fiercely for many centuries in Western and other civilizations (see Rougemont, 1983).

In the twentieth century, the challenge of La Cosa Nostra to the modern state and its institutions of power is nothing else than the struggle between kin and law, between the family and the rule of law, as well as a confrontation between premodern and modern forms of social organization. But clan and relatives we can confront with friends and loved ones. For a member of a clan, friendship or love for someone who is outside of the family's interests, its power and control, may lead only to the disapproval of the family or even great misfortune.

The conflicting objects of loyalty and fidelity will force us to choose either our family (clan, relatives, blood) or freedom and the responsibility for our person and identity (love, friendship, mutual devotion, or joint dedication). In the metaphysical world of tradition and blood, we do not have the freedom to choose the object of loyalty and at the same time be responsible for our identity. We can only be inserted, since both the object of loyalty and the structure of identity exist beforehand. Therefore, love in the modern sense does not exist in the premodern world.

Not only Romeo and Juliet experience unbearable and mortal conflicts of loyalty. Romeo's friend Mercutio, a relative of Escalus, the Prince of Verona, has loyalty to Romeo, which becomes more important than loyalty to the clan, natural in that era. The Prince strictly forbids the settling of quarrels and disputes by duel or armed combat, but his relative Mercutio, who is related neither to the Montagues nor the Capulets, is the first to violate the Prince's order by defending his friend's injured honor.

In the modern world, a person is always faced with a basic choice: you can abandon a blood relative, whom you never have had the opportunity to choose, and freely pick a person not related by blood but dear to the heart and to the mind, a loved one or a friend, or renounce the intimidating principle of freedom and return to your origins in family, relatives, and clan. Whether we like it or not, freedom inevitably takes us farther away from these things. In the life of a free and modern person, a loved one, a wife, and a friend are immeasurably more important than relatives and clan. Traditional, premodern persons, who exist in every modern society, choose forms of inherited social ties and identity. Modern persons, in contrast, have the courage to choose ties themselves.

In this regard, a fundamental conflict between premodern and modern ways of thinking and structures of loyalty occur in the tragedy *Romeo and Juliet*. Romeo, Juliet, and Mercutio are truly modern beings, while the Montagues, the Capulets, and especially the belligerent nephew Tybalt, represent the consciousness of relatives and the clan. Shakespeare's greatness stems from the revelation of this great social transformation.

Reading *Romeo and Juliet*, we start to discern in Shakespeare a modern person of the metaphysics of freedom and choice, who is not recognized by the premodern person of the metaphysics of tradition and blood who feels unbridled hatred for the modern person. This is Tybalt's hatred for Romeo. This is also Tybalt's anguish and despair that for incomprehensible reasons and silly circumstances he ends up clashing swords not with his hated Romeo but with Mercutio, whom he respects, and whose aristocratic, free, and fearless disposition he secretly admires.

Classical literature reveals the organized world's forms of power and authority structures. Writers can achieve fictionally what political philosophers would attempt to do in their theories. For example, the true meaning and purpose of Niccolò Machiavelli's work of political philosophy, *Il Principe* (*The Prince*, written in 1513, and published in 1532), cannot be fully understood without reading his comedy, *Mandragola* (*The Mandrake*, written in 1518, and published in 1524), which depicts the incredible corruption and immorality of Florence.

The young Callimaco, returning to his native Florence after having lived in Paris (an obvious autobiographical element, for Machiavelli had lived in Paris as ambassador of Florence), becomes enraptured by the young but married Lucrezia and seeks her favor by all the means at his disposal. Callimaco, having duped Lucrezia's rich, old, and foolish husband Nicia, who wants to father a child and believes that a potion from the root of the mandrake plant will help him have a child with Lucrezia, succeeds in his efforts to begin an affair with the beautiful Lucrezia. Nicia believes Callimaco's story that a woman who has drunk a potion from the root of the mandrake plant inevitably would conceive, but, unfortunately, the man who has impregnated her will die immediately thereafter.

Therefore, they must find a pickpocket or some other vagrant, make him drink the potion, and let him into Lucrezia's bedroom. She will then be able to be impregnated by her real husband, while the dead vagrant will not be missed by anyone. Not surprisingly, Callimaco disguises himself as the vagrant and ends up in bed with Lucrezia. They truly fall in love and decide to never part. For our purposes, that is not the point. Callimaco easily bribes all the Florentines whom he needs, regardless of social class, not only the crooked Ligurio, but also Lucrezia's mother Sostrata, who for money sings to her married and decent daughter the praises of a stranger and explains to her that an affair with another man is in no way a sin. Lucrezia's confessor, Fra Timoteo, also receives a large sum of money and echoes Sostrata enthusiastically.

This is where everything becomes clear. No brutal military force is needed to conquer the immoral and corrupt Florence. The city has almost completely degenerated. It was not only the fragmentation of Italy and the fierce struggles between the city-states but also the lack of a reliable social and moral order and an utter demoralization that allowed well-organized and centralized powers, such as France or Spain, to conquer easily the Florence that Machiavelli so loved.

Here is the thematic and problematic bridge to *The Prince*. In this medium of such corruption and contract murders, only a leader who has mastered the technology of power can survive, a leader whose goal is not to be power itself, but to restore the order and rule of law of the Roman republic. Machiavelli himself was a humanist of the Renaissance, in spite of the unusual nature of his proposed link between dishonesty and political power, who was satirized or even demonized by sixteenth-century Elizabethan poets and playwrights, such as William Shakespeare, Ben Jonson, and Christopher Marlowe, as well as political thinkers and writers of the eighteenth and nineteenth centuries (see Cassirer, 1974, 116–128).

We would be naïve to think that premodern structures and forms have become extinct in the modern world. They have not gone anywhere. We are continually balancing and choosing between them. The conflict between the premodern and modern forms of power, loyalty, and authority is constant in modern society. La Cosa Nostra, the Mafia in general, and political corruption often illustrate not the abstract faults, the cruelty, or evil of people, but the conflict of loyalties, when family, relatives, or the clan come into conflict with the state, the family, and the law. In essence, the Mafia is a symbol of the struggle of the family and clan against the modern state and its cold, faceless institutions.

2. Machiavelli through the Eyes of Shakespeare

Recently, a noticeable flurry of attempts in the academic literature has reinterpreted Niccolò Machiavelli's (1469–1527) personality and body of work, which had been demonized for so long that the historical and actual Machiavelli has been transformed into a figure we might describe as similar to a modern-age equivalent of the Woland character in Mikhail Bulgakov's novel, *The Master and Margarita* (written in 1928–1941, and published, severely censored, in 1966–1967).

If we refer only to Machiavelli's small book, entitled *The Prince*, which was intended as a means of ingratiation with the Medici dynasty who ruled Florence in his day, then perhaps some basis exists for such an assertion (see White, 2005; Berlin, 1979b, 25–79). All those who have shown an interest in the ideas of this strange and mysterious diplomat, writer, and thinker, will likely recall his notable lion and fox metaphors along with the counsels he proffered in *The Prince*: if you cannot rely on force and act like a lion, become a fox and act with stealth. In truth, Machiavelli was a thinker of far greater complexity than the scheme of his pamphlet may reveal. As Florence's ambassador to France living in Paris, Machiavelli understood perfectly the constant threat posed to a fragmented and divided Italy by powerful centrally governed states, by France, in particular.

As a Florentine patriot, as a humanist in the truest sense, and as someone who believed in the ideals of the Roman Republic, Machiavelli dreamed of a perfect political organism that was incorruptible, un-poisoned, and un-manipulated, which would grasp and then master the entire technology of power along with the repertoire of palace intrigue so that once it had taken root in Florence and spread quickly through all of Italy, it could recreate within it a civilized social and moral order, a republican order. If you doubt this, then read *Discorsi sopra la prima deca di Tito Livio* (*Discourses on Livy*, written between 1513 and 1521, and published in 1531), Machiavelli's work on politics that is of far greater importance than *The Prince*.

Machiavelli secretly admired the appalling treachery, manipulation, cruelty, and cynicism of Cesare Borgia, the son of the famous Pope Alexander VI and the head of the papal army who became a cardinal at the age of twenty-two and later a general. This entire nightmare of nepotism and corruption was possible thanks to the political practices of the Spanish nobleman Roderic Borja, who became Pope Alexander VI in a move that was a serious blow to the reputation of the Church.

Yet Machiavelli admired Cesare Borgia, this dangerous beast, who was a danger to him. Cesare was close to Machiavelli's political and educational ideal of the prince instructed by the teacher who would be *un mezzo bestia e mezzo uomo* (half beast, half man). Machiavelli understood quite well that only someone of the ilk of Cesare could put an end to papal political omnipotence, while putting an end to the untrammeled political banditry of a dysfunctional state, and thereby create a strong centralized state similar to France or Spain.

Some politicians and nobles were shocked by *The Prince* when it was first published. Others thought that Machiavelli was simply cataloguing the behavior of all politicians in a candid way but without affixing labels. Still other interpreters of Machiavelli guessed that he was a satirist and was poking fun at immoral politics while maintaining a facade of seriousness and respect. Incidentally, many other Renaissance humanist writers had done similar things; consider Machiavelli's contemporary, Sir Thomas More's *Utopia* (1523), and Erasmus of Rotterdam's *Encomium Moriae* (*Praise of Folly*, 1509).

Whatever the case, no one was so disgusted by Machiavelli as the great English poets and dramatists of the Elizabethan era, especially Christopher Marlowe and William Shakespeare. In the prologue to Marlowe's play, *The Jew of Malta*, Machiavelli, as if he were the very incarnation of Satan, is made to say the following:

> Albeit the world thinks Machiavel is dead,
> Yet was his soul but flown beyond the Alps;
> And now the Guise is dead, is come to France,
> To view this Land, and frolic with his friends.
> To some perhaps my name is odious,
> But such as love me guard me from their tongues;
> And let them know that I am Machiavel,
> And weigh not men, and therefore not men's words.
> Admired I am of those that hate me most.
> Though some speak openly against my books,
> Yet they will read me, and thereby attain
> To Peter's chair: and when they cast me off,
> Are poisoned by my climbing followers.
> (Cited in Cassirer, 1974, 119)

In Shakespeare's historical drama, *Henry VI* (Part Three, Act 3, Scene 2), Richard, Duke of Gloucester, says:

> Why, I can smile and murder whiles I smile,
> And cry Content to that which grieves my heart,
> And wet my cheeks with artificial tears,
> And frame my face to all occasions.
> I'll drown more sailors than the mermaid shall;

I'll slay more gazers that the basilisk;
I'll play the orator as well as Nestor,
Deceive more slily than Ulysses could;
And, like a Sinon, take another Troy.
I can add colours to the chameleon,
Change shapes with Proteus for advantages,
And set the murderous Machiavel to school.
(*Ibid.*, 118)

The story of Machiavelli's interpretation and demonization is a long and tortuous one, worthy of a separate course in university political science departments. In the nineteenth century, Machiavelli was especially demonized by the French antimonarchists, who associated the restoration of Napoleon III with Machiavelli's nefarious cunning. During the twentieth century, Machiavelli was knocked about by historians and political scientists studying the history of the rise to power of Stalin and Hitler and their régimes, based as they were on overt political banditry.

The Bolsheviks were beginning to be referred to as Machiavellians. This version was popularized by Arthur Koestler, the British writer of Hungarian origin, in his *Darkness at Noon* (1940). We should consider James Burnham in this context. Burnham's book, *The Managerial Revolution* (1941), had a great impact on George Orwell, who also considered as Machiavellians the virtuosos of the twentieth century's brutal *Realpolitik*.

The Carbonari, Italy's nineteenth-century patriots, began openly admiring Machiavelli. He was for them Italy's first modern patriot. Curiously, both Hegel and Marx were among the famous political thinkers who sympathized with Machiavelli. Hegel, who had experienced Germany's humiliation after the battle of Jena in 1806, as well as Napoleon's policies in the German lands, considered Machiavelli a dignified patriot who was the first to have grasped the dangers posed by French imperialism to other nations. While Marx openly postulated that Machiavelli was the first modern political thinker to have demystified politics and power.

Politics cannot exist without that which creates the miracle of sociability, the associative link among people. It cannot exist without norms, beliefs, and values. Technique and mechanics shortly become caricatures whenever they are torn from goals and meaning. Machiavelli never asserted that politics is required to be amoral. He only demonstrated that these spheres have an autonomy and logic of their own, while at the same time they are possible without each other. Yet many writers and commentators were tempted to accuse Machiavelli of almost every dubious tendency of modern politics. Machiavelli was deplored by the great English poets and dramatists of the Elizabethan epoch. He had no shortage of admirers, starting with Johann Gottfried von Herder, Johann Gottlieb Fichte, Hegel, Marx, and ending with the Carbonari and the heroes of the *Risorgimento,* the war for Italian unification.

And so I am re-reading *The Prince*, meant for a legitimate monarch or a despot who has usurped the reigns of state power, at the same time as I read Machiavelli's other work geared for republicans and citizens, especially that work which is far more serious from a theoretical viewpoint, the *Discourses on Livy*. As I read, I see that such a thinker could only have arisen in a country where the Church had far greater political power than any other European country. From this arose his antagonism to the politics of Pope Alexander VI, and his admiration for the activities of the "Duca Valentino" (Duke Valentine), Cesare Borgia, who united Romagna and centralized political power and the state in a formerly fragmented and weak Italy.

As he observed the unfolding of events in Italy, Machiavelli rejected the sacred origins of the state and the idea of the divine right of kings. Ernst Cassirer has remarked accurately that in an era that was so rife with blood and license, only people who were completely disconnected and without any reference point from reality could have been capable of believing that the right to govern was something divinely bestowed (see Cassirer, 1974, 133–139). Machiavelli idealized the ancient pagan Roman Republic, believing firmly that paganism was far more effective than Christianity politically, created as it was for the salvation of the individual soul and not for the consolidation of a political nation and the creation of martial spirit and glory.

Europe, or, more precisely, conservative thinkers and writers have never forgiven Machiavelli for his overt admiration for the pagan world, for his bravery and civic virtues, and, most importantly, for his disqualification of Christianity from politics and his desacralization of political power. Such an era offered only two paths: (1) that of Martin Luther and other religious reformers to rise up against the corrupt political power of the Pope, rife with plays for power, or (2) a radical criticism of Machiavelli's own era, holding it against the light of the wisdom and virtue of the Ancient World. The great majority of humanists chose the first path, choosing not *devotio moderna* and religious reform, but *studia humanitatis* and the rediscovery of the past as an alternative to the broken present. On this path, Machiavelli joined Thomas More, Erasmus of Rotterdam, and François Rabelais.

Compared to these Renaissance thinkers, his contemporaries, Machiavelli's fate was unenviable. Probably no other Renaissance writer has been read letter-by-letter and word-for-word. All who grasp a modicum of the symbolic thinking of the Renaissance, its anti-genres, satires and parodies, its grotesque, its esotericism, and the carnival-like culture of its language and humor, agree that we cannot read More's *Utopia* and Erasmus's *Praise of Folly* letter-by-letter, since these works, just as Rabelais's *Gargantua and Pantagruel* (1532–1564), require especially complex hermeneutics.

Why, then, is Machiavelli, a contemporary of these writers and thinkers who made use of a multitude of devices and symbols of coded language, read letter-by-letter to this very day? Even the lion and fox metaphors are not as clear and simple as they may seem, as is often remarked by those who lack the erudition for a serious reading of Machiavelli.

Even more frequently, Machiavelli is treated unhistorically. Here I do not imply that all ideas need to be wrapped around their historical context and that everything should be explained in this manner. But if you do not pay heed to the situation of a person who threw out a challenge to the Medici family that ruled Florence for over three hundred years (barring a few interludes), that would mean you have not grasped the political life and logic of Florence during his era.

After all, Girolamo Savonarola, the Dominican monk who protested Alexander VI's immorality and cynicism, was killed before Machiavelli's very eyes in Florence's Piazza della Signoria. Piero Soderini, Florence's goodhearted Gonfaloniere, who did not heed Machiavelli's advice to never allow his enemies in place, but to kill them, deport them once and for all or repeatedly, or constantly spy upon their place of abode, was later toppled by the Medici and was forced to flee Florence.

This is the origin of Machiavelli's affixing to the roll call of people who are good, noble, but devoid of political instincts and power (*animo*, *virtù*, and Lady Fortune), the fragile and vulnerable who are poised to become easy plunder for villains. Does Machiavelli's antagonism to the powerful and unscrupulous Medici family really bear witness to his lack of principles and opportunism?

We cannot portray Machiavelli as an angel. He was an ambivalent and dangerous thinker who had lost faith in the instructive powers of politics and who openly professed politics alone as the mechanics of the state. He identified truth with successful practice. In Machiavelli's view, political practice is not constructed of norms and principles, but of its opposite, successful and historically tried-and-true experience. Efficacious truth (*verità effettuale*) is nothing other than successful practice, which is obliged to create a normative dimension in politics and become a recognized form of wisdom.

Machiavelli's roots in ancient historiography are deep and obvious. For Machiavelli, as for Plutarch before him, history and circumstance offer occasions (Fortune) for taking actions (*virtù*). The readiness to act is far more important than theoretical arguments or abstract truth. A profound internalization of politics that allows political problems to permeate your personality and become your existential concerns, suggests Machiavelli to have been close to what might be described as a political existentialism.

Yet we need to admit the breakthrough in the history of political thought, one far greater than the frank counsels offered to Lorenzo de' Medici, to whom *The Prince* is dedicated, which was shocking to Machiavelli's contemporaries. Machiavelli's modern ideas were exceptionally resonant during his era, and they were innovative and inspiring for nineteenth-century thinkers. In simple terms, successful and invincible beasts give rise to institutions and to political and ethical norms and codes of conduct. This was written more than three hundred years before Nietzsche! The idea that truth is accomplished practice that has been tested by history, rather than theorists, could have had impact on Marx.

And that is without considering Machiavelli's insight about religion, which, he says, is essential to a society from a practical viewpoint, as a force that mobilizes, conditions behavior, and provides a useful framework for society. Religion is a social construct, without which any civilized or organized social existence would be impossible. After all, the people do not require complex instruction on faith or, worse, theological disputes. Practical truths help them orient themselves. What could Voltaire have added to this?

3. The Footprints of Machiavelli's Thought in Stendhal's *Les Chroniques Italiennes*

Another book that reveals much of the footprints of Machiavelli's thought in modern Europe is Stendhal's *Les Chroniques Italiennes* (*Three Italian Chronicles*, 1839) (see Stendhal, 1991).

In one of his short novellas, "The Cenci," Stendhal expressed the idea that Don Juan is a *bona fide* Christian phenomenon if only because passion and pleasure are unable to go unmarked by sin and evil in Christian Europe. How many young and wealthy rakes, such as Tirso de Molina's Don Juan and, later, Molière's Don Juan, went completely unnoticed in ancient Athens and Rome? But in those societies, religion was a feast that encouraged people to enjoy life, which, as we know, was something to which Europe was later unable to reconcile itself.

In this context, Callimaco from *Mandragola*, who openly celebrates passion and pleasure revealing Machiavelli's strikingly pagan and un-Christian attitude to love, appears to have been one of those young and wealthy rakes. The character who acts as if he were straight out of an ancient Roman comedy, Callimaco is depicted as a Florentine rake to allow Machiavelli to satirize the human nature and corrupt practices so manifest in his hometown.

According to Stendhal, passion is calamitous, while pleasure is sinful only where it is contrasted to religious sentiment, and the great European Renaissance, especially Italy, sought to reconcile these two sentiments. Stendhal noted that we are forever repeating that Christianity softens traditions and people's feelings. This may be true, but it gives rise to the question whether the ancient world would not have achieved this had it existed longer. According to Stendhal, *The Aeneid* is far gentler than *The Iliad*. Stendhal's insight into the civilizing process and the softening of manners as manifest in literature echoes Giambattista Vico's ideas.

This is how literature approaches a philosophical problem. Were the ideas expressed by Stendhal in this book pasted into works by Niccolò Machiavelli, Giambattista Vico, or David Hume, it would not bring them any shame. Stendhal's thoughts are not out of place in the works of philosophers who were his contemporaries. Stendhal, in this case, can be linked to the debate started by Machiavelli, and continued by Sir Francis Bacon, about what essential advantages modern Europe, with its scholarship and culture, had over the Ancient World. Or, in the end, was modern Europe only a continuous distancing from the great classical period and its ideals? This is one of the major questions whose moral and theoretical tensions formed Europe's identity.

Another novella by Stendhal, which addresses Machiavelli even more, is "Vanina Vanini." It is the story of a nineteenth-century Italian woman aristocrat, who falls in love with the nineteen-year old Carbonaro, Pietro Missirilli, who has escaped from prison, injured, and who has been given refuge in Vanina's father's home. Even though the story is set in 1832, allusions occur to the pre-Shakespearean early Renaissance novella about the beginnings of Romeo and Juliet's love. In Luigi da Porto's version of it, Juliet falls in love with Romeo dressed in women's clothing, or, at least, she cannot take her eyes off him. As we know, Shakespeare based his tragedy not on the version by Luigi da Porto, but the later one by Matteo Bandello.

In Stendhal's work, Vanina falls in love with the wounded pretty girl Clementina or is besotted with her beauty. She is revealed soon after as the wounded escaped Carbonaro Pietro. His innocent nineteen-year-old face, angelic eyes, and long hair allow him to disguise himself as a girl. A passionate romance ensues that sees the madly smitten Vanina reaching the painful realization that for her beloved the *venta* (a unit of the Carbonari) and the fight for Italian independence are more important than her.

After a period of abetting the Carbonari and using her wealth to obtain better ordnance, Vanina learns that Pietro and his unit are preparing an especially risky but clever conspiracy against the government. She betrays his comrades without naming Missirilli. All are arrested; Pietro comes under suspicion and, unable to bear the terrible sorrow and horror of having remained free, turns himself in to the authorities. In an attempt to rescue Pietro, Vanina goes to exceptional lengths. She agrees to marry a wealthy Roman aristocrat who is her devoted admirer and who has influential political ties.

Vanina manages to visit Pietro, but in prison he becomes an even more fervent patriot, while his love for Italy is accompanied by a strengthened religious sentiment with interludes of fatalism. After telling Missirilli that their love has no future and that he is first and foremost an Italian patriot whose life belongs to the homeland, Vanina admits that she has committed a terrible crime by betraying his unit. And because one of Missirilli's cohorts kills himself as he is being escorted to prison, she ends up with the weight of terrible crime on her conscience. The prison guard has to protect Vanina from Missirilli, who attempts to kill his disloyal lover with his chains. The story concludes with Missirilli still in jail, though Vanina manages to save his life, while Vanina marries the Duke Livio Savelli.

During one of his most passionate avowals of love, Missirilli cries out that he loves Vanina even more than life itself, that he would gladly go to America with her and be happy except for the woeful fact that Italy has yet to be liberated from the barbarian yoke. In another place, he vows to devote all of his energies to freeing Italy from the barbarians (Stendhal, 1991, 178). I found myself itching to find out who those barbarians were in the end. What does he mean by barbarians? As a child, I sensed instinctively that all those who sought to hinder noble Italy from achieving its freedom were the veritable barbarians.

Was it Napoleon and the France of his era mentioned in the novella? The Austrians? Those Italians who collaborated with foreign powers, such as the Papal State and its carabinieri? Who, really?

Missirilli, when referring to the barbarian yoke, repeats Petrarch's words about the liberation of Italy from barbarians (*liberar l'Italia de' barbari*) uttered in 1350. Machiavelli was to repeat them at the end of *The Prince*, where he exhorted Lorenzo de' Medici to resolutely unite Italy and liberate it from the barbarian yoke (the French). These words were also repeated by Pope Julius II and eventually, long before George Gordon, Lord Byron, by the eighteenth-century Italian poet and dramatist Count Vittorio Alfieri, who deplored tyranny even more than Lord Byron (see *ibid.*). Count Alfieri called Machiavelli the "divine Machiavelli," *divino Machiavelli.*

Remarkably, Stendhal, a French writer, develops this theme and allows us to retrace Machiavelli's thought and sentiment back to the eighteenth and nineteenth centuries. This may strike you as incredible, until you have read Stendhal's novella, "The Duchess of Palliano," in which the prologue discusses the loss of Italian passion, its disappearance in the eighteenth century when, to their great loss, the Italian aristocracy imitated the cold and wholly indifferent upper classes of France and England. France's calamitous influence consisted in its demonstration of indifference toward everything and everyone and its studied masking of emotions, while England's disastrous influence was a stilted and all-effacing politeness to which one could add the affected boredom of its dandyism and the perfunctory stance toward everyone and anything.

Stendhal, in this superb study of mentalities and the history of customs, demonstrates the manner by which passion vanishes through the imitation of alien modes of aristocratic behavior. It was precisely his desire to discover Italian passion that encouraged Stendhal to study and recount the chronicles of Renaissance Italy. Should we be surprised by this? Italian history, after all, rife as it was with passion, betrayal, and suffering, provided Shakespeare with much inspiration.

Stendhal wrote that fifteenth-century Paris, compared to the life of Italy's cities, was a city of admirable and pleasant barbarians. In the France of the time, women idolized only military leaders who were slated to be forgotten. Meanwhile, in Renaissance Italy a man who knew ancient Greek could be admired as much as any warrior. This happened in Italy, thanks to its passion and not the gallantry that stifles it. This is one more interpretive master stroke by Stendhal.

So, it is Stendhal who emerges as the discoverer of Renaissance Italy in Europe, where no one any longer believes in anything aside from power and prestige. Just as he emerges as the investigator of freedom, honor, and passion, disclosing their fate in periods where the dividing point between civilization and barbarity was quite unclear. As it is in our day.

4. Will Bravery, Glory, and Honor Be Reborn?

Vertù contr' al furore
Prenderà l'arme, e fia il combatter corto:
Che l'antico valore
Ne gli Italici cor non è ancor morto.
(Virtue will take arms against sound and fury
Let the battle be brief
For the ancient valor
In the Italic heart is not yet dead.)

(From *Italia Mia*, by Francesco Petrarch, 1304–1374)
(Cited in Machiavelli, 2003, 134)

Florence, immoral and depraved as it was, did not need brutal military power to subjugate it. Mothers drove their daughters to sell their bodies for money. The same drive was conducted by men of the cloth with money, propelling into sin women who had come for confession. Its own decline and immorality posed a greater threat to Florence than any powerful and centralized state such as France and Italy. An amoral or immoral society cannot in principle be patriotic or self-conscious.

Not even weapons were required to conquer Florence. Florence could be defeated by allowing it to finally degenerate and drown in its internal turmoil and struggles over wealth, power, and prestige. Moral decrepitude inevitably ends in political collapse and the loss of liberty. Machiavelli, to whom all manner of sins are imputed, understood this better than any other political thinker.

In his view, Florence allowed itself to degenerate during the fifteenth century. Not only Italy's fragmentation and the terrible battles between the city-states, but also the absence of a dependable social and moral order, along with utter moral decrepitude, allowed any organized and centralized power to conquer Florence at will.

And this situation provides a thematic and problematic bridge to Machiavelli's *Prince*. Only a sovereign who had a perfect grasp of the technology of power and statecraft could have survived in a realm rife with such corruption and assassins-for-hire. Such a sovereign's goal would not be the power for its own sake, but, instead, the re-establishment of the law and order of the Roman Republic. In the end, Machiavelli was a Renaissance humanist and a passionate Florentine patriot who grasped the full extent of the decline of his native city and the emerging political dangers to which this gave rise.

The last thing I want to do is justify and bow to Machiavelli. All I hope to achieve is to interpret and understand him against the historical and political backdrop. Two Florentines of that era took notice of Florence's decline and of the immorality that was destroying it: Machiavelli and the Dominican friar, Girolamo Savonarola. Savonarola ruled Florence briefly after the toppling of the Medicis, gave fiery sermons, burned books and pictures publicly, destroyed "pagan" objects of art, and sought the creation of a Christian religious republic in Florence.

Even a war against immorality can transform into a hell for those caught in the wrong place or innocent bystanders, which is why what Savonarola's battle with the Renaissance might have led to remains unclear, since Pope Alexander VI put it down brutally. Suffice to recall that the Florentine painter Sandro Botticelli was forced by Savonarola to burn his paintings in public. Savonarola was accused of heresy and burned at the stake. Machiavelli witnessed and recorded his execution.

In this case, I am concerned by the fact that Savonarola believed that the active involvement of the Church in politics could vanquish society's moral decline. Machiavelli rejected this route and placed his faith in a brutal albeit civilized and secular political power that sought to revive the laws and institutions of the Roman Republic. How else could he influence the people that he portrayed in *Mandragola*?

From this does not follow that all people are scoundrels. Those who portray society as a collection of cretins or a rogues' gallery have concealed, or open, tendencies toward brutal politics. From this viewpoint, Machiavelli went too far. In his comedy, Machiavelli introduces the character Ligurio as a parasite. A parasite, as a class or a social mask, was an impossible phenomenon in the New Era, if only because slavery no longer existed. The Parasite is a character in Plautus's comedy, *Miles Gloriosus*, who sponges off of wealthy and free people, a toady who entertains them with gossip, rumor, and jokes. Such freeloaders and hangers-on, stuck midway between slave and freeman, who almost belonged to a separate social class, were referred to by the ancient Greeks as sycophants.

Machiavelli, whom we can consider as having been the first representative of empirical political scholarship in Europe, as a prototype of a political sociologist, and perhaps even as the father of these disciplines, including the foundations he laid for political anthropology and political psychology, by means of the behavior of the actors on his political stage, and analytical model of their tendencies and customs, lays bare an anatomy of human corruption and venality. As someone who treated conspiracies seriously, and who studied them and held them to be inexorable parts of any political machine, Machiavelli raised these to the rank of objects for political analysis and broke ground for later pamphleteers to portray himself as a specialist concerning conspiracy.

In 1864, the French lawyer Maurice Joly (1829–1878) wrote a pamphlet, *Dialogue aux Enfers entre Montesquieu et Machiavel* (*The Dialogue in Hell between Montesquieu and Machiavelli*), which was a landmark pamphlet severely criticizing the despotism and political cynicism of Napoleon III. A brilliant stylist and a thoughtful political analyst, Joly composed his pamphlet in the form of a dialogue between Charles de Secondat, Baron de la Brède et de Montesquieu, and Machiavelli.

Whereas Montesquieu champions the values of liberalism and denounces immoral politics, suggesting that despotism has always been immoral, Machiavelli represents Napoleon III, solemnly and cynically pronouncing that politics has never had anything to do with morality. Joly's *Dialogue aux Enfers* was published after the appearance of Eugène Sue's novels on the Jesuit plot. What Sue described as the Jesuit plot, Joly attributed to Napoleon III: the rise of reaction and religious bigotry, shameless political manipulations, and cynical misuse of democratic institutions for the sake of tyranny.

Maurice Joly was an elegant writer and an original thinker, and he deserved a better fate than what awaited him. The political persecution and imprisonment he underwent, and even his suicide in 1878, were not the worst part of his destiny. The worst, that concerned his essay, was still to come. As we now know, Tsarist Russia's political police, *Okhrana*, forged the notorious *Protocols of the Elders of Zion* (forged between 1897 and 1898, and published in 1917) using Joly's book as a model (see Donskis, 2003, 19–79).

Joly's concern with Machiavelli as representing modern immoral politics was by no means accidental. Machiavelli was surely the most explicit advocate and instructor of what we could well describe as the mechanics of government. Machiavelli was immediately concerned with political mechanics and with the contemporary Italian scene, far more than with abstract political theory.

Although Harvey C. Mansfield suggested that Machiavelli's notion of conspiracies was a logical continuation of his concepts of *animo*, the spirit of self-defense, and *virtù*. According to Mansfield, *virtù*, in Machiavelli's philosophy, is not just another word for manliness, valor, and prowess, as many political theorists suggest. "Machiavelli's virtue is not ancient or Roman manliness" (Mansfield, 1998, 36). Yet it does not mean virtue in the classical sense. Machiavelli stood in sharp contrast to his predecessors, such classical political thinkers as Plato and Aristotle, who, though interested in concrete and practical politics, never abandoned their moral and educational concerns (see Machiavelli, 1998, 218–235; Mansfield, 1998, 36–52).

Mansfield notes,

For Machiavelli, virtue does not consist in having a virtuous character, as for Aristotle. Virtue is alert, on the make; it is not a habit. One must of course get used to the exacting requirements of loose morals and to some extent learn by doing or at least pretending; the main need, however, is not habituation but new and better opinions, or the replacement of inadequate by adequate presumptions. (*Ibid.*, 45)

Machiavelli's major works, *The Prince* and the *Discourses on Livy*, rest on his assertion that historical development is conditioned entirely by the intentions and deeds of those who occupy the limelight on the political stage. This assertion was at the core of modern conspiracy theories, which were all ultimately based on the idea of intentional action as the principal driving force behind the scenes of political life. What is the conspiracy theory of society, if not a theory of political mechanics and of the naked technology of power, a theory devoid of all religious, educational, and moral aspects of politics?

In a way, the modern conspiracy theory of society received its impetus from Machiavelli, who deprived his political theory of all indispensable emphases on religious and moral aspects of politics, and who was least concerned with the *ought to be* as superior and prior to the *is*. Whereas classical political theory rested on, and was derived from, moral theory, Machiavelli emancipated political theory from moral theory.

Since *Quattrocento* Florence was a city of Neo-Platonists, that Aristotle's *Politics* was considered by Machiavelli a serious criterion in constructing a theory of political action and its underlying intentions is unlikely. That Machiavelli even constructed a theory in the classical sense is doubtful, for he made a collection of sketches and insights which had valuable theoretical implications for modern political theory. Yet Machiavelli was a representative of the early historicism who believed firmly in the truth lurking within history. This is not the speculative truth discovered by the mind, but time-tested and efficacious practice. Practical wisdom and the power that crowns it bestow moral legitimacy.

Nonetheless, Machiavelli, as did later Francis Bacon, Giambattista Vico, and David Hume, believed that the truths he discovered do not belong to any single historical period, and are universal. Even if the *Prince* is considered a political document intended first and foremost for all Florence and for the Medicis, it is based on many centuries of confirmed truths about human nature. This is why there is no merit in limiting Machiavelli's analysis of immorality and corruption to his era alone. He addresses all of humanity from a historical perspective.

This supports the claim that Machiavelli was one of the first modern historical pessimists. His belief that the Christian world had lost authentic creative political powers reveals much about Machiavelli the admirer of the Ancient World. He defends that world against the follies of the modern world and its deviations from the ancient canon. Most importantly, he achieved a revolution in politics defending a kind of border-value morality, the priority of successful practice over detached principles, and other phenomena that we associate with modernity. Mansfield suggests,

> ... we are also uneasily aware that Machiavelli was, to say the least, present at the origin of a revolution in morality, which can be defined loosely in our terms as a change from virtue protected by religion to self-interest justified by secularism. The revolution is known to us, again using our word, as "modernity." (*Ibid.*, 7–8)

Machiavelli appears to have been a modern revolutionary and a modern moral and political instrumentalist armed with the universal wisdom of Florentine humanism. This strange fusion gives rise to what we can term the great riddle of Machiavelli.

5. The Genealogy of *Romeo and Juliet*

Shakespeare's *Romeo and Juliet* is one of the works that is most garlanded with mystery and literary legends. At first blush, this tragedy appears to have nothing special about it. Shakespeare encountered the prevalent narrative, involving the unfortunate love between two children of feuding families in Verona during the reign of Bartolomeo I della Scala, in the Italian literature of the Middle Ages and Renaissance. This Italian duke, who ruled Verona and Vicenza in 1301–1304, invited Dante to visit Verona, and is mentioned by Dante in *Purgatorio*, as are the Montague and Capulet families.

The Italian Renaissance writer Masuccio Salernitano was the first to write a short account of the ill-fated love and the death by poisoning of these two young people. Inspired by this novella, Luigi da Porto borrowed the names Bartolomeo I della Scala, Montague, and Capulet from Dante, and set the action in Verona. In Shakespeare's tragedy, the Prince of Verona becomes Escalus. Later, the story is retold by the better-known writer, who was far more talented than his two predecessors, Matteo Bandello, a Dominican priest and a successful imitator of Giovanni Boccaccio's tales. The theme of the Montagues and the Capulets was also used by Lope de Vega in one of his works. Nonetheless, the story would not have become what it did if not for the incomparably more meaningful life bestowed upon it by Shakespeare (see Paster, 1992, 253–265).

Perhaps, as legend has it, Marlowe pointed Shakespeare to the fabula. Whatever the case, the facts tell us that Matteo Bandello's 1554 rewrite of Romeo and Juliet's love story was translated into French five years later by Pierre Boaistuau, and this French version inspired the English poet and translator Arthur Brooke to write the *Tragical History of Romeus and Juliet*, Shakespeare's primary source, which inspired him to write *Romeo and Juliet*.

Furthermore, Bandello's story was translated into English by Sir Geoffrey Fenton in 1567 (when Shakespeare and Marlowe were all of three-years-old). Shakespeare would have needed these translations and adaptations because his education did not place him on the same footing as the erudite Cambridge-educated Marlowe (see Greenblatt, 2005a; Greenblatt, 2005b).

Romeo and Juliet could also have started out as a comedy only to end up as a tragedy. Mercutio's death is the pivotal event after which the story, inevitably, had to become a tragedy. Incidentally, even Lope de Vega consciously united elements of comedy and tragedy in creating his form of *comedia*. Whatever the case, this has no bearing on the heart of the matter: *Romeo and Juliet* remains one of the most marvelous works of world literature.

As we know, Shakespeare was fated to pay a heavy price for this tragedy after his death. Molière was later to reproach him for *Romeo and Juliet*, accusing him of the dubious inability to distinguish comedy from tragedy, and of the jumbling together of genres. During the epoch of Classicism, Shakespeare's name was a general object of derision, while Voltaire, a great admirer of Shakespeare in his youth, was later to describe him as a barbarian. The Prussian emperor Frederick the Great, a devoted follower and imitator of Voltaire, who was also instructed by him, went as far as lamenting that German youths were reading the works of an English barbarian whose kings spoke in the same manner as gravediggers. Only toward the end of the eighteenth century did the young members of the *Sturm und Drang* movement, Johann Wolfgang von Goethe and Friedrich Schiller, espouse the name of Shakespeare as an arbiter of style, historical feeling, and true literature (see Elias, 1994, 3–42).

As is well known, Shakespeare was officially recognized as a major literary genius thanks only to the German Romantics. Even as late as in Victorian England serious doubts remained that an actor of low birth who had never studied at university could have created such peerless works.

What does Shakespeare's *Romeo and Juliet* disclose? First, the work exposes two modern sentiments, love and friendship, at the same time informing us about their sociogenesis. Love and friendship arise here as the feelings of the modern person, and we may easily refer to them as modern feelings.

Thinking sociologically, we always have an itch to offset the statutory law and the family, two concepts that have been struggling fiercely against each other in the West and in other civilizations for centuries. Even the challenge issued to the modern state and its power structures by the Cosa Nostra in the twentieth century is nothing less than the battle between family and law—between clan and state—which was also a form of confrontation in premodern and modern forms of social organization.

Just as with clan and family, we can just as easily counterbalance the friend and the beloved. For the clan person, a friendship with, or a love for, a person on the wrong side of the family's interests, who is beyond its power and control, can only prompt disapproval and far worse. Sooner or later, the conflicting objects of loyalty and fidelity force a person to choose between family (clan, kin, and blood) or freedom and responsibility for the individual's personality and identity (love and friendship). In a metaphysical world of blood and tradition, we are not free to choose our object of loyalty, and it is impossible to be responsible for our own identity in such a world. The object of loyalty and the structure of identity are anterior. We can only be inserted into them. This is why the idea of love in the modern sense did not exist in the premodern world.

Romeo and Juliet are not the only ones in Shakespeare's play who experience excruciatingly painful and deadly conflicts of loyalty. Romeo's friend Mercutio is a relative of Escalus, the Prince of Verona, but Mercutio's loyalty to his friend becomes more important to him than the traditional loyalty to his clan, a holdover from a previous era. The Duke strictly forbids quarrels and rows to be decided by duels or armed conflict, but his clansman, Mercutio, who by lineage is in no way linked to the Montagues or the Capulets, becomes the first to break the Prince's injunction by defending his friend's wounded honor.

People living in the modern world always have two fundamental choices open to them. They can abandon those to whom they are related by blood, and who can never be chosen, freely selecting a friend who is dear to their heart and mind but in no way bound by blood ties—a beloved or a friend; or they can swear off the daunting principle of freedom and return to their roots—kith and kin.

Whether we like it or not, freedom inevitably leads us away from inheritance, ascription, and light categorization. In truth, a person's beloved, wife, or friend is incomparably more important than that person's relatives and clan. Traditional or premodern persons inherited social ties and forms of identity, while modern persons dare to create these themselves.

On this view, in *Romeo and Juliet* a fundamental conflict takes place between the premodern and modern mentalities, along with a conflict within the structures of loyalty. Romeo, Juliet, and Mercutio are truly modern beings, whereas the old Montagues and Capulets, especially their feisty nephew Tybalt, are the representatives of the concept of clan and kin.

Shakespeare's greatness arises out of the revelation of this great social transformation. While reading *Romeo and Juliet*, we see before us the dawning of the age of the modern person belonging to a metaphysical universe of freedom and choice, who is not acknowledged by the premodern person still wedded to the metaphysics of blood and tradition, and who greets this new arrival with tremendous hatred.

Such is Tybalt's loathing of Romeo. This is the reason for Tybalt's disappointment and vexation at being refused the chance to cross swords with the detested Romeo for reasons and circumstances that are beyond Tybalt's ability to grasp, instead having to face Mercutio, whom he respects, and whose free, aristocratic, and fearless nature Tybalt secretly admires.

6. Hatred as Depersonalization: A Name in the Place of a Face

Tybalt's hatred of the Montagues is more than something he has blindly acquired from the Capulet clan, or something that he is aping. His hatred for them, which in its intensity greatly exceeds the longstanding enmity of the Capulets for old Montague, becomes a problem for everyone, even for the Capulets themselves.

By succumbing to the essence of irrational hatred, Tybalt despises the Montague name more than anything else. It is a designation that has become for him an inexorable part of his clan-dynastic consciousness. In himself and in others, he annihilates any natural and primordial spontaneous impulse or desire to commune with another living person, though not with that person's name.

Meanwhile, Tybalt's cousin Juliet, by falling in love with Romeo, overcomes the vicious circle of hatred, despite having been taught to hate the Montague name from childhood. Here are the words of Juliet's balcony monologue:

> 'Tis but thy name that is my enemy.
> Thou art thyself, though not a Montague.
> What's Montague? It is nor hand, nor foot,
> Nor arm, nor face, [nor any other part]
> Belonging to a man. O, be some other name!
> What's in a name? That which we call a rose
> By any other word would smell as sweet.
> So Romeo would, were he not Romeo called,
> Retain that dear perfection which he owes
> Without that title. Romeo, doff thy name,
> And, for thy name, which is no part of thee,
> Take all myself. (Shakespeare, 1992, 71–73)

The separation of a name, or any other sort of appellation, from a flesh-and-blood person is already the path leading away from hatred. Hatred begins with the cognitive relationship with the destruction of the world. People always refuse to get to know or delve deeply into what they hate. At the same time, hatred depersonalizes its object by removing the unique traits that characterize it.

Hatred only begins to dissipate when people hold one another's gaze, or else look in the direction of other objects in the world. A loving person glances quietly at the world, at things, at works of creation, and at people. Those who hate do not want to see, they are always cocked to start speaking of names and designations, but not about individuals.

To begin despising a well-defined individual in a spontaneous manner is quite difficult. In a highly competitive world, this is true up to the point where the person poses no threat, or else becomes a problem. If you want to maintain your loathing successfully, you must first depersonalize the intended object of hatred. This can only be accomplished by bringing language into play to replace a living being and an inimitable face with words and labels. We reduce those we hate to a designation, category, or grouping that reveals nothing about them. Hatred prefers a rich and encrusted language, as well as a refined terminology.

Hatred tends toward active verbalization, because it is only possible where situations involving eye-to-eye or face-to-face contact have been prohibited. When you look people in the eye directly, it is well nigh impossible to despise them or discriminate against them. Most commonly, people are objects of hatred when they are the bearers of a name, or are members of a sex, a type, or a group, but not when they are perceived as unique individuals with distinguishable facial features that allow them not be confused with any other person. This, then, is the metaphysics of the human face. Spontaneously, almost impulsively, the face is respected as a testament to the miracle of the encounter between people. Yet it is also cause for embarrassment in the presence of baseness or atrocity.

Hatred vanishes when real people encounter one another, having cast aside their names and designations. It burrows its way to the place where the battle takes place between recollections, interpretations, narratives, names, labels, and competing memories or sufferings that refute each other radically. People can hate one another, when they are engaged in the acts of speaking, shouting, mourning, and laughing, but they almost never feel hatred when they are looking at one another for extended periods. This is why enemies avoid long gazes.

Gazes pose a danger to hatred, to the resolve necessary in battle, and to feelings of vengeance. A long and silent gaze obliterates intolerance. The only effective manner of prolonging hatred is to isolate physically those who hate from their objects of hatred, which exhausts both sides sooner or later. This organized hatred was well understood, created, and exploited by totalitarian régimes. It has been grasped thoroughly by today's criminal and hate groups.

Human individuality is annihilated by intolerance and by death. Intolerance is death's midwife. Both act as levelers of people. And they both always target that greatest of miracles which the geniuses of Western European art, from Leonardo da Vinci, Hans Holbein the Younger, Anthony van Dyck, Frans Hals, Johannes Vermeer, and Rembrandt to Chaïm Soutine and Amedeo Modigliani, have tried to comprehend: the fragile and vulnerable human face and the individuality of the soul. Love alone can restore a human soul that has been wounded or disintegrated. Not only can love restore, but it can confer a new individuality on a person.

Hatred of the despised is useful in and of itself. It allows people to better orient themselves in the world. Hatred divides those in our vicinity into necessary categories and offers signposts indicating how we should treat people and groups. Hatred creates the illusion of continuity and traditions of respect within a group: despise those whom your ancestors, family, tribe, clan, or nation despised, and you will be naturally loyal to your own tradition while maintaining your identity and sense of history. We find particularly easy to hate those who are trying to topple a world order that is recognizable to some while offering change to others. Uncertainty, unsafety, and insecurity, this unholy trinity of modernity, fuel and instigate hatred.

Tybalt is the perfect incarnation of the form of hatred which prohibits a person from having the merest doubt or stopping to think for an eye blink. In *Romeo and Juliet*, he is a fearless warrior and the caretaker of the clan's morale. He steadfastly refuses to recognize any moral reform or compromise. He knows no fear, and his instinct of self-preservation is especially weak. The equally fearless Mercutio, who is Tybalt's opposite number, takes on the duel, knowing full well its possible repercussions, because he is apprehensive of the soft and fragile Romeo's abilities to defend himself against Tybalt.

Tybalt and Mercutio are like the two faces of Janus, the Roman god of transition: one of them proffers a strict order, respect for tradition, obedience, and a clearly delineated, albeit mandatory, object of loyalty, while the other pokes fun at that order and sees in it only human wretchedness, mystification, and a mask that disguises its hollowness. Order and authority against play and laughter.

Tybalt, with his lack of a sense of humor and his inability to recognize irony, who is as haughty and affected as an expensive purebred dog, and who denigrates those of mixed breed whom he feels to be beneath him, emerges as the guardian of order and authority, while the debonair Mercutio, an ironist by vocation who masks his limitless sensitivity and vulnerability with his wit, throws out a challenge to order and authority, at one and the same time demystifying the world of Verona laden with bombast and vanity.

In his famous Queen Mab speech, Mercutio temporarily casts aside his mask, and, his face exposed in the presence of his friends, holds forth like a true critic of his era and society, deriding its *vanitatum vanitas*. This aristocratic rogue, forever bestrewing obscene jokes, pronounces on human dreams, secret fantasies, aspirations, and visions in such a way that we find difficult to believe the monologue was written more than three hundred years before Sigmund Freud. Worthy in itself is Mercutio's notion that we dream and fantasize about that for which we constantly yearn but which we cannot achieve in reality. Mercutio is a moralist in disguise whose aristocratic cynic's mask allows him to remain in the same state of youthful exuberance and lust for life as his loyal, albeit predictable, friends Romeo and Benvolio.

A good measure of gender-dependent ambivalence and sexual masquerade occurs in *Romeo and Juliet*. This duality permeates all of Shakespeare's work and is a common feature of the Renaissance era in general. This is because male actors in Shakespeare's Globe Theatre and in other London theaters of the day played female roles, and the use of female masks by male aristocrats and their deliberate concealment of gender created massive erotic tension and agitated the ladies' imagination. Luigi da Porto's novella describes how Romeo subjugated Juliet's heart during the ball at the Capulet home by wearing the mask of a young woman.

No one recognizes others in the decisive ball that takes place at the Capulet residence; this is only natural since it takes place during carnival time. The conscious disguising or improvisation of each person's identity creates a short-lived peace. How can you despise the mask of an insect or a pig? You do not see your enemy. The tensions dissipate along with the possibility of exchanging looks. Only that genius of hatred and conflict, Tybalt, is exempted from all of this, since he manages to recognize the masked Romeo by his voice.

The life of a society and of its individual members is created by dipping into a chest of instruments that is not wide or deep. Everyone wears clothing, everyone needs food, everyone thirsts for intimacy and eroticism, and everyone seeks security and recognition. But precisely at this juncture we encounter the inevitable duality of social life: clothing can mean both the tramp's rags and a luxurious silk shirt; wealth can secure people's dignity and increase their freedom, but it can also lead to their debasement; organized and legitimate power is capable of greatly diminishing the level of depravity and violence in a society, but, at one and the same time, it can cause the death of many innocent people; sex can become an act of brutality, violation, and humiliation, but in other circumstances it can liberate persons and make them happy. All of this comes about from that selfsame human material, from that same person's body and its means of self-realization.

Here Friar Lawrence who, in his morning monologue, reflects most rhapsodically on virtually all of the dualities in the phenomena of social existence and most fully understands that the distilled essence of the same plant can heal us yet poison us, and that death is our abiding companion during all of our lesser or greater moments of joy in life. Friar Lawrence's medicines are supposed to save Romeo and Juliet, but they actually kill them.

The Prince attempts to save Verona from the grips of destruction stemming from the discord between two powerful families by using his civilized and legitimate powers, and he seemingly achieves his aim. Yet the question remains: Is Verona the better for this, having liberated itself from hatred, but having lost some of its loving citizens, who were also beloved by the entire city? Is it morally acceptable to engage in social engineering and apply it to the warring clans by using people's souls, as well as their love and attachment, as building materials or instruments of politics?

In the end, even love is something greatly ambivalent and dangerous. It integrates and restores to wholeness the loving personality, but at the same time love can send a person into the ditch of perennial existential deficiency where that same love engages in a predatory exploitation of another person's body and soul to which the exploiter is oblivious. This can lead to the ruin of another human being who has the same right to freedom and happiness as anyone else. Ultimately, the activity of loving always leaves open the bleak possibility of seeing it transform into a hatred which feeds on itself and which annihilates everything.

Love and hatred threaten an individual's autonomy equally. In simple terms, both the person who is consumed by love and the person who is consumed by hatred experience the insufficiency of their own existence. They need another personality, or another person's life, to experience their own identity, to witness their being and their meaning in the world. If that other person becomes for someone merely an extension of the body or a mechanical adjunct to the ego, this leads to destruction in its truest sense, though this is rarely grasped as such.

Beyond any shadow of a doubt, love creates or recreates a personality, integrating it and filling it with bounteous life. But a treacherous boundary exists, as with every passion, which when reached can transform love into its opposite, and which can develop into the annihilation of a personality, seeing it change into another individuality. Passion is dangerous, more so because it always affects the parties and their fate differently. In the case of Romeo and Juliet, passion transforms both of these young people beyond recognition, re-creating their personalities and human identities.

We behold in *Romeo and Juliet*, the manner in which nearly all modern forms of consciousness, identity, and social diffusion can be discovered in Shakespearean tragedy: the birth of the modern individual; love and friendship as foundational forms of modern society; conflicts of loyalty; the collision of elements in traditional and modern societies; a hatred for the unsteady and unclear modern world in which order and hierarchy are being demolished. At the same time, we observe how a world sparkling with the aesthetics of the Renaissance carnival reveals to us the mystery of the birth of the modern individual and of modern society.

The modern individual is created not by the inherited objects of loyalty and not by a ready-made structure of identity, but by the other individuals and other objects in the world that the individual chooses freely. Modern society is created by solidarity, love, and friendship, which are not based on blood ties. Hatred originates most often when people find themselves in no man's land and in barren territory. The modern world of freedom and self-creation is becoming frightening for some—they find it foreign and impossibly distant—while the paradise of kith and kin no longer exists. We have been banished from it, just as puberty sooner or later banishes us from childhood and tosses us into the world of adults.

7. Love and Friendship in *Romeo and Juliet*

Romeo and Juliet pokes fun at sonnets. For good reason, Mercutio, after the ball at the Capulet residence, unaware of the love between Romeo and Juliet, and believing that Romeo, who often changed the objects of his heart's desire, is still enamored with Rosaline, ribs his friend while demonstrating perfect command of classical literary technique:

> Without his roe, like a dried herring. O flesh, flesh, how art thou fishified? Now is he for the numbers that Petrarch flowed in. Laura to his lady was a kitchen wench (marry, she had a better love to berhyme her), Dido a dowdy, Cleopatra a gypsy, Helen and Hero hildings and harlots, Thisbe a gray eye or so, but not to the purpose. (Shakespeare, 1992, 93)

Unquestionably, Juliet surpasses Romeo in the maturity of her feelings. Whereas Romeo has not changed but transfers his love for Rosaline to Juliet, who then becomes his fateful love, Juliet undergoes a metamorphosis. She transforms from a child to a strong-willed woman, who fights for her love. Romeo, because of Juliet, loses the opportunity to do battle with his surroundings. Juliet, meanwhile, is given the chance to live out an entire drama by opposing her parents who want to marry her off to Paris, without having second thoughts or otherwise shaking her belief in Romeo's innocence and justness regarding Tybalt's death.

But the symmetry ceases in the sphere of friendship. As Harold Bloom has remarked accurately comparing Shakespeare and Miguel de Cervantes, "friendship in Shakespeare is ironic at best, treacherous more commonly," yet "the friendship between Sancho Panza and his Knight surpasses any other in literary representation" (Bloom, 2004, 82). Hamlet's ties to Rosencrantz and Guildenstern, or the dramatic relationship between Othello and Iago, reveal the unachievability of friendship, or, at least, its dangerous powers of transformation and the conflicts it can engender.

One of friendship's most unexpected instances occurs between Romeo and Mercutio. In the end, Mercutio dies for his friend not as a hero who knows his fate and is aware of the circumstances leading to his taking of that step, but as knight-joker, hoping for an exploit right up to his last breath, believing in the power of humor and playfulness. Though Mercutio behaves bravely, his friendship with Romeo does not change him. In the face of his own will, Mercutio becomes a tragic figure. Out of this emanates his curse on both quarrelling families: "A plague o' both your houses!" (Shakespeare, 1992, 121).

After the retreat of the injured Mercutio and Benvolio, Romeo, having a presentiment of Mercutio's death, speaks of his loyal friend as of a true knight:

This gentleman, the Prince's near ally,
My very friend, hath got this mortal hurt
In my behalf. My reputation stained
With Tybalt's slander—Tybalt, that an hour
Hath been my cousin! O sweet Juliet,
Thy beauty hath made me effeminate
And in my temper softened valor's steel. (*Ibid.*, 123)

Curiously, Romeo describes the effect of Juliet's beauty and love much in the same way in which Machiavelli, in *Discourses on Livy*, judges Christianity for its dangerous ability to render men weak and effeminate: "This mode of life thus seems to have rendered the world weak and given it in prey to criminal men..." (Machiavelli, 1998, 131). Yet a powerful Christian ethos of fidelity and self-sacrifice distinguishes Romeo and Juliet's love from a manifestly and proudly pagan Callimaco's passion for Lucrezia in *Mandragola*.

Nothing softens valor's steel in Mercutio's temper. Mercutio is a trickster to himself, but his friends recognize in him an honorable and chivalrous friend. The tensions in the clan and in friendship, and, most importantly, the tension between Tybalt and Mercutio, are resolved fatefully in Romeo's soul after Mercutio's demise. This is addressed by Benvolio first in bearing witness to the death of his noble companion:

O Romeo, Romeo, brave Mercutio is dead.
That gallant spirit hath aspired the clouds,
Which too untimely here did scorn the earth.
(Shakespeare, 1992, 123)

For Shakespeare, friendship is not an object of optimism. An honorable and just ruler, such as Escalus who seeks to instill civil concord in Verona, avoiding acts of revenge and clan wars, is more realistic and possible for Shakespeare than friendship in cases where political power is interlaced with it. Consider Escalus's counterpart in Shakespeare's *The Tempest* (written in 1610–1611, published in 1623), Prospero, who uses his magical powers perspicaciously and refrains from exacting retribution. The characters in Shakespeare's comedies find it incomparably easier to be true friends than those of his tragedies. A joke and trick underlie Mercutio's ability to be a friend. He is a foreign body in the gallery of characters who populate Shakespeare's tragedies.

The squire Sancho Panza becomes Don Quixote's one true friend. Sancho manages to overcome his own vulgarity and lack of faith. From the very outset of the novel, Sancho scrupulously represents the principle of reality. Don Quixote, in contrast, represents the principle of imagination. But the servant increasingly takes on the ideas of his lord. Bloom draws attention to the close tie between Shakespeare's Hamlet and Falstaff in *The Merry Wives of Windsor* (1602) and Cervantes's Don Quixote and Sancho Panza: "Hamlet and Don Quixote, Falstaff and Sancho Panza represent something new in the tradition, since all of these are at once surprisingly wise and dangerously foolish" (Bloom, 2004, 98–99).

We could also assign to this group, but only partially, Mercutio who is poised between wisdom and foolishness. Whatever the case, they are all linked by their casting off of serious and dramatic social masks. Something exists for them of greater importance than the monumentality of power and abject strength in the world of people.

The friendship among equals, be they knights or humanists, is well-known to scholars of the Renaissance and of the Middle Ages. Recall the friendships between Tristan and King Mark, between King Arthur and the Knights of the Round Table, and between Thomas More and Erasmus of Rotterdam. In his *Utopia*, More immortalized his friendship with the Antwerp humanist Peter Giles (see Bray, 2003). We can surmise that the friendship between Romeo, Benvolio, and Mercutio has overtones of latent homosexuality and that this was behind Mercutio's jealousy at Romeo's infatuation with Rosaline.

The psychogenesis and sociogenesis of love and friendship in Shakespeare's *Romeo and Juliet* help us to retrace the contours of the birth of the modern world. These two great literary creations are a map of modern consciousness and modern society's moral imagination. Of utmost importance are the works' revelations of the relationship between power and imagination during the transitional period when Europe's entire spiritual universe, which we refer to as the world of the Middle Ages, became extinct.

Not only did the ethics of chivalry vanish, but so did a code of conduct, a constellation of values, and a worldview. The two works discussed portray the birth of the world which we recognize as modernity. An analysis of the relationship between political power and moral imagination, grounded on major works of world literature, allows us to retrace the emergence of the modern form of sensibility, and at the same time the climax of the earlier worldviews and their mental strata.

One of these foundational transformations, which changed in its essence the entire sociopolitical, sociocultural, and mental life of Europe and the Western world, was the end of the medieval era that extended one thousand years. The spiritual cartography of this great transformation is a part of the secret of the creative success of Shakespeare and Cervantes. We can claim that *Romeo and Juliet* and *Don Quixote* reveal the death knell of the medieval personality and the psychogenesis and sociogenesis of the modern individual.

These works are the culmination of a form of moral imagination and mentality. In *Romeo and Juliet*, we can encounter the rudimentary version of friendship that was later referred to as romantic friendship, which the eighteenth-century writer Harriet Bowlder described as the union of souls (Faderman, 1981, 68). This form of sensibility and version of friendship emerged on the grounds of classical examples, among sixteenth-century aristocrats.

Works Cited

Berlin, Isaiah. "The Originality of Machiavelli," Isaiah Berlin, *Against the Current: Essays in the History of Ideas*. London: Hogarth Press, 1979, pp. 25–79.

Bloom, Harold. *Where Shall Wisdom Be Found?* New York: Riverhead Books, 2004.

Bray, Alan. *The Friend*. Chicago & London: University of Chicago Press, 2003.

Cassirer, Ernst. *The Myth of the State*. London & New Haven, Conn.: Yale University Press, 1974.

Donskis, Leonidas. *Forms of Hatred: The Troubled Imagination in Modern Philosophy and Literature*. Amsterdam & New York: Rodopi, 2003.

Elias, Norbert. *The Civilizing Process*. Oxford & Cambridge, Mass.: Blackwell, 1994.

Faderman, Lillian. *Surpassing the Love of Men: Romantic Friendship and Love between Women from the Renaissance to the Present*. New York: William Morrow, 1981.

Greenblatt, Stephen. *Renaissance Self-Fashioning: from More to Shakespeare*. Chicago & London: University of Chicago Press, 2005.

———. *Will in the World: How Shakespeare Became Shakespeare*. New York: W. W. Norton, 2005.

Machiavelli, Niccolò. *Discourses on Livy* (1531). Chicago & London: University of Chicago Press, 1998.

———. *Mandragola* (1524). Indianapolis, Ind.: Bobbs-Merrill Educational Publishing, 1980.

———. *The Prince* (1532). Boston, Mass.: Dante University Press, 2003.

Mansfield, Harvey C. *Machiavelli's Virtue*. Chicago & London: University of Chicago Press, 1996.

Paster, Gail Kern. "*Romeo and Juliet*: A Modern Perspective," in William Shakespeare, *The Tragedy of Romeo and Juliet*, New York: Washington Square Press, 1992, pp. 253–265.

Rougemont, Denis de. *Love in the Western World*. Princeton, N.J.: Princeton University Press, 1995.

Shakespeare, William. *The Tragedy of Romeo and Juliet* (1597). New York: Washington Square Press, 1992.

Stendhal, *Three Italian Chronicles*. New York: New Directions, 1991.

White, Michael. *Machiavelli: A Man Misunderstood*. London: Abacus, 2005.

Two

POLITICS AS TRAGEDY: SHAKESPEARIAN TREATMENT OF MACHIAVELLIAN THEMES

David Coombes

"…This is no world
To play with maumets and to tilt with lips.
We must have bloody noses and cracked crowns,
And pass them current, too. God's me, my horse !"—*Henry IV Part One*, II/5 88

"Alone I did it" *Coriolanus*, V/6 117

The plays attributed to William Shakespeare show an exceptionally realistic awareness of how individuals behave in a political setting. In particular, they reveal poignantly both how the ambitions that drive human beings to engage in the political life inevitably turn out to be frustrated, and that the sentiments which provide the initial pretext for such an engagement become, no less irresistibly, adulterated by experience. No matter how altruistic the ambitions and the sentiments may appear to be, the effects of political engagement invariably prove harmful for both the elected leaders and those—often today in their millions—who follow them.

The essentially tragic nature of politics is as prevalent and observable in our own time as it was in the England of Elizabeth I, and as it was in the earlier periods of history that provided the settings for most of Shakespeare's dramatic works. Those plays are thus of lasting value for any who pursue politics, whether as students or practitioners. They expose the pervasive imperfection of human nature, and the fallibility of attempts to perfect it with a precision and empiricism greater than any self-appointed political science.

Like any tragic revelations worth the name Shakespeare's bear on a central paradox, in this case: that human beings habitually seek a solution to their imperfect condition in dependence on personalised power, when the effect of so doing is to expose themselves all the more to the consequences of man's inherent cupidity, fear and ignorance. For those are qualities that inhere in political leaders—hereditary, appointed or elected—no less than in the rest of us mortals. Indeed, they are likely to be even more pronounced in those who seek a politically active life, if we acknowledge that people are attracted to politics in the first place at least partly out of an excess of those very same defects of character (and in search of a stage where they can be exposed with greater impunity).

On the transition to modernity

Shakespeare's dramatic treatment of politics serves as a vital introduction to modernity as do the much earlier, and far more technical, political writings of Niccolò Machiavelli, who is often regarded as the true forebear of a modern scientific or "comparative" approach to politics. Common to both authors, above all, is a desire to represent their contemporary society as one to which politics is central.

It is at first sight not surprising that both Machiavelli and Shakespeare had this leading perception of the time in which they respectively lived, given that the former was political adviser to the Medici rulers of late fifteenth and early sixteenth century Florence, and the latter more or less official dramatist at the successively Elizabethan and Jacobean courts in England one hundred years later. Indeed, each lived at either end of a secular historical transition, through which previous spiritual sources of authority in human affairs, above all the universal Christian Church, gradually but irrevocably lost credibility and status both as an ultimate arbiter in disputations over political power and as a means of reconciling human beings generally to their own mortality.

Civil society did not thus supersede traditional authority in early modern Europe without prolonged resistance, hesitation and conflict. If Machiavelli was the first modern to offer a more or less coherent theoretical explanation of *political change*, Shakespeare's plays—above all the histories, the tragedies and those with classical themes, but also a few of the comedies—deliberately exploit the dramatic potential of what amounted to a contemporary social revolution. The plays thus reflect a social context in which political authority is always highly precarious, and its efficacy constantly fluctuating. By the end of the sixteenth century a new European system had emerged of sovereign states, governed by highly-personalised despotisms, claiming direct authority from a divine source. Yet the same system was still interspersed by catastrophic interludes of anarchy, famously described later (in 1651) by the English political philosopher Thomas Hobbes as reflecting mankind's natural condition in the absence of a supreme power: "warre of every man against every man."[1]

In fact, the cost of an arbitrary ruler's failure to command strict, universal and unquestioning obedience in such a society of emergent possessive individualism could be, and often was throughout Europe, complete breakdown. We still live in the conditions determined by that same post-medieval transition from communal loyalty to individual responsibility. Only such a radical presumption of the validity of human will could give sense to the famous question, "To be or not to be." The ultimate personification of the dilemma is not Hamlet the Dane, however, but the Roman Coriolanus, trapped in the self-destructive freedom to pick allegiance at will.

> "...Let the Volsces
> Plough Rome, and harrow Italy: I'll never
> Be such a gosling to obey instinct, but stand,
> *As if a man were author of himself*
> And knew no other kin;" (*Coriolanus*, V/3, 22–2. Italics added)

In the new politicised world of modernity, not only do an increasing number of lay individuals find themselves obliged to play at politics for survival, but political engagement becomes a typical pre-occupation of ordained ecclesiastical authorities, whether as in Machiavelli the Pope himself, or pre-reformation ecclesiastics of the Roman Church in England in the works of Shakespeare.[2] The political role of ecclesiastics of the established church was still a major source of public grievance, and ultimately civil war, in England of the seventeenth century.

Machiavelli and Shakespeare, each in his different time and place, prophetically identified the same typical virtues and vices in a social milieu irresistibly absorbed with political controversy. Although we might wonder how Shakespeare could have come to read and understand the fifteenth century Italian Machiavelli, we may assume that his main published works were accessible to most who would have aspired to positions of power in the government of late sixteenth and early seventeenth century England.[3] In fact, Shakespeare's own treatment of politics, and the moral and practical issues thus raised, follows Machiavelli's own with remarkable fidelity. The English playwright was in turn to have an enormous and fundamental influence on how politics is understood, almost wherever politics is recognised to exist and to affect human intercourse. At least some part of the dramatist's work will have been compulsory reading at some stage in the formal education of all those whose main language is English, and even many born where other languages predominate. Whether they will have always realised it or not, their educational—let alone theatrical—exposure to Shakespeare will have thus introduced the educated, and the governing, classes in the now massively-expanded English-speaking world to Machiavelli's own doctrines about the use of public power. We are, therefore, concerned here with perspectives and doctrines that are—visibly or not—part of what determines how we are customarily governed now.

We should now be ready for the main focus of this analysis, which is to reinterpret Shakespeare's opus as potentially subversive of the widespread trust in the personalisation of supreme power that has persisted from his own to our current time.

Political realism

King: "Rebellion in this land shall lose his sway" (*King Henry IV Part One*, V/5, 41)

"Take away kings, princes, rulers, magistrates, judges, and such states of God's order, no man shall ride or go on the highway unrobbed, no man shall sleep in his own house or bed unkilled, no man shall keep his wife, children and possessions in quietness; all things shall be common and there must needs follow all mischief and utter destruction." From: "A Homily on Obedience (1547)" cited in Elton, G. R. (1960) *The Tudor Constitution: documents and commentary* Cambridge : Cambridge University Press, page 153.

One crucial similarity between Machiavelli and Shakespeare is that both are occupied exclusively with what we might call (following the definition suggested by Raymond Geuss) *real politics*.[4] Despite the obvious influence of secularisation, there is little in either Machiavelli's commentaries or Shakespeare's dramas to imply that the task of politics is, ought to be, or even could be, to set out to improve the lives of the masses, either by assuming responsibility for their economic welfare, or by legislating to promote ideals of ethical conduct, let alone to provide their emancipation from either economic or social dependency.

The overriding preoccupation of politics in Shakespeare's work is how to prevent, limit or amend the harmful consequences of civil disorder. Since politics is thus seen as being essentially about the power of one individual or group to enforce its will on another, and since there are always those who are willing to exercise power for selfish ends, then the central problem of politics, and incidentally its value as drama, is the constant struggle between rulers and ruled over access to power (epitomised famously by Lenin as кто кого: Who Whom?). The fact that the same struggle invariably breaks into violence affecting the health and safety of all those dependent on a particular system of rule, has encouraged political "realists" to accept that lasting peace may be possible only when one individual or group is able to assert absolute authority, even if the process of doing so costs the lives and liberty of themselves and others.

This is the *leitmotif* particularly of Shakespeare's two cycles of plays treating the history of the government of England over the previous two centuries of almost continual civil disorder. Always insecure, the legitimacy of rule based on the dynastic principle, itself derived from the monotheistic belief in the direct sanction of ruling monarchs by divinity, collapsed into a long period of civil war in England during almost the whole of the fifteenth century, mainly between rival factions each claiming to be the true descendants of Edward the Black Prince (1327–77). The main subject-matter of Shakespeare's first cycle of historical plays is the outbreak, unfolding and resolution of the "War of the Roses." These works expose most vividly the disastrous consequences that may follow the absence of politically competent leadership. This cycle culminates in the accession to the throne of the Lancastrian Richmond, whose victory in battle ends the tyrannical reign of the Yorkist Richard III, whose dramatic representation in the play bearing his name presages a number of other famous portrayals by Shakespeare of maladjusted and overtly villainous political personalities, done with a psychological, as well as political, insight that is extraordinarily modern. The key significance for our present theme, however, is that the civil war is thus brought to a welcome close by the first Tudor monarch, King Henry VII, grandfather of Elizabeth, at whose court in London the cycle of plays were first performed, seemingly as an extended parable designed to deter rebellion against the then established Tudor dynasty.

The vehemently Protestant government of Elizabeth I was much more stable and secure than its predecessors, though it was also probably even more despotic and indifferent to human rights and to the claims of minorities. Despite the growing influence of a new class of increasingly independent commercial interests, neither political nor religious dissent was tolerated, and those who dared nevertheless to oppose the regime, and risk detection by its secret police, were liable to summary torture and execution. It is very likely, therefore, that the provincial poet and dramatist, William Shakespeare (whose father had been a Catholic), owed his recognition and standing at court, as well as his coat of arms and house at Stratford, to royal favour which had been carefully cultivated.

Reflecting on these biographical factors, but also on the content of the plays, Graham Greene was persuaded to call Shakespeare the "one supreme poet of conservatism, of what we now call the Establishment," and accusing him of cowardly subservience to a dictatorship under which other more courageously dissident literary and intellectual figures met contrasting fates.[5] Greene's iconoclasm regarding Shakespeare seems to have some justification.

The typical and widespread practice of personalised dictatorship in our own age, which Greene must have had in mind when making these claims, tends to be similarly defended by political realists as the only alternative to anarchy or barbarism. Shakespeare's willingness to write publicity for the monarchical despotism of Elizabeth and her successor, James I may well to some degree cast him in the role of precursor to today's political "spin-doctors."

Whatever the genuine reason might be, Shakespeare's history plays are replete with such political realism. The insecurity evidently felt by the Elizabethan court doubtless owed much to the previously notorious instability of the government of England, continually exposed domestically to the depredations of powerful local warlords, and the effects of dynastic rivalry, schismatic religious fundamentalism, and ethnic diversity. Elizabeth's government had to face additionally the overt and militant hostility of neighbouring—predominantly Catholic—European powers, especially the current rulers of France and Spain.

Shakespeare's second cycle of historical plays actually depicts a period of history immediately prior to that covered by the first cycle, but demonstrating the relatively benign consequences of personal rule when the prince is capable of exercising effective political leadership, especially when practiced on Tudor lines and by previous members of Elizabeth's own dynastic lineage.

Much of the dramatic content of these plays revolves around the political formation and maturation of the popular Prince Hal, eventually to become King Henry V, whose debonair invasion of France, culminating in the famous military victory of the English citizens' army at Agincourt, and firm but merciful pacification of domestic strife, had allowed the English people during a substantial part of the fifteenth century to enjoy a rare period of domestic peace, and security against (and prowess over) traditional enemies abroad.

Shakespeare presents Henry V's decision to pursue his popular invasion of France as applying a key Machiavellian precept. In fact, he is following advice previously given by his dying father, whose speeches in *Henry IV Part Two* amount almost to a manual on the practice of government, in which Machiavellian thought is pervasive. The old king is telling his heir of his own efforts to protect his tenure against the rival ambitions of the powerfully militarised English nobility, who were still all too ready to re-open the question of his own legitimacy:

> "...Therefore, my Harry,
> Be it thy course to busy giddy minds
> With foreign quarrels; that action, hence born out
> May waste the memory of the former days." *Henry IV Part Two*, V/5, 213–8[6]

Nevertheless, despite the obvious advantages of such historical representations as propaganda for the contemporary Tudor monarch's own foreign policy, and to justify her demands for total obedience domestically, the dramatist repeatedly hints at evidence in this later cycle that the historical regime in question contained the seeds of its own eventual and tragic disintegration, even with regard to the notoriously triumphal and even jingoistic *Life of Henry V*. The hero of that overtly propagandist political drama did after all, as Prince Harry in both parts of *Henry IV*, betray an indifference to civic responsibility turning at times into sheer delinquency, especially in the famous bawdy scenes with one of Shakespeare's most popular invented characters Sir John Falstaff and his drunken cronies in a tavern-cum-brothel in London's Eastcheap. The crown prince may be represented in this way to be a far more attractive and humane character than his chief antagonist, the rebellious, typical man of action Hotspur (also known as Henry Percy), or for that matter his own younger brother, John, who shows cruelty as both regent and warrior. Seen from the perspective of today's political and social values, however, and especially in the light of what he was to become as ruler, many of us must judge Prince Harry to be no less repulsive (as either inebriate "drop-out" or sober war-monger) than his counterpart Harry Percy. (Both of them, however, would doubtless qualify for Tony Blair's typical approbation as "having balls"!).

Dare we surmise that these are the first revelations of the playwright's own typical ambivalence toward the virtue of political engagement, and his increasingly overt scepticism about the reliability of personalised power, as he must have seen it at unusually close quarters. Indeed, the nauseatingly masculine political realism of the Henries has already been set in contrast to the feminine pusillanimity and idealism of King Richard II himself, in the first play of that name in the later cycle of history plays. There above all the dramatist's own ambivalence is hardly concealed, and when reading or producing *Richard II* today it is surely difficult for anyone with liberal sentiments not to feel more partial to the stoical though neurotic King than the frantic and revengeful Bolingbroke. Moreover, the latter, who becomes King Henry IV in two later history plays, continues to lack both grace and mercy, exposing glimpses of the guilt-ridden paranoia which is to take the full spotlight in the later tragedies.

Much theatrical blood gets spilled throughout both series of history plays. The real violence, both among the ruling elite and the suffering masses, must have been terrible enough—on a par with the modern terrors of internecine violence. The gory melodrama in Shakespeare's historical dramatisations is, nevertheless, accompanied by a remarkably crafted, and highly suggestive discourse of political theorising, in which Shakespeare begins to reveal not only an otherwise concealed subversive instinct but also a prudent concern with a fundamental and enduring problem of modern secularised society: how to insure political authority against the inevitable fallibility and wilfulness of personalised power. In both these respects he mirrors, consciously or not, very similar and characteristic traits of Niccolò Machiavelli.

Legitimacy: Traditional and Modern

"...God knows, my son,
By what bypaths and indirect crook'd ways
I met this crown; and I know well
How troublesome it sat upon my head." (*Henry IV,* Part Two, IV/5, 184–8)

Kent: "...you have that in your countenance which I would fain call master.
Lear: "What's that ?"
Kent: "Authority" (*The Tragedy of King Lear*, I/4, 27–30)

Although he gives a central place to the goddess *Fortuna*, Machiavelli rejects the idea that people should simply submit to their fate in the question of who governs whom. On the contrary his published works on political conduct clearly assume that liberty is the main object of political engagement, and by that he means the liberty of all who qualify for citizenship and not just a privileged few. In this respect he is doing no more than articulating a growing though still radical conviction in his time, one that would continue to grow over the centuries to come: that the legitimacy of those who claim entitlement to govern a political community must depend ultimately on their efficacy in establishing and safeguarding, and even expanding, the liberty of its members.

In the famous book, or manual of advice to princes, *Il Principe* (*The Prince*, published posthumously in 1532) Machiavelli elaborates his view of freedom as self-government—*il vivero civile*—and sets out his conclusion that the prerequisite qualification for success in political life is *Virtù. Virtù* corresponds in English to the modern concept of "virtuosity" more than the conventional understanding of "virtue," which usually carries moral connotations. Part of Machiavelli's purpose, indeed, is to overturn the prevailing ideal of the good ruler as one who essentially abstains from harm, and does good acts, in conformity with Christian ethics. Of course nobody who knew about politics at that time could have reasonably supposed that such an ideal was ever applied in practice even, if not especially, by those ecclesiastics including the Popes who openly engaged in politics for selfish material ends. Nevertheless, Machiavelli's critical point is that political *Virtù*, even when falling short of ethical standards upheld by religion, could still be virtuous to the extent that it enhanced the possibility of self-government for a given community. Indeed, he goes so far as to imply that action with such consequences is even necessary for the attainment of virtue in a broader sense, including the conventional idea of moral goodness, since human beings are so vulnerable in practice to the influence of *Fortuna*—the systematic unpredictability of human affairs, when they are conducted either privately or in the public sphere. The perception of legitimacy that was to become prevalent by the time that Shakespeare wrote his plays was of course greatly influenced by such ideas. Shakespeare could not have written about politics in the distinctive way that he did had that not been so.

As we have seen in the previous section, his intention must have partly been to justify the hereditary legitimacy of Elizabeth I, and to undermine those seeking to challenge it for their own political purposes. In fact, the Tudor despotism had not adequately resolved England's longstanding problem with political succession and was far from completing English subjugation of the whole of the British Isles. Elizabeth's own authority was openly threatened by rival claims, most critically that of Mary Queen of Scots. What is especially significant about Shakespeare's treatment of the theme of legitimacy, however, is his implicit recognition that it is about far more than the need to establish a genuine right of inheritance. That particular aspect was still fraught enough, if only because royal personages so freely availed of the prerogative to sleep with whom they fancied, while Elizabeth's particular claim could be—and was—disputed by devout Catholics on the grounds that her father married her mother (who was already pregnant at the time) only after having been divorced from his previous (Spanish) wife amidst great international controversy and in defiance of papal authority. However, the history plays, and especially those in the second cycle, can be read as admitting an essentially modern, secular criterion of legitimacy as effectiveness in binding a political community together and protecting its integrity in other words: Machiavellian virtue, or "political virtuosity."

In *Richard II*, it is significantly a prelate, the Bishop of Carlisle, who asserts unequivocally the traditional principle of the Divine Right of Kings, when the challenger Bolingbroke seeks to ascend the throne in Richard's absence:

> "And shall the figure of God's majesty,
> His captain, steward, deputy elect,

Anointed, crowned, planted many years,
Be judged by subject and inferior breath,
And he himself not present ?" (*The Tragedy of King Richard II*, IV/1, 116–20)

However, what the bishop invokes as reason for observing tradition is the dire consequences that could follow when "a subject can give sentence on his king." His speech is prophetic, though with hindsight for Shakespeare and his audience, since his first cycle of history plays already described the prolonged and disastrous civil war that was eventually to follow in the fifteenth century:

"And in this seat of peace tumultuous wars
Shall kin with kin and kind with kind confound.
Disorder, horror, fear and mutiny
Shall here inhabit, and this land be call'd
The field of Golgotha and dead men's skulls." (IV/1, 142–5)

The bishop's reward for thus speaking truth to power is to be summarily arrested for treason. The new King Henry IV ultimately withholds the normal punishment of death, hinting thus at an admission of self-doubt concerning his own questionable claim to the throne.

These political dramatisations do, indeed, aptly mark a highly significant turning point of European—and political—history, the "Machiavellian moment." It is the time after the crucial—some would say fatal—question has already been asked. In such a time, and we still live in its aftermath, even the boldest disciples of reason must pause to wonder: what if we do not find an answer to that question or at least one we can all accept; what if the subjects do give sentence but cannot find means to implement it.

The consequences of rationalism in politics are even more adventurously and intensively explored by Shakespeare in the three great plays set in ancient Rome. In this regard, *Julius Caesar* must probably be deemed the apogee of Shakespeare's political theatre. Here we find an early but highly perceptive recognition of the state as a neutral, abstract embodiment of the public interest transcending claims to rule based merely on dynastic legitimacy. Indeed, the Roman plays reveal a legitimate public discourse on the nature of power, in which the transient and inherently untrustworthy nature of personalised power is recognised. The solution for Machiavelli is the establishment of political institutions in the form of a republic, on the contemporary model of Venice or Florence itself, but above all on the model precisely of ancient Rome. It is in his other major political work, the *Discourses on the First Ten Books of Titus Livius*, written almost simultaneously with *The Prince*, and essential companion to it, where Machiavelli describes, with ample reference to those models, the possibility of transforming either tyranny or anarchy into civil order.[7] This is in effect what we now take for granted as the modern state. Machiavelli does not actually employ that concept (describing the kind of political community of which he is writing as a city or *cività*). However, he does conceive the republic as an overarching social institution, capable of embodying legitimacy in a collective and de-personalised form, and representing all the different classes of the people, in accordance with fixed constitutional rules (*ordine*) and procedures (*modi*).

In Shakespeare's version, the republican conspiracy to assassinate the consul Caesar, in order to pre-empt his seizure of absolute power, ends in tragedy, certainly for the conspirators most of whom take their own lives. The existing republic is instead transformed into an oligarchic triumvirate of former Caesar loyalists (including his son Octavius). The real dramatic interest of the play lies in the unwinding of a tangled conflict between, on the one hand, virtue as an objectively calculable set of Machiavellian qualities, such as "honour," rhetorical skill, and valour and, on the other, more inscrutable and discrete emotional attributes like loyalty, fraternity, duty and even love.

The same crisis of civil set against private identity runs centrally through the other two Roman plays, but in them is developed even further in terms of an inner personal conflict and not just an outer public one. The tension is nevertheless still provided by the tragic outcome of vain attempts to use political aspiration as a device to evade personal destiny, *Virtù* to outsmart *Fortuna* in Machiavellian terminology. Thus, Antony is ultimately able to exploit his charismatic authority only to secure the devotion of the fatally narcissistic female ruler of a minor principality of Rome's world-wide empire ("The triple pillar of the world transform'd into a strumpet's fool," as Octavius Caesar nicely puts it, in *Antony and Cleopatra*, I/1, 12) ; and Coriolanus pursues his Nietzschean project of self-liberation only to be humiliatingly disempowered by his subconscious craving for a mother's approval ("There's no man in the world so bound to his mother..." *Coriolanus*, V/3, 158).

However, the key figure to represent the "new politics" of abstract reason, capable of overriding both popular will (what we would now perhaps call "democracy") and traditionally legitimated authority, is Marcus Brutus, whom Antony, comparing him with the other conspirators against Caesar, famously calls "the noblest Roman of them all" (*Julius Caesar*, V/3, 68). Shakespeare makes Brutus's nobility reside not only in his political status as a patrician but also in his resolute pursuit in practice of virtuous qualities of honour and truth, even at the expense of his own personal happiness and that of his own kith and kin (including his wife, Portia, who kills herself rather than continue to face the strain of her husband's political engagement).

Brutus's personal tragedy, as the one who fatally stabs the man he allegedly "loves" (Caesar), reflects his own lack of political realism. Thus despite his constant appeals to honour, and excellent reputation for virtue ("And Brutus is an honourable man" *Julius Caesar*, III/1 95), he turns out to be wanting in Machiavellian *Virtù*. Before the coup he is insufficiently ruthless or tactically smart to let the other conspirators have their way and prudently remove Antony as well as Julius. After it he rejects Cassius's prudent advice to prevent Antony from cynically stirring plebeian sympathy for the deceased Caesar, and then misses the opportunity to exploit divisions between Antony and the other two triumvirs, whose own motives and actions seem anything but honourable. In the outcome Brutus leaves the republic that he claims to love even more at risk than ever. The moral becomes crystal clear to the realist Caius Cassius, who sees too late that Brutus's idealism is fatal for their cause and destined to lead it into defeat in an ill-starred battle against Caesar's self-appointed successors.

However, in their respective ends both Caesar himself and Cassius are shown dramatically to have failed in the primary obligation of political engagement: to respect the natural unpredictability and unmanageability of human affairs in the face of *Fortuna*. Her influence is the great Mystery which Caesar ignores when he mocks the Soothsayer's warning not to venture out on the fateful ides of March, and which Cassius denies with the erroneous and foolhardy rationalist assumption:

The fault, dear Brutus, is not in our stars
But in ourselves, that we are underlings (*Julius Caesar*, I/2, 141)

Thus even a comparatively shrewd and rational actor like Cassius is ultimately foiled by the unpredictability of events: "Alas ! Thou hast misconstrued every thing !", says Titinius as he ironically places a victory garland on his master's corpse (*Julius Caesar*, V/3, 80).

Power: Temporal and Spiritual

Brutus: "There is a tide in the affairs of men,
Which, taken at the flood, leads on to fortune.
Omitted, all the voyage of their life
Is bound in shallows and in miseries." (*The Tragedy of Julius Caesar*, IV/2 270–5)

Aufidius: "... So our virtues
Lie in the interpretation of the time." (*Coriolanus*, IV/7, 49)

"And let the angel whom thou still hast serv'd
Tell thee, MacDuff was from his mother's womb
Untimely ripp'd." (*Macbeth*, V/7, 43)

One method Shakespeare uses to exploit political realism for dramatic effect is his main characters' typical failure to stand up to Fortune at a critical moment.[8]

Another far more significant tragedy is the tendency for people, including those innocent of self-seeking or guile, to get caught up in the sway of political action, often despite themselves. Shakespeare thus gives a foretaste of the totalitarianism nowadays implicit in all forms of the modern state. This may be a reason why Shakespeare continues to be so popular and not only among English-speakers in a world that has become so appallingly experienced in extreme forms of political violence and oppression (and observe in particular his persistent appeal to the Russian intelligentsia).

It is, however, in his great tragedies that Shakespeare fully develops his insights into the personal conflict inherent to lives inextricable from politics. Each of the protagonists in successive plays is found to be in circumstances partly beyond his or her control that are in themselves, to say the least, challenging, but acquire the potential for catastrophe, on account of a particular personal shortcoming, which leads to fatal action or inaction: one who suspects his uncle of having murdered his father in order to marry his mother; a highly successful mercenary soldier whose vulnerability to racial prejudice is exacerbated by his decision to have an affair with his employer's daughter; an irascible geriatric who has rashly turned over his property to two of his three daughters only to find himself viciously abandoned by them; another successful soldier who has been, possibly unjustly, forced to take a subordinate position to socially better-placed relatives, and so face rejection by his concupiscent and probably drug-crazed wife.

Each case could be read as one of personal misfortune, derangement or handicap which, though not certain to cause delinquency, might be considered at least liable to attract attention from the social services. It is nevertheless turned into full-scale tragedy by the degree to which each of the protagonists concerned is obliged to assume some kind of political responsibility, and so to take action, ultimately drastic action, to fulfil what he or she perceives, or is persuaded, to be a moral or political obligation.

Hamlet, the Crown Prince of Denmark, is at first astute in using the passage of travelling players to test, and possibly expose, the guilt of his usurping and adulterous uncle, the new King Claudius. This virtuous ruse turns out successfully, but also leaves Hamlet even more vulnerable to Claudius's devious efforts to remove him as an evident political rival. For his part Hamlet, the "sweet" prince, has no stomach for the political life, and few of the necessary skills beyond wit and eloquence; he cannot even make up his mind whether it is worthwhile and even truly rational to confront outrageous fortune at all. So he basically runs out of time and in the process—as it eventually turns out fatally—provokes the enmity of Laertes, whose not-so-chaste sister he has cruelly (and again fatally) jilted and whose father he has carelessly killed. Laertes is noticeably far less equivocal than Hamlet about his own filial duty and legal rights. His is thus overall the stronger claim to *Virtù* in Machiavelli's sense and the better model of political skill at overcoming *Fortuna*. The invading Norwegian Fortinbras, who makes a brief but highly significant intervention at the end of the play, presents an even greater salutary contrast to Hamlet in terms of political style.

Perhaps the situation of intellectuals in totalitarian regimes in more recent times may be said to mirror Hamlet's pathetic combination of morally-sound dissidence and well-educated hesitation to go into blatant opposition, which would inevitably be seen as political in consequence even if not so in intention. Indeed, one way of interpreting this particular drama may be to see the stirrings in Shakespeare of an early kind of "anti-politics," of which more needs to be said below. Nevertheless, Hamlet's prudence, even if it is usually read more as sheer procrastination, might be considered well justified, given that he represents the perhaps the main threat—other than that of the invading Fortinbras—to what is depicted as a ruthless and powerful regime. To the play's other main characters, including Hamlet's own mother and his girl friend, the rebellion looks like ordinary madness ("O, what a noble mind is here o'erthrown !" See Ophelia's speech in *Hamlet*, III/1, 158.). The same was of course commonly alleged of similarly intellectual dissidents in the USSR.

The playwright is on politically safer ground with the story of the racially-abused and exploited Othello, who is undone ultimately by his own exaggerated piety ("For nought I did in hate but all in honour," *Othello*, V/2) and delusive self-importance ("I have done the state some service, and they know 't'." *Ibid*.). What is most remarkable politically about this play is Shakespeare's most extensive and convincing characterisation of modernist cynicism in the role of Iago. Iago's soliloquies, asides and homilies (especially those spoken to poor Cassio whose role as stooge becomes vital to the plot against Othello) articulate an essentially unprincipled, self-seeking side of political realism, which belongs to a personality that is at one and the same time both manic and manipulative, ever calculating to deceive others but hardly more than it also deceives itself.

> "In following him, I follow but myself;
> Heaven is my judge, not I for love and duty,
> But seeming so, for my peculiar end:
> For when my outward action doth demonstrate
> The native act and figure of my heart
> In compliment extern, 'tis not long after
> But I will wear my heart upon my sleeve
> For daws to peck at; I am not what I am."
> (*Othello*, I/1 58–65)

It is important not to mistake such an attitude, as some have been tempted to do, with Machiavellian realism, of which it is at best mere caricature. Iago's view of the world and of his place in it has nothing of *Virtù*. Othello's, in contrast, does strikingly have many of the prerequisites of that politically supreme quality, but his psychology nevertheless turns out to be crucially flawed, not only by what Machiavelli would have immediately recognised as a detrimental excess of sentimentality, if not narcissism, but also possibly by the same hedonism which lies at the root of Iago's own megalomania. There is simply no other way to explain Othello's vulnerability to Iago's elaborate deception, or his inability to perceive the true dangers of Iago's highly modernist moral relativism ("Virtue ? A fig! 'Tis in ourselves that we are thus or thus. Our bodies are our gardens, to which our wills are gardeners" *Othello*, I/3, 319–20).

Thus Shakespeare creates in Iago (more skilfully than in the earlier and similar character of Richard III) an uncanny model for the political psychopath who was to become so prominent and pivotal in the totalitarian politics of the twentieth century. Rarely then or since has the catastrophic tension in such a personality's perception of self and other been so well encapsulated, along with the consequent impossibility of compassion: "Were I the Moor I would not be Iago" (I/1 57).

In *Macbeth* the horror of such moral relativism, especially when combined with denatured legitimacy, is taken to an even greater extreme. Indeed, the character of the usurping Scottish king would seem almost too fantastic if it did not resemble so alarmingly the beliefs and behaviour of so many political leaders of our own age. We hear and read daily topical examples of Macbeth's characteristic indifference to the effects of his reckless actions on innocent, even accidental, victims, and of his and his wife's insanely persistent denial and desperation to wipe out the evidence of the violence she has persuaded him to perpetrate.[9]

One way of understanding the degeneration of Macbeth and his queen into hallucinatory madness, which in both cases resembles a *delirium tremens*, and in her case leads to suicide, is as a dire warning of the reflexivity of terror as an instrument of power and its capacity to reproduce itself and become endemic even to a whole society. As victims of modern totalitarianism know all too well, in a reign of terror neither retribution nor repentance may be possible without death, while in modern politics the mortal consequences may affect multitudes, and in a manner that is both mindless and pointless. Yet Shakespeare somehow seems to have become aware by the time he writes *Macbeth* of this awful and even inevitable potency in the very nature of modern politics.

It is impossible not to suspect a reflection here of Machiavelli's notorious dictum that, other things being equal, it is better for a prince to be feared than to be loved.[10] Nevertheless, the right way to interpret Machiavelli in this respect is surely as a vital warning about the risks inherent in excessive reliance on personalised power, and above all on the typically modern tendency to regard legitimacy as derivable from mere performance or, even worse, popularity. Macbeth's crucial flaw, as presented by Shakespeare, is what political journalists would nowadays probably call "short-termism": "If it were done when 'tis done, the "twere well it were done quickly." (*Macbeth*, I/7 1–2) What seems impossible for Macbeth and his wife is the necessary prudence of delayed gratification, along with the associated ability to trust other people's honesty, and not least one's own. Appeal to magic or mystery is no substitute for such trust, and will always lose out to simple faith, not of the blind variety but the kind that derives from sober and undistorted perception of the facts. Political leaders who rely on the horoscope are not to be trusted, nor indeed are any who have been convinced that they are the agents of some pre-ordained destiny or infallible instinct.

So even this most fearsome drama, from which all that we recognise as humanity seems otherwise to have been removed, reveals its characters' way to their own redemption, as every tragedy can and must. As so often with Shakespeare, the crucial passage is both short and to all appearances has nothing to do with the main action, which is coming at that point to its final unfolding. It is the sudden, seemingly accidental intervention of the "doctor" in the play's penultimate act, who describes to Malcolm and Macduff his recent observation of the King of England's power to heal an endemic sickness among the local population: "Such sanctity hath Heaven given his hand." Macduff asks Malcolm "What's the disease he means," and gets the reply: "Tis called the evil" (*Macbeth*, IV/3 147–8).

In other words Machiavellian virtue is not to be confused with mere strength and boldness of will or even what Tony Blair likes to call "grip" and George Bush Junior an ability to exploit "decision points." Those particular qualities may be positively helpful to political leadership and, indeed, even necessary in some circumstances. However, Malcolm himself—soon to be the tyrant's successor, and we may assume, Scotland's redeemer—offers to the appointed avenger Macduff a much longer and far more humane list of:

> "... The king-becoming graces,
> As justice, verity, temp'rance, stableness,
> Bounty, perseverance, mercy, lowliness,
> Devotion, patience, courage, fortitude..." (*Ibid.*, IV/3 92–5)

Shakespeare thus shows his capacity to give deeper shade to bare political realism in the Machiavellian mode. His work is replete with examples to demonstrate that politics, in the definition of Geuss, "is about action and the contexts of action, not about mere beliefs or propositions."[11] But he was also remarkably sensitive to the historical context in which his theatre was presented as one where people turned increasingly to political institutions in order to give meaning to human purpose otherwise rendered futile by mortality. The emerging nation-states were designed to act efficiently in real time to suppress or satisfy both internal and external threats to their integrity. They were also to become increasingly objects of the ambitions and fears of ordinary individuals, whose lives *en masse* would gradually become inextricably dependent on states and how they were governed.

National Identity: People and Territory

Although the idea of democracy plays hardly any part in the political perspectives of either Machiavelli or Shakespeare, the former's highly innovative approach certainly relies much on a conception of the people, especially those ordinary members of the political community able and willing to assume a measure of civic responsibility. For Machiavelli, indeed, republican or civic virtue is both a possible and a necessary aspiration for all members of a political community. Legitimacy is thus no longer seen as depending upon a permanently fixed and unquestionable hierarchy of social relationships. Moreover, Machiavelli claims that the ordinary people offer at least as reliable a guarantee of political virtuosity, including respect for the laws (*ordine civile*), as the nobility, and more reliable certainly than those who have accumulated great wealth at the expense of others (what Machiavelli calls *gentiluomini*). Social equality is therefore a necessary safeguard against the corruption to which all political institutions are liable.

Shakespeare does not seem to recognise the people in such a benign or reproductive sense. The politics of the histories and tragedies is essentially court politics, engaging a closed group of characters, all of them privileged and exclusive. The (usually drunken) "common herd" is strictly confined to a role of entertainment, expected either to amuse or to disgust ("mechanic slaves with greasy aprons, rules and hammers" *Antony and Cleopatra*, V/2, 210), or at best confirm the necessary exclusivity of aristocratic rule. Whether as comics, soldiers or spectators ("shouting plebeians") the people's role is subsidiary, and always dispensable.

Even when politics does take to the streets, as it often does in the Roman plays, the people's intervention tends to be ill-informed, disruptive and untrustworthy. *Julius Caesar* opens with a scene in which workers prepare a popular demonstration in support of Caesar, whom the conspirators led by the noble Brutus suspect of preparing a *coup d'état* with popular backing. It seems that Coriolanus and his mother are not alone in finding the masses both unworthy of respect and incapable of sound political judgement: "Cats, that can judge as fairly of his worth as I can of those mysteries which heaven will not have earth to know," *Coriolanus*, IV/3, 33. Democracy thus seems alien to the whole Shakespearean conception of government. The state as a political organisation exists to secure territory rather than people.

Therefore, while the historical plays provide a formidable literary foundation for an emerging nation-state, it is constructed primarily of an invented idea of "Englishness." The chief beneficiaries of any consequently increased security are the English ruling class, exercising right of possession claimed through inheritance. Shakespeare's imagery gives to English nationalism what has continued to be an enriched sense of linguistic identity, while it also provides plenty of rhetoric to legitimate the appropriation of physical space already occupied by others. Both contributions have provided English nationalism with a substance that it would otherwise lack: the first helps create the myth of English exclusionism, and the second excuses the territorial imperialism that has been the primary, and in some ways only, means available to integrate such a mongrel population of immigrants of diverse origin as the so-called English.[12]

Shakespeare willingly endorses the myth that the first destiny of this imagined race is to impose itself on the unruly, mysterious and largely Celtic tribes belonging to the rest of the British archipelago[13]. Justification is then provided (especially of course in *Henry V)* for military expeditions to reclaim French territory on the neighbouring mainland. Subsequently of course the English were to impose themselves wherever else in the world they could find land inadequately claimed or defended by others. Although that more expansionist project had only just begun when Shakespeare wrote, he has been aptly described as the supreme exponent in English literature of the "Imperial Theme."[14]

That theme reaches its apogee in the intoxicated exuberance of world domination which distinguishes *Antony and Cleopatra* both as narrative and as poetics. There is something extraordinarily redolent of our own post-modern age in that late play's obsessive repetition of imagery associated both with what we nowadays call globalisation ("His legs bestrid the ocean ... Realms and islands were as plates dropped from his pocket," V/2, 82) and with politics as a contest for total domination: Cleopatra describes Octavius, after the demise of Lepidus and Antony, as "Sole sir o'the world" V/2, 120. Similar language is often used today in relation to an American president.

Such global imperialism certainly makes the Florentine republicanism of Machiavelli seem almost parochial. Although the latter was a strong and early advocate of Italian unification, and a famous admirer of the Roman empire, he would hardly have approved of the far-flung ambitions of conquest and exploitation that have since inspired Anglo-Saxon imperialism. Indeed, he would surely have considered it a dangerous threat to republican virtue. In this respect perhaps more than any other, Shakespeare's politics betray a significant difference from Machiavelli's, above all in the former's lack of a sense of distributive justice, and habitual tendency to treat public authority as inseparable from political will, seen as the pure will of opportunistic individuals, and thus a matter subject to pure contingency, and prevailing force. The difference helps to indicate how already in the sixteenth century the Anglo-Saxon individualism, which is given such resonant and enduring voice by Shakespeare, had begun to diverge from the main European political tradition, to which Machiavelli gave essential foundation in his espousal of political self-determination as the noblest aspiration of modern man, of civic responsibility as its primary condition, and of the citizens' army the best instrument of its realisation and defence.

Beyond Politics: Power as Truth and the Truth about Power

"Take physic, pomp,
 Expose thyself to feel what wretches feel,
 That thou mayst shake the superflux to them
 And show the heavens more just." (*King Lear,* III/5, 30)

"I have a journey, sir, shortly to go:
My master calls, and I not say no." (*King Lear*, V/3 116)

A further, and in some ways even more interesting, divergence is revealed by comparing the responses of Machiavelli and of Shakespeare, respectively, to the core problem of personalised power. Machiavelli's ultimate remedy is, in short, republican politics, which offers a kind of general sublimation of the human character through deliberate political engagement: the *"vivere civile"* or public life. Shakespeare's—at least in the late plays—is rather a withdrawal into private reflection and remorse, if not into silence[15].

Those same later works offer a very different perspective on politics from the fatuous patriotism criticised by Graham Greene. It does seem that Shakespeare himself must have eventually recognised, far ahead of his time, that to glorify nationalism and ridicule the commons was in itself self-contradictory and no solution to the catastrophic tendency of public power when vested in a single individual.[16] *King Lear*, which must have seemed almost seditious when performed at the court of King James I, is surely far ahead of its time in undermining the idea of sovereignty as well as that of property, hence that of the state itself. The imagery of this late play is far more egalitarian and subversive than anything that went before. In *Coriolanus* we see the people actually rise up with consequence with even Coriolanus's patrician wife and mother on their side.

Even more interestingly, however, from *King Lear* through *Timon of Athens* to *The Tempest*, Shakespeare seems to be moving into a much more profound and even skeptical view of the real human condition as transcending politics and maybe not susceptible to remediation by human power alone, even, and perhaps especially, the heroism of exceptional individuals. One indication of this anti-heroic revelation is the increasing use of domestic servants to play key roles in the action, of which they are invariably wiser and more compassionate observers than the political protagonists themselves, especially in the Roman plays (Lucius, Enobarbus, Charmian) but also in the tragedies (most notably Emilia in *Othello*, but also the unnamed servant who tries, fatally for himself, to prevent the blinding of Gloucester in *King Lear*). The crucial motive of their intervention is always some degree of compassion, a human quality that cannot be constrained by distinctions of race or class.

On the stage the outcome for the protagonists themselves is invariably death, usually violent and often self-inflicted. The fear of annihilation, which is a predominant motif in *Macbeth* with its accompanying dread of future time, is transformed in *Lear* into pure nihilistic despair: "Nothing shall come of nothing." As the most pathetic victim in this play, Cordelia (rather like Hamlet) is condemned essentially by her refusal to act politically, in other words, her actual indifference to time. Yet that abstention is also her unique beauty, and what attracts her future protector, the King of France:

"Fairest Cordelia, that art most rich, being poor,
Most choice, forsaken, and most loved, despised,
Thee and thy virtues here I seize upon.
Be it lawful to take up what's castaway." (*King Lear*, I/1, 250)

Cordelia's more or less accidental death is meaningless and unnecessary as that of the millions murdered on state authority in our own age—probably why it stirs us so severely. This portrays a terrible *untimely* intervention by a relentless and unforgiving fortune. It poignantly demonstrates the truth eventually realised by Lear himself, in his monologues on the heath, with the fool, the madman and the vagabond for audience, that in such a world of arrogant human creation, justice is itself empty of meaning and incapable of palliative effect.

The preponderant role of death throughout the tragedies not only ridicules aspirations to immortality, but also renders space non-proprietary, as in the homelessness of both Lear and Timon. At the same time *Virtù* is transformed into something even more important, yet also more pervasive, than what Machiavelli defined. As observed by Kent and other impartial witnesses Lear himself, though too late to save his own life, learns as harshly as possible how to feel compassion, to take the side of the wretched of the earth.[17] Is this perhaps another moment, just like Richard II's prison soliloquies, when Shakespeare openly admits the riddle of what a more recent playwright has called "the power of the powerless"[18], and glimpses the importance of what lies beyond both time and space ?

If Kent's mysterious last words in *King Lear* (cited above as a motto for this section) suggest a sense of resignation that is spiritually inspired, he surely provides a model of stoical endurance for one of Graham Greene's typical anti-heroes; in a much later age Kent would surely have been a radical Latin American priest.[19] Shakespeare's own public persona should perhaps be seen, therefore, not as the fawning apologist of Tudor despotism, but rather dissident closet intellectual, posturing as loyal servant to the Crown when overt opposition to power is simply too dangerous.[20] Machiavelli faced, and survived, a similar ambivalence in his own time under the Medicis. It seems to re-appear in the confessions and biographical accounts of similar famous survivors of despotic regimes, no less unfairly accused of sycophancy by later critics. Dmitri Shostakovich must be a leading musical counterpart, and the irony, subtlety and innuendo of his music, along with its intensely tragic perception, show qualities similar to both the later dramatic writing of Shakespeare and the political discourses of Machiavelli.[21]

The acceptance of powerlessness, even the celebration of its realisation, is completed in *The Tempest*[22]. Shakespeare's ultimate resolution of what might well have been a painful inner conflict seems to exemplify what John Keats, writing two hundred years later, with explicit reference to Shakespeare, would describe as "negative capability," which can be also defined as the wisdom of compassionate disengagement.[23] Machiavelli, who faced a similar predicament, but one more devastating personally, when he was tortured and banished by the state he had loyally served, was not discouraged from continuing to regard positive and well-reasoned political engagement as necessary. This divergence, therefore, looks very like the juxtaposition, which the late Harold Pinter noted in his Nobel lecture of 2005, of the dramatist's compulsive search for a truth that is immanent, however fugitive in practice, and the politician's conviction that the only real truth is power itself.[24] Juxtaposed, possibly irreconcilable, these different views of truth must nevertheless have the space to co-exist in any society in which there is a genuine aspiration to liberty. Therein lies the tragedy and the task of politics.

Notes

1. Hobbes, Thomas (1996) *Leviathan* (edited by Richard Tuck) Cambridge :Cambridge University Press, page 90.
2. See the role of the Archbishop of York, as leading dissident, and hostile reactions to that role, in *Henry IV Part One*, and how in *Henry V* (I/2) it is the Archbishop of Canterbury who goads the reluctant king into war against France.
3. For an indispensable account of the reception of Machiavelli in the English ruling class of Shakespeare's time, see Pocock, J.G.A (1975) *The Machiavellian Moment: Florentine political thought and the Atlantic Republican tradition* Princeton NJ : Princeton university Press, pp. 330–60. On Machiavelli's wider relevance for political thought and action, see Crick, Bernard (1970) "Introduction" in *Niccolò Machiavelli: The Discourses* Harmondsworth: Penguin, pp. 11–71.
4. Geuss defines "real politics" as "concerned in the first instance not with how people ought ideally (or ought "rationally") to act, what they ought to desire, or value, the kind of people they ought to be, etc, but rather with the way the social, economic, political, etc, institutions actually operate in some society at some given time, and what really does move human beings to act in given circumstances." (Geuss 2008 *Philosophy and Real Politics* Princeton University Press, p. 9)
5. Greene, Graham "The Virtue of Disloyalty" in Adamson, Judy, ed, (1991) *Reflections* New York: Viking Penguin. I am grateful to Thomas Coombes for having drawn my attention to this text of an address given in 1969 upon the award of the Shakespeare Prize by the University of Hamburg.
6. With at least temporary success in electoral terms, Thatcher, Bush and Blair have each consciously applied the same policy in recent times. Under the administrations of the younger Bush , it became indeed a leading official tenet of US foreign policy.
7. Probably the most accessible English versions of the two works mentioned here are: Machiavelli, Niccolò (2005) *The Prince* Translated by Bondanella, Peter, Oxford :Oxford University Press ; and Crick, Bernard, editor, using the translation of Walker, Leslie (1970) *The Discourses* London :Penguin Books. Most of what I say about Machiavelli here is based on my reading of two vital works of criticism, which greatly elaborate the implications of Machiavelli's work for political theory, and also for the understanding and practice of government in England and elsewhere: Pocock, J.G.A. (1975) *The Machiavellian Moment : Florentine Politi-*

cal Thought and the Atlantic Republican Tradition Princeton: Princeton University Press ; and Skinner, Quentin (2002) *Visions of Politics, Volume II : Renaissance Virtues* Cambridge : Cambridge University Press.

8. See Geuss 2008 pp ; 31–4. Geuss uses the classical Greek concept of καιρός , as the crucial opportunity for action that will not re-occur and must be seized immediately, to describe the nature of this particular political skill.

9. For example, the reckless decision-making that led the leaders of USA and UK to order the invasion of Iraq in 2005, in defiance of international law, and their desperate attempts then and subsequently to suppress the evidence of their real motives, together with their persistent denial and self-delusion in face of their own mismanagement of the conseequences, are all present in this notorious play, from which their typical rhetoric might even have been borrowed.

10. The chief reason given by Machiavelli himself is that : "Men are less hesitant about injuring someone who makes himself loved than one who makes himself feared, because love is held together by a chain of obligation that , since men are a wretched lot, is broken on every occasion for their own self-interest; but fear is sustained by a dread of punishment that will never abandon you." Machiavelli (2005) pp. 57–9.

11. Geuss, *op.cit.* p.11

12. On the role of imagination in the invention of national identity, see Anderson, Benedict (1983) *Imagined Communities :Reflections on the Origin and Spread of Nationalism* London : New Left Books.

13. Henry IV is constantly having trouble with the Welsh, particularly; the future Henry VII takes advantage of Richard II's engagement in putting down Irish rebellion to mount his own *coup d'etat;* and the Scots are a repeated threat to English peace, especially when allied to rebellious northern barons.

14. The appropriate title of a celebrated work of literary criticism by G. Wilson Knight (1931) *The Imperial Theme* London :Routledge.

15. "Let my gravestone be your oracle. Lips, let four words go by and language end." *Timon of Athens* V/2, 105.

16. It was of course quite different from the nationalist ideology that was to inspire the French Revolution two centuries later.

17. For the blinded Gloucester the cruel lesson is that it may be better, and even necessary, not to see, so that true love may enter in. As Lear advises him "Robes and gowns do hide all. Get thee glass eyes. And like a scurvy politician, seem to see the things thou dost not." IV/5, 160.

18. Vaclav Havel in Vladislav, J, ed, (1986) *Living in Truth* London: Faber and Faber, pp. 36–123.

19. Compare Henry VII's decision at the end of *Richard II* to join the crusades: "To wash this blood off from my guilty hand." The priest appears in Greene, Graham (1940) *The Power and the Glory* London :Heinemann.

20. On the critical distinction between dissidence and opposition in the politics of the totalitarian state, see Vaclav Havel, *loc.cit.*

21. See Volkov, Solomon (2004) *Shostakovich and Stalin : the extraordinary relationship between the great composer and the brutal dictator* Translated by Bouis, Antonina W. New York ; Little, Brown.

22. See above all the Epilogue spoken by Prospero: "Now my charms are all o'erthrown, And what strength I have's mine own, Which is most faint..."

23. Gittings, Robert, editor (2009) *John Keats : Selected Letters* Oxford University Press, pp. 35–7 and pp. 41–2. "I mean *Negative Capability*, that is when man is capable of being in uncertainties, Mysteries, doubts, without any irritable reaching after fact and reason." (Letter to Geroge and Tom Keats 21 December 1817.) I am grateful to Sarah Hosford for having first explained this reference to me.
24. Nobelprize.org :literature/laureates/2005/index.html

Part Two

CIRCUMSCRIBING THE POLITICAL

Three

OTHELLO, THE SECRET OF THE POLITICAL

Cory Stockwell

The Secret Sharer

We begin with a text that aches to reveal its secret. We begin with its dark passenger.

We begin with *Othello*, Act 2, Scene 3, a scene deeply concerned, like the entire play, with the question of beginnings. The setting is Cyprus, at the palace of Montano, the governor; yet in fact the palace functions more like a courtroom.[1] Someone will be judged here, and he will be judged wrongly. The judgments commence at the very beginning of the scene. Othello commands his lieutenant, Michael Cassio, to stand watch during the night, giving this task to his first in command as though he already sensed the approach of danger. This watching is crucial.[2] As we shall see, it comes up again and again in this scene, which is fitting for a place in which judgments are to be made—what is more central to a courtroom, after all, than testimony, the reporting of what one has seen? Cassio, of course, obeys the command, responding to Othello thus: "Iago hath direction what to do;/But notwithstanding, with my personal eye/Will I look to't."[3] The slippage between I and eye is of course very interesting here, reinforcing the importance of testimony: the very ability to speak (to say "I") in this scene will depend upon the ability of the respective characters to see, and to report what they have witnessed. But rather than focusing on this, let us give some thought to the position of Iago, Othello's ensign, in this exchange between general and lieutenant. Othello tells Cassio to stand guard—to watch, in other words; Cassio responds that Iago has already been given this task. Iago, however, ultimately answers to Othello—and we must therefore ask if it is not the latter who has given Iago the task, and who nonetheless decides to "double up" the task, to command Cassio to also keep watch—to keep watch over the watcher, as it were. Of course, the command could have come from somewhere else. Yet it is interesting in this regard that Cassio so immediately acquiesces to the general's wishes. Even though Iago has already been given this order, Cassio seems to say, he will also "look to't," as though Iago's watch were not enough, as though the latter were not completely trustworthy.

How does Othello respond to Cassio's assurance? He seems satisfied, and immediately retires with Desdemona, followed by their attendants, leaving Cassio all alone (but only for a brief moment, as we shall presently see). Before taking his leave, however, he states: "Iago is most honest" (6). Othello thus seems to concur with Cassio regarding Iago's honesty; indeed, his words complete the line begun by Cassio's last words. And he concurs in more ways than one. For despite the fact that he judges Iago honest, Othello does not for all that change his command: Cassio is still to keep watch, even though Iago is to keep watch. Othello's real agreement with Cassio, therefore, is on the need to keep watch over the watchman: Cassio's injunction is not lessened by the fact that it is identical to that of Iago. It is almost as though Othello were telling Cassio to watch himself, to be careful in the presence of Iago.

And this presence is not long in coming. Immediately after Othello, Desdemona, and everyone else depart—before Cassio can speak a single line (for with rare exceptions, it is only Iago, in this play, who speaks when alone)—Iago comes upon the scene. He is greeted warmly by Cassio, who tells him "Welcome, Iago. We must to the watch" (12). We will have more to say about the first sentence of this line below, but for now, let us return to the watch (for which, the ensign informs the lieutenant, it is "not yet" the hour [13]). Iago and Cassio spend a few moments conversing about, among other subjects, Desdemona ("What an eye she has!" [21], states Iago; "An inviting eye" [23], concurs Cassio). Iago convinces Cassio to have a drink, to celebrate the averted battle with the Turks, and Cassio, provoked by Roderigo (as per Iago's plan), soon loses his temper, first attacking Roderigo, and then Montano. Bells are rung in alarm, Othello is called, and Iago once more remarks upon the watch: "Help, masters!" he cries, "Here's a goodly watch indeed" (150).

And it is at this point that Othello, who shall come to act as judge of all that has happened, makes his return.

His first words upon his return are among the most famous lines of the play:

> Why, how now! Ho! From whence ariseth this?
> Are we turned Turks, and to ourselves do that
> Which heaven hath forbid the Ottomites?
> For Christian shame, put by this barbarous brawl! (160–3)

Words of admonishment, therefore, that seek to separate, on ethnic and religious grounds, those present from their enemies. In the first line of the passage we have just cited, Othello asks: "From whence ariseth this?" It is telling that he immediately poses this question, since for the remainder of this scene—until he departs once more, leaving Iago alone with Cassio—all of his efforts will be with the intent of answering this question: how, he asks again and again, did this begin? In his attempt to get to the bottom of what has happened, he will adopt several different strategies: he will make speeches on the need for order and discipline in a time of war; he will exhort the men to be honest, and laud this quality as among the most important a military man can possess; and finally, he will interrogate each of the "defendants" individually, putting each of them on the stand, as it were: over the next ninety or so lines, until the moment he departs, he will direct specific questions to Cassio, Montano and Iago.

It is this last series of questions that interests us here, the questions he poses directly to his ensign. He speaks to Iago exactly four times. And on each of these occasions, I shall argue, his speech does more than what it says it does: on each of these occasions, his words, at the same time as they demand clarification from Iago, or give him orders, or compliment him, also *accuse* him—they charge him with crimes-in the very act of purporting to do otherwise.

Let us look more closely, then, at these utterances. Immediately after the lines we cited above, in which Othello commands all present, in the name of Christianity, to "put by this barbarous brawl!", he continues thus:

> He that stirs next to carve for his own rage
> Holds his soul light: he dies upon his motion.
> Silence that dreadful bell; it frights the isle
> From her propriety. What is the matter, masters?
> Honest Iago, that looks dead with grieving,
> Speak: who began this?–On thy love I charge thee! (164–169)

We will focus here on the last two lines of this passage, where Othello turns his attention specifically toward Iago. On the one hand, the meaning of these lines is clear: Othello looks to Iago for the true version of what has happened; he asks Iago to speak in the name of the love he purports him to possess. Yet clearly the statement states more than just this. When we hear the words "Speak: who began this?", must we not also hear, if we are listening attentively, "Speak, who began this"; or, put slightly differently, "Speak, you who began this"; or again, with only a slight variation, "May the one who began this be the first to speak!" Othello, in other words, as he himself states in the very next sentence, can be seen to *charge* Iago with the crime here, with bringing about—beginning—the entire situation.

Perhaps this interpretation is a bit far-fetched; perhaps, given everything we know about Othello's trust in Iago, we are reading too much into his words. But what, then, should we say about the fact that Othello continues to make accusations—what should we make of the fact that as the scene continues Othello continues to accuse Iago? Let us return to the text. After Iago has responded to Othello, stating that he "cannot speak/Any beginning to this peevish odds" (175–6), Othello turns his queries first to Cassio and then to Montano; finding their responses inadequate, however, he becomes angry, and states: "Give me to know/How this foul rout began, who set it on" (200–1), before turning once again, at the very end of this speech, to Iago. He exclaims to the latter: "Tis monstrous! Iago, who began't?" (208).

Again, this seems to be a simple demand for clarification, and yet if we shift our standpoint just slightly, it is not difficult to hear in these words an accusation. First, can the words "who set it on" not be read, rather than as an interrogation of the identity of this "who," as an address *to* this very "who"? From this standpoint, Othello would seem to say: "you who set it on, tell me how you began it," or, "may the one who set it in motion tell me how it began." A reading that is supported by the last line of this speech, for the words "'Tis monstrous! Iago, who began't?", at the very same time as they ask this question, also utter this accusation: "'Tis monstrous Iago who began't!"[4] In Othello's second address to Iago, then, we find a second accusation, one that reinforces the first.

The third address follows in much the same vein. After a long speech by Iago, in which he gives Othello a version of the events in question that is at once true and false (true, inasmuch as he relates exactly what has happened; false, inasmuch as he omits the fact that he knows the man who has fled, Roderigo— omits, in other words, the very fact that would prove that he himself "began't"), Othello states the following: "I know, Iago,/ Thy honesty and love doth mince this matter,/Making it light to Cassio" (237–9). And in speaking thus, Othello seems at the same time to say: "If anyone knows Iago, it is I. He has minced the matter completely, forcing it to light upon Cassio. Therein lies his true honesty, his true love."

Othello then dismisses Cassio from his service—convicts him, as it were. And after uttering some very interesting and ambiguous words in the direction of Desdemona, and ensuring Montano that he will receive the best care for his wounds, Othello speaks to Iago for the fourth and last time: "Iago," he says, "look with care about the town,/And silence those whom this vile brawl distracted" (246–7). Yet again, it is as though two Othellos spoke here, one issuing the most banal and predictable command possible, and the other giving Iago a blunt warning, telling him that he knows exactly what he is up to, and that Iago would best watch himself wherever he goes.

We are thus witness in this scene to a very strange turn of events: Othello, who elsewhere in the play charges himself with a lack of eloquence,[5] here proves himself to be an incredibly dextrous speaker, finding the very words that allow him to say two things at once. And I mean this in the most literal way possible. One is tempted to say here that Othello "says one thing and means another": in saying, for example, "Tis monstrous! Iago, who began't?", Othello would *really* mean that he knows Iago is guilty. But this is not the reading I am proposing here. What I am trying to say is this: Othello *both* knows that Iago is honest and that he is absolutely dishonest; the one knowledge does not hide, dissimulate or pervert the other; Othello affirms both sides of this seeming opposition at once, saying yes to each alternative, even though each seems to cancel out the other. It is not that he withholds judgment—on the contrary, he affirms both contrary judgments, holding them in suspension beside one another.

The question then becomes: why would he do such a thing? What is his motivation? In response to these questions, the hypothesis I want to propose is quite simple: what Othello wants to do here, even if unbeknownst to himself, is keep a secret, a secret that he both keeps *to* himself and keeps *from* himself (that he seeks to both *garder* and *se garder*, we might say with Derrida). In each of these utterances, Othello places himself squarely on the terrain of the secret (though we will have to wait a while before we can understand the specific nature of this secret).

How, then, can we understand this motivation, this seeming need for the secret? For we are definitely on the terrain of necessity here, as one of the greatest contemporary readers of Shakespeare, Stanley Cavell, has noted. Toward the end of his book *Must We Mean What We Say?*, in the midst of a reading not of *Othello* but of *King Lear*, Cavell writes:

Of course if Othello had not met Iago, if Lear had not developed his plan of division, if Macbeth had not listened to his wife… But could these contingencies have been prevented? If one is assured they could have been, one is forgetting who these characters are. For if, for example, Othello hadn't met Iago he would have created another, his magnetism would have selected him and the magic of his union would have inspired him.[6]

And Cavell argues, on the basis of these examples, that "a radical necessity haunts every story of tragedy."[7] This necessity, I want to argue here, is what we might refer to as a *need for the secret*, whether on the part of Othello, or the play itself. From the very beginning, the play is invested in a secret, a secret "belonging" to Othello but also shared out among its various characters, a secret that, by its very nature, cannot be revealed (for it would thereby cease to be a secret), but that, as we have just seen in our examination of Othello's statements, is not exactly concealed either (lying, therefore, like every secret, somewhere between concealment and revelation). And the name of this secret, of course, is Iago.

Who, then, is Iago?[8]

Iago, the Dark Passenger[9]

The question is difficult to answer, for the simple reason that Iago is anything but a stable figure—he seems to continually change, to be in a constant state of metamorphosis, and the ways he is described reflect this unstable character.

The question "Who is Iago?" has of course been the object of much debate. And the first place to look for an answer, as is always the case when thinking about the identity of a person, would seem to be the adjectives used to describe him. There is of course one adjective that is used more than any other when describing Iago. He is referred to again and again as "honest Iago," and not only by Othello: restricting ourselves only to the scene we examined above, Cassio employs the adjective on several occasions, and Iago even joins in, referring to himself as honest. Our conclusion here, as in any case in which a word is used too often, is obvious: the very fact that Othello must incessantly refer to his ensign as honest is the surest possible proof that he knows the opposite to be true; in repeating "honest Iago" ad nauseam, what Othello is trying to do, above all else, is convince himself that this is indeed the case—convince himself, in other words, of something he knows not to be true.[10]

We will look at the term "honest" from a very different perspective below; however, for now let us turn to a second adjective that is used to describe Iago. "Welcome, Iago" (12), states Cassio early in this scene, and welcome, as we know, in addition to its use as an interjection, a noun and a verb, can also function as an adjective. Indeed, this is possibly the most interesting of all the adjectives that are attached to Iago: the *OED* tells us that the origin of the word welcome is the Old English *wilcuma,* denoting not so much the one whose arrival brings forth joy or causes pleasant surprise, as the guest or "newcomer" whose arrival is *willed,* desired, hoped for in advance (we are closer here to the terrain of *wilkommen* than *bienvenu*). Iago, therefore—to refer to a very different yet uncannily similar "text"—is very close to the "Mystery Man," Robert Blake's character in David Lynch's film *Lost Highway,* who, when asked by the protagonist (played by actor Bill Pullman) how he got into the latter's house, responds: "You invited me. It is not my custom to go where I am not welcome." Is this not a perfect definition of Iago's place in *Othello*?

"Honest" and "welcome" are not, however, the only adjectives used to describe him. Cassio refers to the ensign, for example, as "good Iago" (30); and in passages we have cited above, Othello names love as one of the qualities he possesses. Are we to take from this plethora of descriptions that Iago simply possesses many good qualities? Or must we, on the contrary, conclude that he possesses no qualities at all? The fact that he is described in such different ways from one line to the next—he literally seems to stop language in its tracks, as the other characters alight on one word after another without ever finding the right one—reveals something essential about Iago: he is *pure semblance*; there is no essence, no truth, that lies behind his appearances, his various masks. To turn to a near contemporary of Shakespeare—one with whom it cannot be doubted that Shakespeare is in conversation for the entirety of this play—Iago, it could be argued, is a perfect Machiavellian hero: rather than adhering to a single quality that he would impose on every set of circumstances, he changes from one nature to the next depending on the demands of the given situation.[11] He is the perfect shape-shifter, and the adjectives that attach to him—or rather, that slide right off of him—show that everyone knows this, even if they do not want to admit to this knowledge.

We have seen, therefore, three of the levels on which Iago works. He is first of all the one to whom the wrong adjective—"honest"—attaches, and as such, he is made into something that he is not by all the other characters of the play.[12] Second, he is the one who is "welcome," whose coming is willed by the play. Third, he is the one to whom *every* adjective attaches, and as such is pure semblance, or the perfect shape-shifter—a kind of "joker,"[13] a universal equivalent or empty signifier. But there is yet another level on which Iago works, a level on which his entire being seems to be a kind of fantasy projection, on the part of Othello, but also of the play itself. To understand this, we need to turn to Iago's name. It is a name that tells us, on the one hand, that he is no more Venetian than Othello, and indeed, his provenance is key here, given that the most important relationship in the play for our purposes is between Iago and the *Moor*. The Oxford Edition of the play[14] reminds us that Iago is a Spanish name, recalling Spain's patron saint, Tiago—Saint Tiago, *Santiago*, known as *Santiago Matamoros* (Saint James, Hammer of the Moors, or literally, Moor-killer), or, as we might improvise, *Sant Iago Matamoros* (and from the perspective of this name, Othello's need for Iago would reflect nothing less than a/the death drive). Yet on the other hand, this foreign name speaks a distinct familiarity: Iago, I-ago, what I myself was a few moments ago; or even I-ego, the one who is twice me, in me more than me, to paraphrase Lacan. It is no exaggeration to say that death, his own death, passes through his mouth every time Othello utters the name of his ensign.

The question of Iago's identity, or lack thereof, leads us to a distinctly political point. In the final section of this essay, I want to argue that the play holds a political lesson[15]: namely, that secrecy is essential to politics, that there is no politics without the secret—without the semblance, without the mask, without dissimulation, without saying one thing and meaning another. And the moment in *Othello* at which this lesson unfolds, the moment at which this is truly revealed to us—revealed without, for all that, becoming any less concealed—is the play's final scene: Act 5, Scene 2, which, much in the manner Act 2, Scene 3, reads like a trial in a court of law. It is to this scene that we now turn, in order to understand the play's *need for the secret*.

Hush

Let us note first, however, that in the scene immediately preceding this final scene—Act 5, Scene 1—yet another skirmish occurs, in which Cassio, Roderigo and Iago are again present. And once again, Iago, here, is invisibly pulling the strings. 5.1 ends with these famous lines from Iago, spoken as an aside: "This is the night/That either makes me, or fordoes me quite" (5.1.127–8). Iago, in other words, is preparing for his final judgment, the judgment that will render him either hero or villain. A judgment, of course, especially in a court of law, depends on a truthful presentation of *all* the pertinent facts, in order that these facts may be considered rationally by the one who judges; and at the beginning of the play's final scene Othello believes he finally has all the facts: he believes, in other words, that he is finally in a position to think clearly about what "began't," about the source of all that, in his mind, has gone awry; he believes himself, in other words, to finally understand the *cause*. He says as much three times in the first three lines of the scene: "It is the cause, it is the cause, my soul–/Let me not name it to you, you chaste stars:/It is the cause" (5.2.1–3). So terrible is this "cause"—he is of course referring to Desdemona, to her supposed tryst with Cassio[16]—that Othello dares not even speak it in the presence of the "chaste stars."[17] Refusing to name that of which he believes himself to be in possession, Othello jealously guards his secret. The repetition of the word "cause" echoes an earlier repetition, that of "honest"; and yet if previously repetition was a sign of anxiety for Othello, in this case it seems that the opposite is true: Othello seems to savour his repetition of this word, believing that he is finally able to speak—to judge—with certainty (as when, a little later, this judge gives Desdemona her death sentence: "thou art to die" [5.2.58], he says).

This seeming certainty begins to unravel, of course, immediately after Desdemona's death. In response to the question, put to him by Emilia, of why he has killed his wife, Othello responds that he did so based on information supplied to him by Iago—by her husband. "Thy husband knew it all" (5.2.139), he tells Emilia, to which she responds with the question: "My husband?" (140)? And here begins another series of repetitions. "My husband?" she states again at line 144, and then yet again at 147. The word "husband" appears nine times in the space of fourteen lines, and this repetition brings to a halt any certainty Othello might have considered himself to possess. Indeed, this word—another "h" word[18]—*intrudes* on the text here, so much so that Othello becomes annoyed, indeed anxious or disquieted, finally responding: "What needs this iterance, woman? I say, thy husband" (148). And Othello yet again proves his extraordinary eloquence here, choosing what must be the perfect description or definition of the coming of this word, "husband," to the text. It is precisely, as Othello says, an *iterance*,[19] a word that comes to us from the Sanskrit root *itera*,[20] from which we derive our words "other" and "alterity." What this iterance, this husband, announces is the opening of a gulf or a chasm in knowledge, a space opening up in knowledge that is other to knowledge itself. This honest husband, he, him, Iago.

The last sentence is very close to what Othello himself says, at the beginning of his disquiet. In response to Emilia's "My husband say that she was false?" (150), he states: "He, woman;/I say thy husband—dost understand the word?–/My friend, thy husband, honest, honest Iago" (150–2). The "He" with which Othello opens his response, this "He" that comes to join the other h-words, is indeed interesting. Just as "honest" has been a kind of empty signifier throughout the play, and "husband" has just announced the coming of an other to knowledge in what Othello had hoped was at long last a realm of certainty, the word "he" seems decidedly unsure as to what it is supposed to designate (unsurprising, perhaps, given that we have moved from proper name to pronoun). This seemingly insignificant word calls to mind Blanchot's remarks upon it in his essay "The Narrative Voice (the 'he,' the neutral)": Blanchot argues that the word "he," in Kafka, marks the precise point (marks it without marking it, one might say—announces that to which no stable location can ever be assigned) at which the *other* enters the text. For Blanchot, Kafka's "he," rather than signifying a character, person, proper name, or even "proper initial" (K., for instance), would constitute what he calls a "void in the work," a kind of "absence-word" (he borrows this term from Marguerite Duras) at which the work, rather than speaking, "falls silent." Yet "silence" is not quite the right word here, for Blanchot insists, again borrowing from Duras, that this absence-word or "hole-word" is not simply silent: "one cannot speak it, but one can make it resound," in the manner of "an empty gong."[21] Such is the case for this "he" in this passage from Othello: it no doubt refers, quite simply, to Iago, and yet there is something else in this word, as with the other h-words we have looked at, that seems to resound or resonate, something that would lie beyond its most obvious signification.

This beyond of signification comes to the fore most perfectly in the next h-word we will look at, since this word is not really a word at all. When Emilia, in response to the lines from Othello we have just looked at, says of her husband "He lies to th' heart" (154) (and "heart" is another word that appears on several occasions in this scene[22]), Othello's dumbfounded response is of the simplest variety: he states, simply, "Ha?" (156). This response could mean many things: a demand for clarification (as in "what?" or "huh?"), an expression of surprise or simple misunderstanding, a simple grunt or murmur, or even an uncomfortable laughter. Yet even in the meaninglessness of this seeming non-word, there is a meaning that makes itself heard here, a meaning that resounds, a meaning that speaks in the very impossibility of its utterance. What, then, does this utterance—"Ha?"—state?

What it states, I want to argue here, is Othello's betrayal of his own secret.

The narrative returns here to Emilia, who, understanding what has occurred, immediately cries out: "help, help, ho, help!" (164). The call is soon heeded, by Montano, Gratiano, and of course Iago ("O, are you come, Iago?" [167], states Emilia). What is striking about Iago's presence in this final scene, however, is his decided lack of eloquence compared to the rest of the play: his words serve only to clumsily threaten Emilia as she reveals his plot;[23] he makes a few implausible excuses, tells lies that are immediately seen through, and then, toward the end of the play, simply falls silent, refusing to speak—"From this time forth," he states, "I never will speak word" (302). This is not, however, an indication that his words have ceased to work. On the contrary, these stammerings and silences of one who had been so eloquent to this point are simply indications that the play has come to an end, that there is no more left to be said because all the necessary work has been done. Or, to put it a different way: if Iago no longer needs to speak here, it is because he has ventriloquized all of the play's utterances to such a degree that his words move about without him even having to speak them. Where, then, after Iago has begun to stammer and eventually falls silent, are his words at work?

They are at work precisely in that which Othello has always believed to lie behind his own speeches, his own utterances. They are at work in Othello's *honour*. At the moment Othello finally understands everything for what it is, it is to this quality that he turns. "But why should Honour outlive Honesty?/ Let it go all" (244–5), he states; and, a little later: "An honourable murder, if you will,/For naught I did in hate, but all in honour" (292–3). *H*onour and not *h*onesty, *h*onour and not *h*ate: this is the *virtue* of which Othello has been guilty, from the very beginning of the play, even if unbeknownst to himself. Othello's plight, however—and here we return to Machiavelli, to the play's dialogue with Machiavelli, and to the specifically *political* nature of the play—is simply this: for him, as many have noted, honour is a stable, unchanging quality, a quality that serves him and that he seeks to deploy in each and every situation. What Othello knows, without quite knowing, what Othello has kept secret to himself and must finally admit, concerns the very essence of the political: for the prince, indeed the general in this instance (hasn't Machiavelli told us that the *only* art of the statesman is war;[24] indeed, isn't Machiavelli's prince always already a general of sorts, a man of war?), it is not enough to have the honour or the valour of a lion—he must also have the qualities of a fox. Put in slightly different terms: for the statesman and for the general (unlike, say, for the philosopher, who can claim a stability for the qualities good, just, etc.), there can be no overarching or transcendent quality to act as guide; for the prince, and this is perhaps the main point of Machiavelli's treatise, *everything is situational*. Even if honour never disappears, the *way* in which it is defined will change from one situation to the next—and necessarily so. This is what Iago—who, all fox and no lion, is the perfect accomplice or the perfect foil for Othello, the reverse of the same coin as it were—understands, and this is why, to return to Cavell's words, the play would have brought him about if he didn't already exist: Iago is quite simply the name of the political in this play, the name of that which can never have an absolutely fixed quality, the name that, and the name of that which, changes from one moment to the next. Iago names that which cannot be predetermined or foreseen, that which arises only in the instant, and then, as quickly as it came, is gone.

And this, of course, is what Othello has known all along. This is the reason for which Iago is welcome, for which Othello wills his coming; the reason for which Othello admits his knowledge of Iago as "cause" from early in the play; the reason Othello *needs* (without desiring) this other who is more self than the self, who is in him more than him, his I-ago, his I-ego. In the final scene, Emilia begs Iago to reveal the truth, to reveal what he said to Othello. Iago's response, as always, is succinct and—it must be said—absolutely honest: "I told him what I thought; and told no more/Than what he found himself was apt and true" (174–5). And when Othello asks him, a little later, why he did what he did, he responds: "Demand me nothing: what you know, you know" (301). In each of these responses, Iago tells Othello what he already knows: that the answer is to be found not in Iago but in Othello himself; that Othello heard what he wanted to hear, that he knows what he already knew and what he has already known from the very beginning. Iago is not somehow other to Othello; he is, rather, the other of Othello's knowledge, that which Othello knows without knowing. Iago is quite simply the capacity of Othello to keep a secret, the capacity of Othello to keep a secret *even from himself*…and his betrayal of this secret, in his all-encompassing need for revelation. In the midst of this necessity, the secret resists; it could not do anything but.

It could not do anything but, for the simple reason that there is no "content" to this secret. The secret, what we might call the secret of the political that is kept by this play, is pure movement: as soon as we think we know what it is, it is already something else. Not honesty, not honour, none of these virtues, none of these causes. Nothing but a breath of wind, whispered or murmured but never quite revealed in these words that approach Iago, all the while moving away from him: honest… husband… he. *Ha.*

Notes

1. Many critics have remarked upon the juridical structure of the play. In his essay "Representing Othello: Early Modern Jury Trials and the Equitable Judgments of Tragedy," Nicholas Moschovakis remarks upon "the play's saturation with juridical episodes, language and implications" (293), and writes, quoting Heilman's famous study of *Othello, Magic in the Web*: "*Othello*, critics have long recognized, 'advances by a series of scenes analogous to trials or court actions'" (295).
2. The predominance of watching or looking in *Othello* has also been studied by many commentators. The references here are too numerous to mention, but see, for example, Patricia Parker's *Shakespeare from the Margins*, especially the book's final chapter, "*Othello* and *Hamlet*: Spying, Discovery, Secret Faults," where she writes of the early modern period's "fascination with the ocular, with exposing what lay hid to the scrutiny of the gaze" (237).
3. Shakespeare, *Othello*, 2.3.4–6. All further references to this play will be made parenthetically in the body of the text.
4. The reading of these words as, in part, an accusation, is supported by the words that follow immediately upon this speech, words not from Iago but from Montano, who says to Iago: "If, partially affined or leagued in office,/Thou dost deliver more or less than the truth,/Thou art no soldier" (209–211). On the one hand, it is natural for Montano to be suspicious of someone he barely knows, especially in so delicate a situation. On the other hand, it is as though Montano picks up on the accusation that is in the air—as though he can sense, from Othello's two-pronged statements, that Iago is not completely trustworthy.
5. "Rude I am in my speech" (1.3.82), he states earlier in the play; and a little later, he ties this lack of eloquence to his "race": "I am black/And have not those soft parts of conversation/That chamberers have" (3.3.266–268). Note, however, that Othello has won Desdemona over precisely with his eloquence, i.e. with the stories of his adventures: he speaks of how, with a "greedy ear," she would "Devour upon my discourse" (1.3.149–150).
6. 341.
7. Ibid. It should be noted that Cavell's argument is more complex than this. The next line of his text states: "It is the enveloping of contingency and necessity by one another, the entropy of their mixture, which produces events we call tragic" (ibid.).
8. A question that dates at least back to Coleridge (and no doubt before), and has been taken up on many occasions since: *Qu'est-ce qu'Iago?*, the Duc de Broglie famously asked in 1830. Some thirty-four years later, Victor Hugo provided this response to Broglie's question: Iago "est le mal." See the appendix to *Othello*, ed. Furness, pp. 451–2.
9. I borrow this term from the television series *Dexter*, which revolves around a blood spatter analyst—the Dexter of the series's name—who works for the Miami police,

and who is also a serial killer (whose victims are killers the police have been unable to apprehend). Dexter views himself as an addict (at one point he even begins to attend Narcotics Anonymous meetings) who acts on an irresistible urge to kill, and the name he gives to this urge is the *dark passenger*, a passenger who cannot be seen by others, but who is always present, pulling Dexter this way and that, whom Dexter cannot defeat and with whom he must therefore learn to live.

10. I do not claim, of course, to be the first to have made such claims about the play. On the contrary, many of the most interesting readings of *Othello* are those that have called into question Othello's trust in Iago. Stanley Cavell, for example, states: "However much Othello...believes Iago's tidings, he cannot just believe them; somewhere he also *knows* them to be false...we must understand Othello to be wanting to believe Iago, to be trying, against his knowledge, to believe him" ("Epistemology and Tragedy," 38). Indeed, one reading of the play, that of Julian Willis Abernethy, is entitled "'Honest Iago'"—the words are placed within quotation marks—and begins thus: "I do not believe that I am abnormally sensitive or aesthetically perverse, yet whenever I read or hear of the play of *Othello* my soul is tormented by the endless iteration of the word 'honest'" (336).

11. Recall that for Machiavelli, virtue has no positive content, and the attributes or qualities that a prince must employ are defined only situationally. "In the actions of men," he writes, "and especially of princes, where there is no tribunal to which to appeal, one must consider the final result. Therefore, let a prince conquer and maintain the state, and his methods will always be judged honourable and praised by all. For ordinary people are always taken in by appearances and by the outcome of an event" (*The Prince*, 62).

That Shakespeare makes constant and unmistakable references to Machiavelli in *Othello* is evident; we can observe as much even if we confine ourselves to this particular scene. The word virtue is debated on several occasions, including, most tellingly perhaps, in a certain speech of Cassio. After the latter is relieved of his duty by Othello, Iago advises him to plead his case to Desdemona, at which point Cassio compliments Iago on his good advice; when Iago protests in the name of modesty, Cassio insists: "I think it freely; and betimes in the morning I will beseech the virtuous Desdemona to undertake for me. I am desperate of my fortunes if they check me here" (315–7). In a single speech, Cassio not only names the two driving forces of Machiavelli's thought—virtue and fortune—but speaks of them just as Machiavelli does, as being in conflict with one another (only Desdemona's virtue can bring about a change in his fortune). A little earlier, Iago says the following to Cassio: "You are but now cast in his mood—a punishment more in policy than in malice, even so as one would beat his offenceless dog to affright an imperious lion" (263–6). Do we not hear, in this passage—and a little later, when Roderigo refers to himself as a "hound" (348)—a reference to Machiavelli's statement that a prince must know "how to play the role of the lion and the fox, whose natures [he] must imitate" (Machiavelli, 68)? And finally, Iago himself is described in the following terms by Cassio: "I never knew a Florentine more kind and honest!" (3.1.40).

This is not to say, of course, that Iago is some sort of Machiavellian prince. Speaking schematically, we could say that in Iago we see a lot of fox and not much lion—Iago, in other words, is extremely cunning, but cannot be said to be truly glorious. Should we conclude from this that Shakespeare's dialogue with Machiavelli is at the same time a criticism of the latter? Iago, it could be argued, is Shakespeare's vision of the Machiavellian prince gone wrong, or of the prince carried to its absurd yet logical extreme.

12. Unless he is in fact the most honest character of all, insofar as he is the only one, among all of these politico-military figures, who assumes a truly political character (in the Machiavellian sense). We will return to Machiavelli and the question of politics below.

13. Bradley notes that the clown in this play is one of the least interesting clowns in all of Shakespeare (*Shakespearean Tragedy*, 177), and perhaps the presence of Iago explains this: a clown is unnecessary when this joker-figure (who, like a clown, tells truths that no one wants to hear) so dominates the play. It is indeed interesting that the clown, who appears twice, is never on stage at the same time as Iago, who is almost always present—on his first, brief appearance, the clown exits just as Iago arrives on the scene (see 3.1.29–30).

14. See p.94.

15. I therefore disagree slightly with Cavell, who writes that "compared with the case of Shakespeare's other tragedies, … [Othello] is not political but domestic" ("Epistemology and Tragedy," 35).

16. Though things are far from simple here. In her essay "Othello's Lost Handkerchief: Where Psychoanalysis Finds Itself," Elizabeth J. Bellamy makes very interesting remarks on the psychoanalytic concept of the cause, and its relationship to Desdemona's handkerchief…

17. Much could be said about these stars: they constitute a motif that recurs often in this final scene. The fact that Othello refers to them as chaste indicates, to a certain degree, that even a few hundred years on, we are very close to Dante here, to a conception of the stars as truly "heavenly" bodies. Hence the truly disastrous nature of his referring to his dead wife, later in the scene, as "ill-starred" (5.2.271; the Oxford Edition notes that this is the first recorded use of this term by the *OED*): something much worse than bad luck is at play here.

18. This letter, and specifically words beginning with it, is of extreme importance throughout the play, but especially in the last scene. Several commentators on *Othello* have called attention to the prevalence of another letter—the letter "o"—in the play, seeing in this letter a marker of the play's, and especially Othello's, intimate relationship with nothingness. Joel Fineman, for example, adopting a Lacanian framework, writes the following: "I understand the sound of *O* in *Othello* both to occasion and to objectify in language Othello's hollow self" (86). Daniel J. Vitkus, on the other hand, argues that "[f]or Shakespeare, the 'O' is a transcendent signifier" (347), and concludes his essay by stating Othello's "name, beginning and ending in 'O,' becomes a cipher signifying nothing" (360). I think, however, as I will try to show in this final section of my essay, that it is just as interesting to think about the workings of the letter h in *Othello*—of this letter perhaps even closer to nothingness than the "o," often not even pronounced (as in "honest"), not really representing any sound at all but simply an aspiration, nothing more than a breath.

19. The Oxford Edition tells us that this is yet again, according to the *OED*, the first recorded use of this word.

20. Derrida has of course made very interesting remarks about this root.

21. All quotations here are from Blanchot, *The Infinite Conversation*, 385. Translation slightly modified. Blanchot borrows the terms "hole-word" *(mot-trou)*, "absence-

word" *(mot-absence)*, and "empty gong," and the phrase "one cannot speak it, but one can make it resound," from Duras's novel *The Ravishing of Lol V. Stein.*

22. As in the very last words of the play, which belong to Ludovico: "Myself will straight aboard, and to the state/This *h*eavy act with *h*eavy *h*eart relate" (5.2.369–70).

23. While it is beyond the scope of this essay to enter into this discussion, it seems quite clear that Emilia, no less than Othello, has known the "truth" about Iago from the very beginning. This is not to indict her, for is any word less accurate regarding Iago, this master of masks, than the word "truth"?

24. The beginning of the fourteenth chapter of *The Prince*, entitled "A prince's duty concerning military matters," reads thus: "A prince, therefore, must not have any other object nor any other thought, nor must he adopt anything as his art but war, its institutions, and its discipline; because that is the only art befitting one who commands" (50). We are obviously very close here to Schmitt's definition of the sovereign as "the one who decides on the state of exception": for Schmitt, as for Machiavelli, the very definition of the sovereign is tied up at its most intimate level with the "art" of war.

Works Cited

Abernethy, Julian Willis. "'Honest Iago.'" *The Sewanee Review* 30.3 (1922): 336–344.

Bellamy, Elizabeth J. "Othello's Lost Handkerchief: Where Psychoanalysis Finds Itself." *Lacan, Politics, Aesthetics.* Ed. Willy Apollon and Richard Feldstein. Albany: State University of New York Press, 1996.

Blanchot, Maurice. *The Infinite Conversation.* Trans. Susan Hanson. Minneapolis and London: University of Minnesota Press, 1993.

Bradley, A.C. *Shakespearean Tragedy: Lectures on Hamlet, Othello, King Lear, Macbeth.* London: Macmillan and Co., 1964 (1904).

Cavell, Stanley. "Epistemology and Tragedy: A Reading of Othello." *Daedalus* 108.3 (1979): 27–43.

—. *Must We Mean What We Say?* Updated edition. Cambridge, UK: Cambridge University Press, 2002 (1976).

Fineman, Joel. "The Sound of *O* in *Othello:* The Real of the Tragedy of Desire." *October* 45 (1998): 76–96.

Machiavelli, Niccolò. *The Prince.* Ed. and trans. Peter Bondanella. Oxford, U.K.: Oxford University Press, 2005.

Moschovakis, Nicholas. "Representing Othello: Early Modern Jury Trials and the Equitable Judgments of Tragedy." *Othello: New Critical Essays.* Ed. Philip C. Kolin. New York and London: Routledge, 2002. 293–323.

Parker, Patricia. *Shakespeare from the Margins: Language, Culture, Context.* Chicago and London: University of Chicago Press, 1996.

Shakespeare, William. *Othello.* Ed. Michael Neill. Oxford, U.K.: Oxford University Press, 2006.

Vitkus, Daniel J. "The 'O' in *Othello*: Tropes of Damnation and Nothingness." *Othello: New Critical Essays.* Ed. Philip C. Kolin. New York and London: Routledge, 2002. 347–362.

Four

DECEPTION, NATURE AND NIHILISM IN POLITICS: *KING LEAR* AND KUROSAWA'S *RAN*

Bartholomew Ryan

Even so, I'm somebody.
I'm the Discoverer of Nature.
I'm the Argonaut of true sensations.
I bring to the Universe a new Universe,
Because I bring to the Universe its own self.
—Alberto Caeiro[1]

"It is hard to prevent oneself from believing what one so keenly desires"
—Jean Jacques Rousseau[2]

The drama of *King Lear* moves from an unstable, ominous purgatory to a merciless hell. Yet unlike Dante's stumble into the dark wood halfway through his life, Lear is thrown into the darkness in his winter years, and his gift, or curse, is the very torment he creates for those around him. This is perhaps the darkest of Shakespeare's plays and one of his most political in the arena of power, authority and legitimacy. Like all of Shakespeare's greatest works, the play goes well beyond the trivialities of politics. But Shakespeare's "politics" as such represents human beings in all their life actions, and the battle against and in nature in the quest for legitimacy, power, authority and control. Nowhere is this more intense than in *King Lear*. I want to show how this interpretation of Shakespeare's politics is also transferred to the medium of cinema by the filmmaker Akiru Kurosawa in the release of *Ran* in 1985. Firstly, I will analyze the use of the force of nature and its impact on the political figures. The meaning and role that nature plays in politics in Shakespeare is manifested brilliantly in *Ran*. Secondly, I explore the dilemmas that lie between deception and honesty, tenderness and barbarism, vision and flattery; also, the theme of legitimacy is touched on where parent and child, identity and the problem of authority are teased out. Finally, through interweaving *King Lear* and *Ran* I show the connection that comes about between politics and nihilism, and the reverberating nothing that pervades all.

1. Nature and Politics

The eighteenth-century critic Samuel Johnson called Shakespeare "above all modern writers, the poet of nature."[3] Part of what Johnson means by this is that Shakespeare involves nature in everything we do as human beings. When Lear is anxious, the air around him is overcast and oppressive; when he is angry, the weather is stormy and thunderous; when a kingdom is poorly ruled, the land itself starts to decay. It is at once symbolic and existential. This is what brings out the brilliance of not only the performance on the stage in the combination of heavy symbolic imagery and larger-than-life characters as forces of nature, but also in the writing itself as we read from the written page. Johnson is also simply responding to one of Shakespeare's many declarations on this matter such as when Prolixenes says that "the art itself is nature" in *The Winter's Tale*[4], or to read the line from *Lear* isolated: "Nature is above art in this respect." The art is a pale imitation of nature, or at its best it is a manifestation and power of nature and this applies especially to Shakespeare. The central point for my purposes is that figures of political authority are in deadly combat with nature, at once a part of and at war with it. But when we speak of "nature," we are entering a foggy realm in which it represents the natural world, the instinctual element of human beings and the cycle of inevitable birth and death. The philosopher Baruch Spinoza gave a famous example in a letter to Henry Oldenburg to clarify the nature of parts to wholes, where each of us is like a little worm in the blood. This can be viewed as analogous to the political human being like a worm in the blood that is nature—at brief moments aware but for most of the time ignorant, determined by one's own passions, and blinded by limitations. In other words, at times unaware of our connection to it, at other times at war with it, and usually finally consumed and swallowed up by it. We, as humans, are stuck inside the blood while the universe in its infinitude is so much larger, unknown and ultimately overwhelming:

> That worm would be living in the blood as we are living in our part of the universe, and it would regard each individual particle of the blood as a whole, not a part, and it could have no idea as to how all the parts are controlled by the overall nature of the blood and compelled to mutual adaptation as the overall nature of the blood requires, so as to agree with one another in a definite way … Now since the nature of the universe, unlike the nature of the blood, is not limited, but is absolutely infinite, its parts are controlled by the nature of this infinite potency in finite ways, are compelled to undergo infinite variations.[5]

This is a quintessential problem for Lear as a force of nature and as king over a people. He is aware and yet tragically unaware, described at one point as "Oppressèd nature" (See Quarto text: sc.13, 90). Of course, the tragedy is disclosed when he realises the necessity of maintaining the balance between politics and nature only when he has thrown himself outside the political realm, and when he overreaches himself. Pride does come before the fall, and political flattery is put before natural love and the bond between the father and youngest daughter.

The greatness of Kurosawa's *Ran* is that it successfully brings out Shakespeare's "politics" and "nature" through the medium of cinema. The opening scenes set the stage in impeccable fashion. Let us take a look at the fusion of Shakespeare and cinema in the coming together of politics and nature as both symbol and actuality. The opening shot of *Ran* looks like a painting: so still are the four horsemen on the hill in the countryside, the colours so vibrant, continuing Kurosawa's radical departure from his black-and-white trademark. Each of the four horsemen is looking in a different direction. These four horsemen of death symbolize a foreboding future. The camera also pans across the countryside, showing the vastness of nature (the film ends with a similar motif of showing nature in its full scope in contrast to the miniature size of man, as the shot goes further out). In one fell swoop in the opening minutes of the movie Kurosawa masterfully transfers Shakespeare's vision of the apocalypse we are about to witness, the insignificance of man and the expanse and indifference of nature to our woes. This opening scene is a hunt for a wild boar led by Kurosawa's Lear, the Great Lord: Hidetora Ichimonji. The first shot of the grizzled Great Lord is with bow and arrow hunting the beast who is also old, followed by the word "Ran" coming up on the screen. The film sharply cuts to the first dialogue of the film of the sharing and distribution of power. Film director Chris Marker has said of Kurosawa's movie: "It is King Lear, yet it is not King Lear, more like Lear's echo, reverberating across the castle walls built by Kurosawa at Mount Fuji."[6] The image of the volcano Mount Fuji is also another indicator of Shakespeare's fusion of politics and nature: ominous, unpredictable, powerful and mightily destructive. From the four horsemen to the king hunting in nature to the first dialogue, Kurosawa has condensed the central themes of *King Lear* in the first three minutes.[7]

The first dialogue is between the Great Lord, his three sons (Taro, Jiro and Saburo) and the two visiting guests Lord Aabe and Lord Fujimaki. The visitors have come to offer their daughter in marriage to Hidetora's youngest son Saburo, in an attempt to forge alliances and consolidate power, just as in *King Lear* with Cordelia and the King of France and Duke of Burgundy. Throughout this scene an unsettling wind blows and Hidetora falls asleep, revealing his tiredness and old age. We see the robust Saburo make a shelter out of shrub for his sleeping father outside in a matter of minutes—an indicator that he is the only one of the three sons who actually cares for his father in a practical manner. This is the first of only very few indications of the possibility of using nature to control nature. For the rest of this film nature is mostly presented as fierce, hellish and unforgiving, but only for the very reason that political human beings are corrupt, dishonest, greedy and careless. Ultimately, following the vision given to us by Shakespeare and translated by Kurosawa, all we can do is watch in horror as political man goes to war with himself.

It is worth mentioning briefly the tie between nature and the impending madness of Lear and Hidetora, if only to show again the symbiosis between kingship and nature, and the great Hobbesian *Leviathan* (1651) of England's tumultuous sixteenth century calling for strong rule over land and subjects, and warning of a world without rule where life is "solitary, poor, nasty, brutish and short." Nature is always watching, and never more intently as when the collapse of humanity is underway. In *Ran*, the first sign of madness is accompanied by shots of the sky, sun and the moving clouds; the second moment of madness is accompanied by the sound of birds, and the third time again we have shots of the moving clouds. Nature also offers hope: in the meeting of father and son towards the end of the movie in the moment of reconciliation, the clouds are moving again. The question is whether they are parting to clear the mess that we have travelled through or warning of more destruction. Equally, the image of the picking of flowers in the windy field after the burning of the third castle can be interpreted negatively or positively. And then the carnage of war, the continuation of politics for some[8], is accompanied by sun and mist and furious winds. As ruined pieces of nature Lear and Hidetora are consumed and, with nature's eyes, they see in their disintegration the folly and blindness of human beings.

A final point in the interlinking of nature with politics is this sense of abandonment that drives the principle characters in *Lear* such as Edgar, Edmund, the Fool and Lear himself. As Edmund has his eye on power and usurpation, he declares that he will use nature to get what he wants. That "nature" is the brilliant demonic quality of Edmund, the bastard son, who will betray his half-brother, deceive and cast out his father and seduce both Regan and Goneril. We rarely encounter such seductive, powerful figures of the dark except perhaps with Iago in Shakespeare's *Othello* or with Stavrogin in Dostoevsky's novel *Demons*. Like a sorcerer, Edmund proudly calls up nature to guide him through his pillage for power: "Thou, nature, art my goddess. To thy law / My services are bound" (1.ii, 1–2).[9] Meanwhile his father responds indirectly to the demonic surge of Edmund as he reflects on the supposed betrayal of Edgar his legitimate son:

> These late eclipses in the sun and moon / portend no good to us. Though the wisdom of nature / can reason it thus and thus, yet nature finds itself / scourged by the sequent effects. Love cools, friendship / falls off, brothers divide; in cities, mutinies; in countries, / discord; in palaces, treason; and the bond cracked / 'twixt father and son. (1. ii, 101–108).

This passage also expresses in a nutshell the dark political vision that *Lear* gives us in the form of a work of art. As politics enters a *ran*-like state, nature rises up in fury too, and the demonic element breaks out, in the Kierkegaardian sense of the term, as the "anxiety about the good"[10] that burns within such charismatic figures as Stavrogin or which drives Kierkegaard's merman into a furious rage of despair. We can perceive this also through the words and images of Lear leading up to and during the storm. Beginning with an attempt to reason and understand nature, Lear metamorphoses into nature as his words become the sounds of thunder itself. Beginning with lines such as "Allow not nature more than nature needs / [...] Why, nature needs not what thou gorgeous wear'st," Lear starts again with "Blow, winds, and crack your cheeks! Rage, blow, / You cataracts and hurricanoes, spout / Till you have drenched our steeples, drowned the / cocks" (2.ii, 440, 443; 3.i, 1–4). The demonic is only a hair's breath from the divine: both are spiritually powerful, one the destroyer, the other the redeemer. It is Cordelia who "redeems nature" (4.v, 202) while the demonic element (which is potentially in all of us) abandons it. This pathos theme is brilliantly depicted by Kurosawa at the end of his film when Kyoami (Kurosawa's Fool) cries out in despair and anger at the gods: "Are there no gods, no Buddha? If you exist, listen to me! You are mischievous and cruel! Are you so bored up there that you must crush us like ants? Is it fun to see me weep?" It is Tango, Kurosawa's Kent, who clarifies who is actually abandoning whom:

> It is the gods who weep. They see us killing each other again and again since time began. They can't save us from ourselves. Don't cry. It's how the world is made. Men prefer sorrow to joy, suffering to peace. Look at them in the first castle. They revel in pain and bloodshed. They celebrate murder.

It is not the gods who have abandoned us; men are the ones who have abandoned themselves. The passion of fury and rage is stronger than peace and serenity. Here, men abandon themselves under the guise of politics and it is significant that the Japanese word "Ran" can be translated as "rebellion," "revolt," and sometimes as "chaos." Both *King Lear* and *Ran* represent the madness of the king in the realm of nature and the madness of desire for political power in the realm of public life.

2. How to Rule: Identity, Deception and Legitimacy

This second section explores the ways to rule and the role of identity, deception and legitimacy in *Lear*, and notes how it is transformed into feudal Japan onscreen. In regard to ruling, this brings us to the Machiavellian dilemma. In *The Prince*, Machiavelli famously writes: "it is better to be feared than loved if you cannot have both."[11] This statement haunts both Lear and Hidetora. In the dilemma between being feared or loved, the relationships between compassion and ruthlessness, and deception and honesty, emerge.

Firstly, let us look at the dilemma that Shakespeare poses and Kurosawa attempts to present on screen in the choice between compassion and ruthlessness in positions of power, no less than the power of a king, and how others' conceptions of how to attain that power and rule. Even though Lear commands love from his daughters when he is in the process of ceding his power, it is falsely reciprocated and he fails to see it, and it is with flattery and ruthlessness that the two elder daughters are able to attain power and annihilate love and compassion. But the message also is that this method creeps into the two elder daughters' private lives too and that will be the death of them politically and personally. We follow the rise to power of Goneril and Regan with their respective husbands, and of Taro and Jiro, while also seeing what the servants Tango, the Fool, Kent and Kyoami have to face and the suffering that they have to experience as a result of their duty. And most of all, we have to witness Saburo and Cordelia's deaths which are the most meaningless. What does this all ultimately imply? It is in trying to answer this question that we see the pessimism in Shakespeare and Kurosawa's vision of the political world. The problem is that the rulers and those who strive after power and authority fail to find the balance between ruthlessness and compassion. They sway like a pendulum from one to the other *in extremis*. Lear veers towards sentimentality that is easily exploited by Regan and Goneril, and his ruthlessness turns to stupidity in his banishing of Cordelia. At other moments he acts like a demonic, misdirected wizard in his cursing of Goneril in that incredible tirade against her in the first act (I.iv, 254–269). Gloucester is also short-sighted in his love for Edmund, Goneril and Regan's lust drives them to their doom, and even the enigmatic Edmund, when he is about to die, feels strangely "moved" by Edgar's words. In typical hyperbolic fashion Harold Bloom remarks: "Shakespeare remorselessly makes loves itself both outrageous and outraged, in a cosmos centred upon Lear's greedy greatness."[12] Should one leave love out of politics? Is the kind of love that we see depicted in the political dramas of *Lear* and *Ran* extreme, unreal, wild and outrageous?

It becomes a question of judgment and how to wield one's authority. The opening line of *King Lear* is a statement of political judgment by Kent, the loyal and honest servant. Goneril and Regan abuse their power, when they have been given rites of passage from their father and king, and they know no compassion or love and are destroyed as a result of their ruthlessness and lust for power without moderation or tenderness. Hidetora's rise to power is a story of making war, destroying his enemies without mercy and finally bringing peace to all the land, but as a result of great butchery. We do not know the history of Lear and his ascent to power. Lear and Hidetora, once stripped of their power, which at the beginning is of their own doing, find their humanity out in the wilderness like the prophets of old. Interweaving fear and love, the madness they experience on the heath and the plains only finds peace through the daughter and son that they rejected.

Sexual politics drives *Lear*, and Kurosawa intensifies this aspect through the female character of Kaede, a startling addition that synthesizes elements of Edmund, Goneril, Regan and Cornwall into one character. She has a more valid excuse for her ruthlessness and treachery. She has suffered mightily from Hidetora's tyranny, as he had her father and brother murdered after she had married his oldest son Taro, and her mother subsequently killed herself in the first castle that Kaede grew up in. Her ultimate goal is the destruction of the house of the Great Lord combined with total power. She moves from taking charge of the first castle with Taro, to becoming a widow, to effortlessly seducing the second son Jiro and sending him and his army to their doom regardless of care for military strategy. She is the cunning fox that the loyal soldier Kurogane indirectly warns Lord Jiro of in her very presence:

> There are many foxes about here. It is said they often play tricks on people. Beware, my lord. They often impersonate women to play tricks. In Central Asia, a fox seduced a king Pan Tsu and made him kill 1000 men. Later in China, the fox married King Yu and ravaged the land. In Japan, as Princess Tamamo, the fox caused great havoc at court. And it became a white fox with nine tails. Then they lost trace of this fox, but some peope say it settled down here. So beware my Lord, beware.

We can see the shades of Edmund here in her enigmatic quality of being able to seduce almost all those around her and of being an outsider who lusts for power; and she resembles Goneril in having no qualms about loyalties in her ease in moving from one husband to another; and there are parallels with Regan in her lustful urges towards powerful men and her violent nature in demanding the head of Jiro's wife Sué. We can see that the different characters so far have overstepped the mark in their ruthlessness, "sharptoothed unkindness" and barbarism or by their trust and sentimentality.

Let us take a brief look at the role and use of honesty and deception in the political arena of ruling and serving. Cordelia spells it out clearly when her father accuses her of being so untender while being so young. Her reply is simply: "So young, my lord, and true." The last lines of the play reconfirm this affirmation of being honest rather than using flattery or deception when Edgar closes with: "Speak what we feel, not what we ought to say." And yet these lines by Edgar are a double-edged sword. Is this not how Lear acted? Although Edgar is speaking with good intentions, it is honesty without impulsion that might have saved Lear, and it is Edgar's disguise and deception that helped him survive and triumph. This difficulty and confusion in politics drives both *Lear* and *Ran*. When the drama of *Lear* and *Ran* begins, it is not love and honesty that Lear and Hidetora listen to, nor is it merely a show of instilling fear on their subjects; rather, it is flattery and vanity that is their initial downfall. Edgar is bonded with Cordelia: both love and are loyal to the father but have been rejected in favour of other dishonest and disloyal siblings. Instead we have examples of loyalty in Kent and Kurosawa's counterpart in Tango, and of course the Fool and Kyoami. Again, it is the loyal servants who see the shortcomings of their masters, and suffer as a result in attempting to tell the truth, as Gloucester ponders on Kent: "And the noble and true-hearted Kent banished, his offence honesty!—'Tis strange!" (1.ii, 114–115). Tango also expresses the same sentiment in *Ran*: "And yet all we did was say what we honestly thought." Even Kurogane maintains his dignity, loyalty and honesty in relation to Jiro, when he berates the middle brother for succombing to Kaede's power: "You are a mouse posing as a mastiff," or when he tells him: "Wars are won by strong leaders," or when he stays with his master until the end: "Lord prepare to die. I will follow you." Like the wonderfully witty squire of infinite resignation in Bergman's *The Seventh Seal,* The Fool knows that it is folly to follow the disintegrating king but he also understands the notion of loyalty and his duty to the king even when he has lost everything.[13]

So there are two kinds of loyalty here: to those who are the strongest and to those to whom they have a duty. The tragedy of this drama is that both kinds suffer: the former turn out to be traitors, the latter misunderstood, punished or murdered. Jiro remarks on the upstarts Ikoma and Ogura, who are loyal to whoever is stronger: "Men who betray one master may betray another" and casts them out from his kingdom. Jiro is being a good Machiavellian in the fact that he maintains his honour even though he uses these two advisors to out-manoeuvre his older brother. But we can also see how loyalty is twisted with the use of deception and, in its cheapest form, flattery that most of the characters are consumed. Throughout this drama indeed, "the prince of darkness is a gentleman" (III.iv146). Saburo sees this deception right from the start from listening to his brothers' speeches: "What a pretty speech … I cannot use such honeyed words." Tango defends Saburo to Hidetora: "Master Saburo is blunt, perhaps even disrespectful, but his words are honest, and they come from the heart. Think about it, and you will find that he is not wrong." (19.39). Saburo and Tango are both cast out into exile. Machiavelli does warn the prince of the flatterers (Chapter XXIII), and through his madness, Lear realises his short-comings: "They flattered me like a dog" (4.v, 96). It is the honesty of others that allows Edmund to play everyone so easily: "[…] on whose foolish honesty / My practices ride easy" (i.iii, 170–171). The deceiver is always adapting to whichever situation, and even those who are honest and loyal must learn how to deceive. Thus Tango, Kent and Edgar must all take on new guises in order to preserve any chance of restoring order. Tango clearly expresses the motive: "Whatever disguise I must adopt, I shall not abandon the Great Lord."

Deception and the art of seeing are masterfully woven into *Lear* in the symbol of the eye. Gloucester's blindness is the physical parallel to Lear's mental madness. We have a vision of a return to nature when the mad king and the blind Earl meet on Dover Cliff (the layers of depth in this play continue in the fact that Edgar, has led his father Gloucester to the heath, disguised as the mad Poor Tom). Lear was not able to see through his daughters' flattery, Gloucester never guessed Edmund's demonic quality; both are punished as a result. Lear loses his mind; Gloucester his eyes. As a result both begin to "see" more clearly. "I see it feelingly" (4.v, 145), the blind Gloucester tells Lear. And so we have the apocalyptic image of the mad leading the blind through the wilderness. The irony, of course, is that Goneril had already told her father the truth in her declaration of love for the king: "Sir, I love you more than word can wield / the matter; / Dearer than eyesight, space and liberty" (1.i, 56). Such is the strength of the great deceiver in telling the half-truth, as the Western tradition has witnessed from *Genesis* to *Faust*. The symbol of the eye is also used by Kurosawa in the character of Tsurumaru, brother of Sué. Kurosawa presents the ying and yang of coping with suffering: the despairing and bitter nihilist and the enlightened, accepting Buddhist. Kurosawa plays it in such a way that Tsurumaru becomes a tool for Hidetora to see. Tsurumaru's blindness and contempt highlights Hidetora's same characteristics in his judgment and distribution of power.

The political dilemma remains unresolved in *Lear* and *Ran*: how does one strike a balance between tenderness and becoming the sword, and to being able to detect deception and trickery. Machiavelli has already tried to aid us and goes as far as to say that when we have to make a choice between fear and love from our subjects, it is better to choose fear—at least with fear the subject cannot and does not dare to demand. However, this is what distinguishes Shakespeare and Kurosawa from Machiavelli, in that as much as it means impending doom and suffering, it is still better to choose love over fear. This is bad politics perhaps, but supreme virtue? Spinoza confirms this controversial position in stating: "Minds, however, are conquered not by arms, but by love and nobility."[14]

In moving through deception and honesty, one comes before the idea of identity itself. In a first viewing of *Ran* one can be bewildered by the large cast of characters, each with their own story, each struggling to assert their identity as a fine line is drawn between being forced and deciding to become a new persona. The climactic line on this point in *Ran* is when Saburo asks his broken father: "Don't you recognise me?" Throughout the film Hidetora becomes more and more a wraith-like creature, at once turning into a shadow of his former self and at the same time more aware than ever before. The other shadow is Lear's Fool—the mirror and conscience who tells the king what he is and also sees what he himself has become: "Who is it that can tell me who I am." The Fool responds: "Lear's shadow" (1.iv, 236). The Fool becomes more serious and the king more ridiculous. There is so much to play with here in the interchanging identities of (*inter alia*) Edmund and Edgar, Lear and the Fool, Edmund and Gloucester, Gloucester and Edgar, and Lear and Cordelia.

In *Ran* the plot thickens with fantastic additional identity changes and mirrors occurring between Sué and Kaede, Jiro and Taro, Hidetora and Tsurumaru. It is through these reflections on each other that one is revealing the other for what they really are. But it comes with a heavy price. In the first act of *Lear*, it is Regan who astutely remarks about her father: " 'Tis the infirmity of his age; yet he hath ever but slenderly known himself" (1.i, 295). Kent perseveres in trying to guide the lost Lear and to attempt to expose the lie from the truth when he declares: "I'll teach you differences" (1.iv, 91). And yet Kent, in exile, decides to be not what he is, in order to carry out his duty. To make matters more complicated, the question of identity is connected with legitimacy. Edgar becomes the elusive and incredible character of Poor Tom, the mad seer who makes his long and arduous journey towards restoring legitimacy and honour in the state of nature. Such are the cruel ways of politics that one becomes something other in order to restore oneself and the state. Our opposites more often than not turn out to be ourselves.

The identities of *Lear*'s Edgar and *Ran*'s Tsurumaru are the most curious. Kurosawa picks up on this reversal of fortune, and twisting of identity to place the mirror on the king and great lord who stumble upon their new identity. Edgar concludes his soliloquy on his mutation into Poor Tom: "Edgar I nothing am," and upon confronting Edmund towards the end of the drama still declares: "Know, my name is lost." Tsurumaru is a fascinating addition by Kurosawa fusing again characters from *Lear* into one, an audacious fusion of Gloucester and Edgar. When Hidetora, Tango and the Fool seek shelter in the little house in the wilderness, they are not welcome, as the voice from within tells them: "My house is too poor for visitors." They enter regardless, and it is difficult to see if this person inside is a man, woman or even supernatural creature—so twisted and torn has his identity become. And in allusion to Gloucester he apologises in the form of saying: "I'm sorry I must be alone" / "I have no light. I have no need of one." In the deception and identity meltdown that has occurred the eyes are no longer needed, or the eyes that we need in politics must be everywhere and yet hidden. Edgar, the Fool and Kaede know this and Edmund too, although his arrogance ultimately gets the better of him. We then witness the great importance of mirroring identity when Kyoami turns to Hidetora (that "ruined piece of nature") in Tsurumaru's shelter, "You shelter in the very ruins of the castle you burned." Kurosawa is getting to the bottom of identity and showing the history of the protagonist, and the remorse and redemption that lies behind the madness and misery. In *Lear*, we have the space for infinite poetic imagination; in *Ran* we experience the full cinematic effect of a great lord whose history we discover only when he has no future. Kurosawa himself said in an interview: "What has always troubled me about *King Lear* is that Shakespeare gives his characters no past. ... In *Ran*, I have tried to give Lear a history."[15]

In reflecting again on what we have unfolded above we see that deception moves in two directions: deception as a form of betrayal to usurp power, or becoming something other in order to bring out the truth. We have seen the latter used to full effect in the Western tradition by Socrates and Jesus as incognitos *par excellence*, as the messiah and wisest man in Athens respectively and yet appearing as vagabond and wastrel. Identity is changing all the time as a result, and as politics disintegrates, identities become blurred and legitimacy and loyalties become uncertain. Kaede is acutely aware of the significance of legitimacy and warns Taro early in the film: "Without them [his father's banner and insignia], you are but a shadow." And there is the question of loyalty and how that has been linked with deception and identity. Saburo, a moment before being exiled, asks: "What kind of world do we live? A world that is barren of loyalty and feeling... We too are children of this age, weaned on strife and chaos." And that is the moment when his father disastrously casts out his son due to misunderstanding and vanity: "Since you say there is no bond between parents and children in this world, I cut the bond between us! You are a stranger to me."

We now weave our way to the closing section in order to confront and work through the challenges that *Lear* presents to us, and which Kurosawa depicted on screen. The complexity of politics, in as far as we understand it to belong to the art of governing, intensifies and progresses to destructive consequences, which the final section details.

3. Political Nihilism and the Nothing

In his first line of the play, King Lear says: "Meantime we shall express our darker purpose." He is referring to the game of politics and the distribution of power that is about to occur; and, on a greater level, he points to the nihilism of politics. When I speak of the nihilism of politics, I am referring to, on the one hand, the transient nature of politics that rises and falls, that out of vanity and audacity builds great palaces, laws, cities, countries and empires, but which also easily crumbles and is swept away by the indifferent winds of oblivion, like Shelley's poetic memorial to Ozymandias, whose lost and broken statue was found half-buried in the lone and level sands. On the other hand, I am referring to the word "nothing," which is oft-repeated in *Lear*, as well as the nothingness that pervades our actions.

The "darker purpose" of Lear also refers to the division of the kingdom. Gloucester, in his opening line, has already mentioned the division that is to come, and, together with Kent's opening lines, the central political themes of the play are given: disintegration and questions of judgment and loyalty. The division of the kingdom in this case can be read in reference to the *Gospel of Matthew* (24: 7): "For nation shall rise against nation, and kingdom against kingdom: and there shall be famines, and pestilences, and earthquakes, in diverse places." The division alludes to civil war, the catastrophic moment of politics that drove Hobbes to write *Leviathan* during the turmoil of the civil war in England. Lear can also be likened to Solomon, the wise king who as an old man is supposed to have written that most nihilistic of texts, *Ecclesiastes*, and who declares at its beginning: "Vanities of vanities; *all* is vanity." *Ecclesiastes* is a vision of the world without God; *King Lear* is a vision of a political world divided against itself, where loyalty is washed away, and identity has been shattered. Lear himself is aware of what he will do somehow, whether consciously or unconsciously: "I will do such things—/ What they are, yet I know not; but they shall be / The terrors of the earth." Kurosawa transforms this prophesy into the form of a dream that Hidetora tells to his three sons upon waking after the first discussion in the film:

I was in a strange land. A wilderness. I went on and on but I saw no one. I called. I shouted, but no one answered. I was by myself. Alone in the wide world. I felt a chill... such stupidity! Taro's voice pulled me back. I saw my beloved children right before my eyes. Taro, Jiro, Saburo.

This time however there is a shift: Hidetora has now found himself in a post-apocalyptic world. Throughout the film, his dream becomes reality: his sons are far away from him, his kingdom is divided, at war and soon to be destroyed. The nihilism of politics is intensified when Hidetora declares in the wilderness that he is lost. His fool Kyoami responds: "Such is the human condition." The dialogue gets to the heart of the nihilism in politics. Hidetora continues in his by now fragmented manner: "This path … I remember. We came this way before." Again Kyoami replies: "Men always travel on the same road. If you're tired of it, jump off the wall." Hidetora does indeed jump, but even then he cannot die. This is Hidetora's hell, in despair not even able to die nor get away from his violent past that comes back now in the wilderness to haunt him: "The ruins of a castle… Why am I here? Why is Sué here? And Tsurumaru too. Is this a dream? No, this is hell. The lowest level of Hell." No longer in purgatory, and far from any salvation, the barrenness of the plains in the latter stages of the film reflects the barrenness of his political life. Hidetora flees into the barren Azusa plains and Kyoami loses him. He is bound upon Lear's "wheel of fire," where "All's cheerless, dark and deadly" (5.iii, 266).

Kurosawa is direct in showing the viewer the horrors of war, and the consequences not just of bad politics but the inevitable outcome of politics when we look around us. This is indeed a very pessimistic outlook from Kurosawa but one that has been moving that way through his previous two films in *Dersu Uzala* (1975) with the death of the "good man," and in *Kagamusha* (1980) with the death of political identity and legitimacy. In *Ran*, we cross these deaths again and also then the death of the state. After five minutes of unrelenting images of the carnage of war, we see Hidetora's concubines either kill each other or be killed, while one of the Great Lord's soldiers makes his last statement: "We are truly in hell." The final battle in its organisation and destruction takes up nearly thirty minutes of the film. We are being reminded in this nihilism of politics that passion masters reason once again. It is after all Lear who declares: "Death on my state" (2.ii, 284) and total war ensues. And Kurosawa himself reflected: "All the technological progress of these last years has only taught human beings how to kill more of each other faster. It's very difficult for me to retain a sanguine outlook on life under such circumstances."[16]

On a final note, there is the use of the word "nothing" in *Lear*. It is interesting to see where this word is used throughout the text. The first use of "nothing" comes from Cordelia's lips at that pivotal moment when the king asks his favourite and youngest daughter how much she loves him. The dialogue proceeds:

Lear: […] Speak.
Cordelia: Nothing, my lord.
Lear: Nothing?
Cordelia: Nothing.
Lear: Nothing will come of nothing. Speak again. (I, i, 86–90)

We do not have to go that far down the road of deconstruction to recognise that the use of the word "nothing" is of significance here. This is a pivotal moment of the play, when at once we have the demand for speech, which Cordelia responds with "nothing." She does speak, and all too clearly and eloquently. She responds to a demand to play the political game in public, but she refuses. Instead, she, as a powerful mouthpiece for Shakespeare, reveals the kernel of politics itself. At the same time, she speaks of her father as king and man and of her future. With "nothing" appearing five times in the first of Cordelia's few dialogues, nothing certainly does come of nothing. It is no accident then that the first dialogue that the Fool partakes of is also about (the) "nothing." In response to the first speech that the Fool gives, Lear says: "This is nothing, Fool" (1.iv, 127). And again the king repeats the formula with a slight change: "Nothing can be made out of nothing." Then the Fool delivers the central line: "I am a Fool; thou art nothing" (1.iv, 175–176). The king has become (the) nothing, and the fool goes on to become wiser and more serious as the play unravels. The nothing is the result of politics, and this is the nihilism that drives at the heart of the text and which Kurosawa shows to devastating effect. The third powerful appearance of the nothing is in Edgar and his transformation into Tom O'Bedlam, where all is bedlam and having reached the "worst" (4.i, 28). Once cast out and on the run, he gives that remarkable soliloquy about becoming Poor Tom and closes with the line: "That's something yet: Edgar I nothing am" (2.ii, 184). This line gives significance to the "nothing," as it is indeed something: though his political life seems finished, the rawness and violence of his exile, like Lear's and Cordelia's, and later Gloucester's, becomes part of the nothing that ultimately pervades all politics. Later he embraces this nothingness and that becomes his strength as he begins to rebuild himself and prepare himself for revenge and restoration: "Welcome, then, / Thou unsubstantial air that I embrace: / The wretch that thou hast blown unto the worst / Owes nothing to thy blasts" (4.i, 6–9). The unravelling of the tale of *Lear* and *Ran* to a wretched end reflects the vortex that governs their political world. Only the wild beast of nature remains. Walter Benjamin, another exile and victim of the 20th century political world, wrote in an enigmatic fragment that "to strive for such a passing away [...] is the task of world politics, whose method must be called nihilism."[17] He is alluding to the messianic element that his thinking is moving towards, but he is also referring to the very transitory quality of politics that fuels Shelley's vision of Ozymandius. Nihilism is that transience, and the nothing drives the nihilism that we can see in the form of politics in the vision of *Lear* and *Ran*. There is something infinitely intriguing about the following line taken out of its immediate context: "Nothing could have subdued nature" (3.iv, 66).

In conclusion, even after close analysis of a profound work, one can go in infinite directions and be infinitely surprised. The political pessimism of a work such as *Lear*, and its offshoot *Ran* (which in the context of post-war Japan was not ready nearly unwatchable), remains. What I have attempted to show in this essay is the friction between political humanity and nature. I have also teased out this lust for political legitimacy and identity and the dilemma between honesty and deception and its connection with identity. Finally, there is the elusive nihilism infiltrating politics relentlessly hurled at us by both Shakespeare and Kurosawa . Perhaps the only heroes left are ones like Edgar, who have to become nothing in order to find some—any—resolution. It is not solely the stars that govern our conditions, as Kent muses[18], but also the chaos or *Ran* within us that becomes either a symptom of our disease or something affirmative, perhaps in the Nietzschean sense of giving birth to a dancing star.[19] Both Lear and Hidetora tragically try to express this ambiguous tension at one and the same time.

Notes

1. Original: "Ainda assim, sou alguém. / Sou o Descobridor da Natureza. / Sou o Argonauta / das sensações verdadeiras. / Trago ao Universo um novo Universo / Porque trago ao Universo ele-próprio." (1914). Fernando Pessoa; *A Little Larger than the Entire Universe. Selected Poems*, trans. by Richard Zenith, London: Penguin Books, 2006, XLVI, pp. 43.
2. Rousseau, Jean-Jacques, *Reveries of the Solitary Walker* (1782), trans. by Peter France, London: Penguin: 2004, pp. 54.
3. From "Preface to Shakespeare" and "King Lear" (1765), *The Tragedy of King Lear*, edited by Russell Fraser, New York: Signet Classic, 1963, pp. 212.
4. *The Winter's Tale*, 4.iv.
5. Spinoza's Letter 32 to Henry Oldenburg (1665), *Spinoza: Complete Works*, trans Samuel Shirley, Indianapolis / Cambridge: Hackett Publishing Company, Inc., 2002, p. 849.
6. See *The Making of Ran* by Chris Marker in the special features of DVD edition of *Ran*.
7. This is not the first time that Kurosawa has loosely adapted Shakespeare to the screen and brought out this connection between "nature" and "politics." He did it with great artistic success in *Throne of Blood* (1957), an adaptation of *Macbeth*. Interestingly, while much of *Ran* was filmed along the barren plains of Mount Fuji, the castle exteriors of *Throne of Blood* were built high up on the mountain.
8. See for example Carl von Clausewitz (*On War* (1832), London: Penguin Books, 2003, Book VIII): "War is nothing but a continuation of political intercourse with a mixture of other means."
9. I quote from the folio version of *King Lear* unless otherwise indicated.
10. See Søren Kierkegaard; *The Concept of Anxiety* (1844), trans. by Reidar Thomte, Princeton, New Jersey: Princeton University Press, pp. 118–154.
11. Machiavelli, Niccolò; *The Prince* (1513), tr. by George Bull, London: Penguin Books, 2003, XVII, pp. 54.
12. Bloom, Harold; *Shakespeare: The Invention of the Human*, New York: Riverhead Books, 1998, pp. 510.
13. In another moment of lucidity within ruined walls of another castle, Kyoami reveals not only the switching of roles between himself and Hidetora, but also the desperate

reality of deception, betrayal and differences in generations: "Everything is a mess. I used to be a fool that made him laugh. Now the coin has been flipped. Don't be a mute. Say something. You speak some nonsense and I'll speak some truth. We'll see what comes of that. A serpent's egg is white and pure. A bird's is speckled and spoiled. The bird left the speckled egg for the white. The egg cracks. Out comes the snake. The bird raised the snake and is eaten by it. Stupid bird."

14. Spinoza, Baruch; *Ethics* (1677), trans. by Edwin Curley, London: Penguin, 1996, IV, Appendix XI, pp. 156.

15. Cardullo, Bert; *Akiru Kurosawa: Interviews*, Mississippi: University Press of Mississippi, 2007, pp. 125.

16. Bock, Audie; "Kurosawa on His Innovative Cinema." New York Times, 04/10/1981, pp. 21.

17. Benjamin, Walter; "Theological Political Fragment" (date disputed,), *Selected Writings Volume 3*, edited by Howard Eiland, and Michael W. Jennings, Cambridge Massachusetts: The Belknap Press of Harvard University Press, 2006, pp. 306.

18. See Quarto edition sc.16, 33–34: "It is the stars, / The stars above us govern our conditions."

19. Nietzsche, Friedrich; *Thus Spoke Zarathustra* (1883–85), trans. Walter Kaufmann, New York: Viking Press, 1954, Prologue 5, pp. 129: "One must still have chaos in oneself to be able to give birth to a dancing star."

Works Cited

Benjamin, Walter; "Theological Political Fragment" (date disputed), *Selected Writings Volume 3*, edited by Howard Eiland and Michael W. Jennings, Cambridge Massachusetts: The Belknap Press of Harvard University Press, 2006

Bloom, Harold; *Shakespeare: The Invention of the Human*, New York: Riverhead Books, 1998

Cardullo, Bert; *Akiru Kurosawa: Interviews*, Mississippi: University Press of Mississippi, 2007

Clausewitz, Carl von; *On War* (1832), ed. by Anatol Rapoport, London: Penguin Books, 2003

Kierkegaard, Søren; *The Concept of Anxiety* (1844), tr. by Reidar Thomte, Princeton, New Jersey: Princeton University Press, 1980

Kurosawa, Akiru; *Ran*, film release 1985

Machiavelli, Niccolò; *The Prince* (1513), tr. by George Bull, London: Penguin Books, 2003

Marker, Chris; *The Making of Ran*, documentary, from Extras in DVD edition of *Ran*

Johnson, Samuel; From "Preface to Shakespeare" and "King Lear" (1765), *The Tragedy of King Lear*, edited by Russell Fraser, New York: Signet Classic, 1963, pp. 212

Nietzsche, Friedrich; *Thus Spoke Zarathustra* (1883–85), trans. Walter Kaufmann, New York: Viking Press, 1954

Fernando Pessoa; *A Little Larger than the Entire Universe. Selected Poems*, tr. by Richard Zenith, London: Penguin Books, 2006

Rousseau, Jean-Jacques, *Reveries of the Solitary Walker* (1782), tr. by Peter France, London: Penguin: 2004

Shakespeare, William; *The Complete Works*, General editors Stanley Wells and Gary Taylor, Oxford, Clarendon Press, 1988

Spinoza, Baruch; *Ethics* (1677), trans. by Edwin Curley, London: Penguin, 1996

Spinoza, Baruch; *Complete Works* (containing Spinoza's 32nd Letter to Henry Oldenburg from 1665), trans. by Samuel Shirley, Indianapolis / Cambridge: Hackett Publishing Company, Inc., 2002

Five

PLATONISM AND POLITICS IN
THE TEMPEST

Ervin Beck

For many years it was customary to assume that Shakespeare wrote tragedies, comedies, history plays and romances that somehow supported "the Elizabethan world view." But, then, there were also several "problem plays"—notably *All's Well That Ends Well, Measure for Measure* and *Troilus and Cressida*—that, despite their presumably satisfactory endings, left too many personal, social, religious and political issues unresolved.

However, with the recent development of various political literary critical theories from about 1980 on—notably Marxist, feminist, queer and postcolonial—seemingly every Shakespearean play has become a problem play, or at least traditional interpretations have become problematized by new insights from these approaches. One result is the destabilization of conventional notions of dramatic genres and an acceptance of many unresolved issues at the ends of the plays.

This development is especially true of *The Tempest* (c. 1610–11), which for so long was regarded as the ultimate statement of Shakespeare's final, accumulated wisdom. The play boasts a rather unique status within Shakespeare's career: it was one of Shakespeare's last plays before he retired to Stratford in 1613; it probes highly contemplative themes such as the fundamental tendencies and qualities of human nature; and, with *Love's Labour's Lost*, it has a plot that is entirely Shakespeare's creation, not borrowed from other writers, unlike all of his other plays' origins. Perhaps this justifies regarding the play as a more "personal" statement by Shakespeare.

This essay will first sketch the interpretation of *The Tempest* that dominated critical reception for nearly three hundred years, then it will summarize the most recent consensus on the play's meaning, and finally it will consider whether the text can be "rescued" from inherent contradiction by some kind of integration of these opposing interpretations.

Prospero and Neo-Platonic Humanism

The Tempest is probably the best example in English drama of what E. M. W. Tillyard called "The Elizabethan World Picture" in his seminal book of the same title (1942), and as specifically applied to Shakespeare's works by Theodore Spencer in his book *Shakespeare and the Nature of Man* (1942). This world view is also articulated by Ulysses in Act 1, Scene 3 of Shakespeare's *Troilus and Cressida* (c. 1602). It is essentially a Renaissance humanist synthesis of

Christian and classical views of the human and the divine. In classical literature it is found most explicitly in Plato's *The Symposium*. In late Renaissance English literature it pervades Alexander Pope's *Essay on Man* (1735). In various forms, it is universally found in most cultures. Although Tillyard's thesis is very useful in studying Renaissance English literature, scholars following him have qualified his claims and shown that it is a scheme that is tested— sometimes discredited, sometimes affirmed—in literature of Shakespeare's day and later.

Renaissance Neo-Platonism saw the universe as structured according to a hierarchy of material, moral and spiritual values, ascending from the basest material to the highest spiritual levels: from the mineral universe, to plant life, to the animal kingdom, to humanity, to angels and to God. Within the human realm the ascent rose from the basest slave, to free laborers, to lower nobility, to aristocracy and to kings and queens, who were God's representatives in human affairs. In each level, further distinctions were perceived. Hence the universe was full of divine intention and meaning—implying dire consequences for violating the hierarchy.

The application to the range of characters in *The Tempest* is clear. Caliban, as "deformed monster" and slave, is at the bottom of the human chain of being, barely human. Above him, in ascending order, are the servants Trinculo and Stephano, the gentleman Gonzalo, the lords Adrian and Francisco, the minor nobility Sebastian and Antonio, the heirs Miranda and Ferdinand, and above them all are their rightful rulers, Prospero as Duke of Milan and Alonso as King of Naples. By implication, the chain extends further downward from Caliban to the witch Sycorax, who was Caliban's mother, and, finally, to the bottom of the universal hierarchy, the Devil himself, who fathered Caliban on Sycorax. The chain extends further upward, too, with Ariel and the other spirits that serve Prospero, and culminates in the arrival of the heavenly goddesses Iris and Ceres and their queen Juno, who is at the top of the universal hierarchy in Shakespeare's imagined universe.

On the literal level of the play Prospero is a "white" magician, in that he uses his magical powers to do good, not ill. He is cast in the platonic mode, since his special powers derive from his superior intellectual mastery of the wisdom found in the many books that he has read, and that have sustained him in his lonely fifteen years or so on the desert island. We may guess that, in the philosophical allegory of the play, Prospero's books included Homer, Plato (especially his *The Republic*), Virgil, the Bible, Augustine, Dante, Thomas More (especially his *Utopia*) and Montaigne. For Plato, like so many after him, knowledge was power. Caliban himself recognizes this fact in Prospero when he says, in Act 3, Scene 2: "Burn but his books, for without them he is a sot, as I am."

On the level of political allegory Prospero becomes Plato's "philosopher-king," that is, the person most qualified to rule others because of his intellectual achievement, based on the humanist assumption that the person who knows what is true and good will also act effectively and morally.

These ideas lead to a traditional reading of *The Tempest*, which sees the main problem as the pervasive personal, moral and political usurpations of acceptable "order" or "degree" in the play—as symbolized even by the storm in scene one whereby the waves threaten to usurp the heavens and the landlubbing nobility from below usurp the work of the sailors on the deck.

Some of the minor usurpations are that Sycorax had imprisoned Ariel in a tree, that Caliban tried to rape Miranda, and that Ferdinand moves too quickly (Prospero claims) in courting Miranda. The major usurpation driving the plot is the original usurpation of Prospero as Duke of Milan, which was carried out by his own brother Antonio, with the aid of Alonso, the King of Naples. This political treachery is parodied in the low comedy plot of Caliban, Trinculo and Stephano as they aim to kill Prospero, seize Miranda and rule the island.

Given this context, Prospero's task is to restore order and degree to a chaotic situation by using his superior intellect, power and moral sense. Indeed, the play tests the degree to which education, or "nurture," as exercised by Prospero, can overcome base "nature" in Caliban and base human nature in Prospero's enemies. Notice the frequent and telling use of the words *nature* and *nurture* throughout the play.

Prospero's first challenge on the island was to restore proper order. First, he liberated Ariel and productively harnessed Ariel's spiritual powers. His second task, of humanizing Caliban, was less successful. He taught Caliban "language," which led to Caliban's finer awareness of himself, the island, the sky, music and the spiritual world. But, in the last analysis, nurture could not "stick" on Caliban, as witnessed by his attempt to rape Miranda. In punishment of this deed, Prospero used his power to make Caliban his kitchen slave. The implication of Caliban's experience is that there are limits to which one's station in an orderly universe can be improved.

Prospero's greatest challenge is coping with his enemies from Italy, i.e., his brother Antonio as well as Alonso and his brother Sebastian. To that end, Prospero draws their ship to his island and creates the storm that will shipwreck them and put them under his control. His dilemma thereafter is whether to punish them for their perfidy or find a way to reform them or forgive them. Although the plot seems rather undramatic, since we are always aware of Prospero's superior power over everyone in the play, the most interesting action of the play is Prospero's dynamic internal conflict, which can be seen in carefully reading Prospero's psychology throughout. Some of the psychology is overt, but a careful reading of correspondences in the play suggests that the moral psychology is also allegorized in Caliban (=cannibal/flesh) and Ariel (=aerial/spirit) and the way they embody impulses toward physical revenge or spiritual forgiveness within Prospero himself.

In the beginning, Prospero seems Calibanic in his impulse toward revenge, as suggested by the anger in Scene 2 that he directs against Caliban, Ariel, Ferdinand and even his beloved daughter Miranda. By Act 3, Scene 3, as stated in Ariel's magnificent speech, "You are three men of sin…," he has decided to enact no revenge if his enemies repent and reform. Ariel's speech on behalf of Prospero does move Alonso to repent, but not Sebastian and Antonio. Urged by Ariel in Act 5, Scene 1, Prospero renews his decision to forgive them if they repent. But later in the same scene he forgives Antonio even though Antonio has not repented. At the very end of the play, Prospero even is willing to pardon Caliban. The Ariel, or spirit, in him has prevented the usurpation of his spiritual self by his baser, fleshly nature.

Prospero has righted the political situation by bringing Alonso to repent and to return to Prospero the dukedom of Milan. He has guaranteed the future peace by marrying his daughter and heir Miranda to Alonso's son and heir Ferdinand. He promises to liberate Ariel from his term of enforced service and, by implication of his leaving the island, will also release Caliban from his slavery. Prospero will return to his beloved library and to meditating on his own mortality.

The "happy ending" of this comic romance brings about the restoration of rightful order in the moral and political universe. Yes, there are some loose ends in the plot and some contradictions in moral character and theme. The most obvious problem is that the unrepentant conspirators Sebastian and Antonio return to Italy with a weakened Prospero. More profound questions also remain. For instance, does Prospero himself acknowledge that his use of spiritual power was a kind of human usurpation of the divine, as evidenced by his promise to free Ariel, break his [magic] staff, drown his [magic] book (Act 5, Scene 1) and return to his weaker condition in Italy? In his control of the spiritual world, did Prospero become too close to being a Superman hero, to the extent of even being able to bring down goddesses from heaven? And what will become of Caliban, whose character and insights were elevated by Prospero beyond what will make him truly content on his to-be empty island?

Such details lend complexity to the play, but do not much undermine the traditional view that a good, divinely ordained order—the great chain of being, the Elizabethan world picture—has been implied, challenged and re-affirmed by *The Tempest*. That the play is a "summing up" of the rather positive wisdom that Shakespeare had gained from his life and study is a satisfying assumption, but one that is undermined by the same powerfully felt skepticism that pervades his great tragedies.

Caliban, Ariel, and Postcolonialism

Literary theory and literary criticism are very much related to historical context. Notice, for instance, that the Tillyard and Spencer books that consolidated the interpretation above were published in 1942, during the dark years of the Second World War. The books can be seen as literary intellectuals' attempts to re-affirm the historic classical-Christian values that Fascism and the war were so seriously challenging.

So, too, with postcolonial theory and criticism, which is even more explicitly related to historical events. Postcolonial approaches to literary study emerged with the post-Second World War liberation movements that ended the European empires and resulted in the political and cultural independence of indigenous peoples from their erstwhile overlords. Beginning especially in the 1960s, newly educated writers from formerly colonized people began writing their own stories from their own point of view, as for instance with R. K. Narayan from India (independent 1947), Chinua Achebe from Nigeria (independent 1960), and V. S. Naipaul from Trinidad (independent 1962). Postcolonial political and literary theory, heavily Marxist, came from thinkers like the psychiatrist Franz Fanon from Martinique and Algeria, who wrote *The Wretched of the Earth* (1957), and the Palestinian Edward Said, whose *Orientalism* (1978) has become seminal in the field.

Overtly postcolonial studies of *The Tempest* stem mainly from about 1988 and remain the dominant interpretation of the play today. One important book in this field is Eric Cheyfitz's *The Poetics of Imperialism: Translation and Colonization from* The Tempest *to* Tarzan (1991). However, such studies have their true origin in a 1964 essay, "Shakespeare's American Fable," published by Leo Marx in his book *The Machine in the Garden*, where Marx claimed that *The Tempest* is the first literary work about America.

Although the setting of *The Tempest* is literally in the Adriatic Sea somewhere between Tunis and Milan, its historical subject matter is clearly linked to the colonization of North America. In 1610–11, when the play was apparently written, London was abuzz with news of English commercial ventures in the New World, which included the capital investments of some of Shakespeare's friends. The text refers to Bermuda in Act 1, Scene 2. And Caliban's odd name derives from colonists' contacts with indigenous people in America. It apparently is related to the Spanish word *canibal*, which came from the language of the Arawaks, the original inhabitants of Caribbean islands, for whom it meant "strong man," although in English it now refers to humans who eat human flesh.

Caliban's character and experience—and Ariel's, to a lesser degree—is the touchstone for the postcolonial interpretation of the play. If the humanist interpretation sees the play from Prospero's point of view, the postcolonial interpretation sees the play from Caliban's and Ariel's point of view; or, rather, from the point of view of critics from formerly colonized countries who identify with Caliban, as victim, rather than with Prospero, as foreign master. For instance, Derek Walcott, the Nobel Prize winning poet from St. Lucia in the Caribbean, calls himself a "Caliban" and says he views the world from a "calibanic" point of view.

The analogies are persuasive. Prospero may have landed on the "desert island" accidentally, but once there he took it over as his province, re-ordered and subjugated the indigenous population of Ariel and Caliban, and proceeded to impose his will and culture on the island. That background history of colonization is replicated by the Italians who land on the island following the storm. Even the good man Gonzalo expresses in his long speech in Act 2 Scene 1 what he would do if he had command of the island: "Had I plantation [colonization] of this isle, my lord—." Although the speech has always been admired for its utopian idealism, it is actually the fantasy of a European who imagines powerful control over a land that is not his to command. This colonizing impulse is literally, and foolishly, duplicated by the impulses of the comic characters Trinculo and Stephano, who aim to rule the island by themselves. However, in league with them is Caliban, who rather pathetically sees their murderous scheme as his own war of independence to regain control of the island, which he claims was originally his.

Caliban's point of view as subjugated native is most forcefully expressed very early in the play, with his angry address to Prospero over being his slave. Act 1, Scene 2, contains the testimony and complaint by Caliban that wins sympathy even from those in the audience who identify with Prospero:

> This island's mine, by Sycorax my mother,
> Which thou tak'st from me. When thou cam'st first,
> Thou strok'st me and made much of me, wouldst give me
> Water with berries in 't, and teach me how
> To name the bigger light, and how the less,
> That burn by day and night. And then I loved thee
> And showed thee all the qualities o' th' isle,
> The fresh springs, brine pits, barren place and fertile.
> Cursed be I that did so! All the charms
> Of Sycorax, toads, beetles, bats, light on you!
> For I am all the subjects that you have,
> Which first was mine own king; and here you sty me
> In this hard rock, whiles you do keep from me
> The rest o' th' island...
> You taught me language, and my proifit on 't
> Is I know how to curse. The red plague rid you
> For learning me your language.

Here, in marvelous poetry and rhetoric, is a brief summary of the universal process of colonization and of the native's declaration of war on his oppressor.

Like a typical colonizer (according to Cliban's complaint), Prospero first seized land that was not his from a native of the island. He feigned kindness to the native and, with his superior education, taught the native many things he did not know, including language. The native reciprocated by teaching him what Prospero needed to know in order to survive, and ultimately prevail. But then the colonizer used a pretext to enslave the native and take over the island completely. In the humanist interpretation, Caliban's attempted rape is a sign of his inferior, immoral nature. The postcolonial interpretation of the rape instead uses feminist theory, which sees rape not as mere lust but as a power play. That is, Caliban, in his politically and physically inferior relation to Prospero, can resist Prospero only by attacking Miranda, a weaker stand-in for her father. It is no surprise, then, that he quickly joins Trinculo and Stephano, who offer him a kind of "army" to carry out his violent resistance to his oppressor. One reason he is so quick to join them, of course, is the alcohol that they offer him to drink, which was another means whereby colonialists undermined natives and their culture. In turning Prospero's gift of language into cursing, Caliban resembles other colonized people who used the gifts of their European education to theorize and implement their own revolutionary movements.

Of course, all kinds of details in the play militate against a fully sympathetic interpretation of Caliban (as also with Shylock, Falstaff, and many other comic characters in Shakespeare). But Shakespeare clearly gives him some of the finest poetry in the play, and Caliban emerges as a more complex character than any other besides Prospero. In scolding Trinculo and Stephano in Act V for being diverted from their militant campaign by gaudy clothes, Caliban also becomes their superior in intellect.

He even becomes a kind of tragic character. In his Act 1 manifesto, he indicates that Prospero has elevated his personal awareness, through language, of himself and his universe. And later in the play (Act 3, Scene 2) Caliban utters a haunting speech that expresses the awareness of beauty that Prospero's liberation of the spirit world on the island has brought to Caliban:

> Be not afeard. The isle is full of noises,
> Sounds, and sweet airs, that give delight and hurt not.
> Sometimes a thousand twangling instruments
> Will hum about mine ears, and sometimes voices
> That, if I then had waked after long sleep,
> Will make me sleep again; and then, in dreaming,
> The clouds methought would open and show riches
> Ready to drop upon me, that when I waked
> I cried to dream again.

Caliban may have used Prospero's "language" in order to curse him, but he also can express himself now in a poetry that matches, or even excels, that of Prospero and Ariel.

Like other colonized natives, Caliban has become a kind of split personality, suffering from the kind of "nervous condition" analyzed by Franz Fanon, a psychiatrist. Caliban is a product of two cultures—the primitive island culture of his mother and the more worldly, sophisticated culture of his foreign master. "Nowhere man" is the name that Kamala Markandaya of India gives to such a culturally divided person. "Half-caste" is the term used by Camara Laye, of Guinea, to refer to a person of such mixed cultural background. The ending of the play implies the haunting image of Caliban, the only physical creature left on the island, enjoying his springs and berries but frustrated by being unable to fully express himself or communicate with the foreign-imposed language that he is now the master of.

The play lends itself to many possibilities when staged. In light of its connection with the original colonization of America, Caliban can be depicted as an American Indian who originally welcomed European immigrants but eventually was killed or herded into reservations by them. Or, also in America, Caliban can be conceived of as an African enslaved in pre-Civil War culture. A refinement of that interpretation sees Caliban as a field slave, who remained less cultured and more exploited by slave masters, and Ariel as a house slave, who took on whites' culture and enjoyed more privileges than a field slave. Of course, for instance, in Lithuania (or in Eastern Europe more generally) Caliban can be seen as a native exploited by his Soviet overlords, and Ariel as a collaborator who enjoyed special privileges during the occupation.

There are obvious limits to the postcolonial interpretation. Caliban is certainly no "noble savage," ruined by colonialists through no fault of his own. The attempted rape is one stroke against him. So is his too easy joining with Stephano and Trinculo. Yes, that association is fuelled by drink, but Caliban's ludicrous act of falling to his knees and worshiping Stephano as his "god" undermines Caliban's dignity and authority. It even suggests an inherently inferior intellect and will in the native, who therefore needs the benevolent discipline of an inherently superior Prospero. Caliban comes to this self-knowledge in the final scene, saying to his master and others:

> ... I'll be wise hereafter
> And seek for grace. What a thrice-double ass
> Was I to take this drunkard for a god
> And worship this dull fool.

Caliban, the would-be revolutionary, decides to accept Prospero's "pardon" and meekly follows his instruction to return to Prospero's "cell" and tidy it up for his return.

Finally, Shakespeare also complicates the question of who really owns the island. Who is the occupier and who is the native? According to the background story of the play, Ariel was the original inhabitant, not Caliban, who nevertheless claims ownership. The first invader of Ariel's island was "this damned witch Sycorax," who by her black magic imprisoned Ariel in a pine tree. On the island was born her son Caliban, whose father was the devil himself. With this history and genealogy in mind, one can see the positive outcomes of Prospero's work on the island: the restoration of rightful ownership to Ariel and the improvement of Caliban, the spawn of witch and devil.

Reconciling the Interpretations

How can a single play, which is so successful when staged, contain two such opposing meanings?

For a postmodern audience, that is not a problem. Postmodernism tends to accept, and even assume, contradictions, indeterminate genres and open-ended, even baffling endings. But neither the humanist nor the postcolonial approach to literature is postmodern in its expectations. Instead, the humanist reading looks for a kind of moral consistency and the postcolonial reading assumes a kind of political correctness, especially a Marxist perspective that emphasizes exploitation at the level of class.

The best way to resolve the contradictions is in performance, through a director's choices. Characters and events in *The Tempest* are so amorphous, so "unrealistic" that they lend themselves to symbolic interpretations. In fact, *The Tempest* is Shakespeare's most symbolic play. Obviously, a director who gives Caliban a costume of animal skins encourages a humanist reading. A director who gives Caliban an American Indian costume encourages a postcolonial reading. Directors can also emphasize one event or character over another, omit lines, rearrange scenes, and so forth.

However, if one finds both readings equally attractive and seeks a unity of idea, to match the two other neo-classical "unities" of time and place that the play respects, there are two developments in the plot that offer opportunities to emphasize things about Prospero, as both philosopher-king and colonialist, that can help integrate the moral and the political implications of the play.

The first, major one is Prospero's decision in Act IV to give up his magical powers. At the conclusion of his magisterial speech in Act 5, Scene 1, "Ye elves of hills, brooks, standing lakes, and groves," he vows to "break my staff" and "drown my book"—by "staff" referring to his power over nature and by "book" referring to the knowledge that gives him that power. In the humanist reading of the play, that relinquishment indicates that Prospero, at last, chooses to be human rather than superhuman, to forgive rather than to take revenge on others, to release both Ariel and Caliban rather than hold them in bondage, to return to fallen Milan rather than live in a remote utopia. He will re-join the human race.

But Prospero's relinquishment of his moral and spiritual powers can also include the idea that he has also relinquished his political power over the island and its inhabitants. He may not consciously understand or admit that he has been acting like a colonizing tyrant, but by giving up his power and leaving the island he, in effect, repudiates that role and gives independence to those that he earlier lorded over. The gesture recalls that of de Klerck in South Africa, who reversed *apartheid* by decree; also, although perhaps less willingly, Gorbachev in Russia, who reversed the course of the Soviet regime. The text does not call for an actual on-stage burying of the staff and drowning of the book, but a director can introduce an appropriate symbolic action at the right moment in the play.

The second moment of opportunity occurs near the very end of the play when Prospero and his Italian compatriots confront Stephano, Trinculo and Caliban, the failed conspirators. Stephano and Trinculo shrink back to Alonso, after which Prospero speaks the astounding words, referring to Caliban: "This thing of darkness I acknowledge mine."

When I have directed the play, I have tried to make this a culminating moment of the play, by instructing Prospero to help raise a crouched Caliban to a tiptoed height of human dignity, close to him, with their faces in profile, and with that position held for moments longer than would be natural.

In the humanist reading, that gesture by Prospero indicates that he has accepted his limitations as a human being, made of flesh, limited by mortality, capable of moral failure. He has attained full self-knowledge. In the postcolonial reading, the gesture indicates that Prospero has accepted as his equal the creature that he had exploited and regarded as his inferior. In postmodernist terms, he has acknowledged the "Other" and come to terms with himself through coming to terms with it (i.e., the otherness which helps determine his own identity). It becomes both a moral and a political achievement for Prospero.

Some may still want to rewrite the play in order to make an unalloyed postcolonial point. Aimee Cesaire of Martinique, who was a leader in postcolonial thought and literature and an influential teacher of Franz Fanon, did just that in his play, *A Tempest* (1969). He has been joined by literally hundreds of other writers who have, in a postmodern way, re-written *The Tempest* in their own image or written dramatic, fictional or poetic responses to it. Probably no other play by Shakespeare has been so often re-envisioned by other writers.

That, of course, is hardly a negative comment on *The Tempest* as a failed play. Rather, it is clear evidence of the imaginative hold that it continues to exercise as a seminal, defining text in today's global culture.

Works Cited

Cesaire, Aimee. *A Tempest.* New York: Ubu Repertory, 1986. (*Une Tempete.* Paris: Seuil, 1969. "adaptation pour un theatre negre")

Cheyfitz, Eric. *The Poetics of Imperialism: Translation and Colonization from* The Tempest *to* Tarzan. New York: Oxford University Press, 1991.

Fanon, Franz. *The Wretched of the Earth.* New York: Grove Press, 1963. (*Les Damnes de la Terre.* 2nd ed. Paris: F. Maspero, [1962]. First edition Ahwaz, Iran, 1957.)

Laye, Camara. *The Dark Child.* Trans. James Kirkup and Ernest Jones. New York: Farrar, Straus and Giroux, 1969. (*L'enfant Noir.* Paris: Libraire Plon, [1953].)

Markandaya, Kamala. *The Nowhere Man.* New York: John Day, [1972].

Marx, Leo. *The Machine in the Garden: Technology and the Pastoral Ideal in America.* New York: Oxford University Press, 1964.

Said, Edward. *Orientalism.* London: Routledge and Kegan Paul, 1978.

Spencer, Theodore. *Shakespeare and the Nature of Man.* New York: Macmillan, 1942.

Tillyard, E. M. W. *The Elizabethan World Picture.* New York: Random House, 1942.

Six

CURRENCIES OF LOVE: POLITICAL AND ETHICAL ECONOMIES OF LANGUAGE IN SHAKESPEARE

J. D. Mininger and Jason Michael Peck

In "Interim Report on Recessional Aesthetics," Simon Critchley and Tom Mc-Carthy dissect the ontological status of money as represented in Shakespeare's *The Merchant of Venice*.[1] Quoting Shylock's assertion that Antonio is a "good man," Critchley and McCarthy point out that Shylock's meaning is not that his character is morally good, but that "he is sufficient" (40), i.e. he is "good" for the money: he has a sound credit rating and is therefore "good." This leads to their conclusion that "what is going on in the drama of *the Merchant of Venice* is the transformation of the language of courtly love into that of commerce, the moneying of desire." (Critchely and McCarthy 40)

To what extent, however, does this "moneying of desire" extend beyond the specific dramatic work in question? Is this transformation inherent in Shakespeare's larger body of work? Is it merely the symptom of this play about the Jewish moneylender Shylock that allows us to mistake money for love? Critchley and McCarthy also have other topics in mind, so they may be easily forgiven for only offering a cursory (albeit richly provocative) reading of Shakespeare's play. However, a closer reading of this particular passage in the play can help to elucidate *how* this transformation takes place. Moreover, to move from *The Merchant of Venice*, wherein the register of courtly love is merely suggested, to Shakespeare's sonnets, wherein the register of courtly love is explicitly referenced if not fully manifested, would make the transformation of both linguistic registers complete. Our essay aspires to charting this transformation through close readings of parts of *The Merchant of Venice* and several sonnets.

Of Kindness and Mercy; or, from a Restricted to a General Economy in *The Merchant of Venice*

The movement between the metamorphosis of money and desire in *Merchant of Venice* and the sonnets circulates around two terms that link the play and the poems: namely, the twin figures of sufficiency and constancy. In Shakespeare's play, the two terms are in a state of tension with one another. Characters who can demonstrate their sufficiency suffer from a lack of constancy (Antonio), and characters who remain constant throughout the play are marked as insufficient in both material and spiritual wealth (Shylock). What is ultimately needed to transform the language of love into the language of money is a character who both embodies the sufficiency of material goods with the constancy of value (Portia). The irony of this situation is, of course, that Portia (disguised as the lawyer Balthazar) is seemingly removed from this system of exchange by rendering absurd Shylock's constancy and superfluous Antonio's original claims of sufficiency. The third term, mercy, would seem to be a way out of this system of exchange, yet, as Critchley and McCarthy point out, "mercy" is the global system that encompasses both. This makes Portia—keeper of the three caskets, it should be added here—a de facto I.M.F., able to set the unimpeachable standard of value for the entirety of the play.

Of all the characters in the play, it is worth noting that Shylock seems the most removed from the romantic intrigue that frames the play. Aside from a brief mention of a family ring which it is rumored his daughter Jessica trades for a monkey, a ring which Shylock mentions "I had it of Leah when I was a bachelor. / I would not have given it for a wilderness of monkeys" (III.i.121–123), the language of love seems to be absent from Shylock's discourse. However, in contrast to this very intentional absence on Shylock's part to any affinities with other human beings, thus allowing ostensibly his abject portrayal by the end of the play, the word love occurs multiple times within Shylock's introduction in the play.

This scene introduces the terms of Shylock's "bond" with Antonio—the famous "pound of flesh" that Shylock will take from Antonio should he fail to pay Shylock his three thousand ducats. This is also the scene that Critchley and McCarthy cite at the beginning of their recessional report. As Shylock and Bassanio discuss the money that Shylock will lend to Antonio, Shylock mentions:

> *Shy.* Antonio is a good man.
> *Bass.* Have you heard any imputation to the contrary?
> *Shy.* Ho, no, no, no, no! my meaning in saying he is a good man is to have you understand he is sufficient (I.iii.12–17)

Sufficiency here means that he will be able to repay Shylock, though "his means are in supposition" (I.iii.17). Critics have tended to read this scene as the first instance of Shylock's deception: he knows very well that Antonio will not be able to repay him and, thus, he will be able to exact his revenge upon him. This is seemingly borne out by the comments Shylock makes as an aside when Antonio enters:

> *Shy.* [*Aside*] How like a fawning publican he looks!
> I hate him for he is a Christian;
> But, more, for that in low simplicity
> He lends our money out gratis, and brings down
> The rate of usance here with us in Venice.

If I can catch him once upon the hip,
I will feed fat the ancient grudge I bear him (I.iii.41–47)

In this scene, Antonio—according to Shylock—demonstrates "sufficiency," although he does not demonstrate "constancy." To be good in the world of the play is to be sufficient, yet not constant. In the aside quoted above, the audience learns that Antonio "lends our money out gratis," thus avoiding the system of usury "here with us in Venice." Further on, after Antonio initially agrees to borrow money for Bassanio from Shylock, Shylock remarks: "Well then, your bond, and let me see—but hear you, / Methoughts you said you neither lend nor borrow/ Upon advantage" (I.iii.67–69) To which Antonio responds: "I do never use it" (I.iii.70).

Here the split between sufficiency and constancy is clear—one is good only insofar as one is sufficient to repay debts. One need not be constant to be "good" as is proven by Antonio's answer in this scene. So what of the Jew? Where does the Jew's ethics rest in this scene? In the secondary literature on the play Shylock is generally presented as "consistent," insofar as he refers to his "bond" throughout the play and will not be swayed by the "mercy" Portia famously implores at the end of the play:

Port. Do you confess the bond?
Shy. I do.
Port. Then must the Jew be merciful.
Shy. On what compulsion must I? Tell me that.
Port. The quality of mercy is not strain'd.
It dropeth as the gentle rain from heaven
Upon the place beneath. (IV.i.181–186)

Critchley and McCarthy turn Portia's Christian apologia against the Jew as a mere echo, a repetition of all that had come in the play previous:

Portia, cross-dressed as the young lawyer Balthazar, announces a mercy that "droppeth as the gentle rain from heaven'—that is, without measure, infinitely. Portia (an impostor, let's not forget) supplants economic law with a "higher," moral order. And yet Shakespeare, good etymologist that he is, is all too aware that the mercy that cannot be strained, that should season justice, that the Jew Shylock should show, and that is even— according to Portia—an attribute of God himself, is derived from *merces*, meaning "payment," "price," or "fee." Mercantile revenue is *revenu* in moral talk of mercy. Christianity (and, by extension, the moral rhetoric of liberalism into which it has mutated) is the hypocritical spiritualization of the originally material. (Critchley and McCarthy 41)

Thus, in the play, all forms of love, even Christian love, mutate into their material opposites as a system of exchange. To be good in the sense of being *merciful* is to exact a payment (in this case from the Jew). Many commentators have noted that the very mercy the Christian characters wish to employ at the end of the play is not very *merciful* insofar as they force conversion on the Jew, refuse him his principal and take hold of his possessions. Again, to be "good" in this sense means to be "merciful"; however, as demonstrated by Critchley and McCarthy's reading of the play, to be merciful is neither to be good (in the sense that there is a secret "repayment" expected for the limitless supply—i.e. a demand made by mercy's supply) nor is it to be very consistent. Of course, given the consistency with which the Jew has insisted on "his bond," he will not be "sufficient" to repay the debt demanded by mercy by the end of the play: "Therefore, Jew,/ Though justice be thy plea, consider this,/ That in the course of justice, none of us,/ Should see salvation" (IV.i.197–200). Therefore, in this transvaluation of all values hitherto (which, as Critchley and McCarthy have correctly pointed out, bears a striking resemblance to liberal capitalism), it is not Shylock that comes to represent the emergent form of capitalism through mercantilism and usury, rather the Christian value of mercy that produces sufficiency and goodness.

Where does Shylock fit in this constellation of sufficiency, constancy and goodness? Returning to the scene wherein the initial transaction between Shylock and Antonio takes place, it appears as if Shylock is neither consistent (due to the fact he speaks in an aside of his hatred of Antonio and his desire for revenge) nor is he sufficient in either the material exchange of money (he mentions that he "cannot instantly raise up the gross/Of full three thousand ducats" but that "Tubal, a wealthy Hebrew of my tribe,/Will furnish me."), or the immaterial exchange of justice for mercy (Antontio notes—after Shylock has cited the story of Jacob and the ewes from Genesis—that "An evil soul producing holy witness,/ Is like a villain with a smiling cheek,/ A goodly apple rotten at the heart."). Therefore, Shylock, the character that would seem to be the signifier for exchange, somehow stands outside of the system of exchange constructed by the play.

The text appears to highlight the duplicitous nature of Shylock by presenting us with an aside ("If I can catch him once upon the hip,/I will feed fat the ancient grudge I bear him.") that stands in contrast to what Shylock explicitly states to Antonio ("I would be friends with you, and have your love,/Forget the shames that you have stain'd me with,"). However, what is ingenious about the wager, the exchange, that Shylock proposes is that it is truly ambivalent (ambivalent) in its meaning, an ambivalence that can be compared to the language Shakespeare uses in Sonnet 105.[2]

Antonio initially accuses Shylock of offering to lend him money because it is advantageous to "lend it rather to thine enemy,/Who if he break, thou mayst with better face/Exact the penalty" (I.iii.135–36) Shylock appears to take offense, stating:

Shy. Why, look you how you storm!
I would be friends with you, and have your love,
Forget the shames that you have stain'd me with,
Supply your present wants and take no doit
Of usance for my moneys, and you'll not hear me.
This is kind I offer. (I.iii.137–142)

Again, were Shylock to be valued by his constancy, perhaps he would be found lacking. Yet, Shylock never deceives Antonio in the terms of his agreement—he lends him the money without taking "usance" for his services (something that Antonio had complained of in the past). He mimics Antonio's earlier claim that while he neither lends nor borrows money, he will make an exception "to supply the ripe wants of a friend" (I.iii.63). Here, Shylock would not ordinarily refuse usance for his money but, that Shylock "would" be friends with Antonio and "have his love," he makes an exception. It is from this exceptional state that both Shylock and Antonio may "meet" one another in "kindness."

The text goes on to play with the word kind/kindness in brokering the deal between Shylock and Antonio. As mentioned above, Shylock believes the terms of the agreement to be "kind," with Bassanio commenting: "This were kindness" (I.iii.143). Bassanio's suspicion is still present in the use of the conditional: i.e. were we to believe that the Jew could be "sufficient" (i.e. good) enough to demonstrate kindness (much like mercy), then this deal would be kind.

Almost as if anticipating Bassanio and Antonio's skepticism, Shylock elaborates on the deal he wishes to make:

Shy. This kindness will I show.
Go with me to a notary, seal me there
Your single bond; and in merry sport
If you repay me not on such a day,
In such a place, such sum or sums as are
Express'd in the condition, let the forfeit
Be nominated for an equal pound
Of your fair flesh, to be cut off and taken
In what part of your body pleaseth me. (I.iii.143–151)

Antonio agrees that, "there is much kindness in the Jew" (I.iii.153) after hearing the terms of the loan, assenting to seal the bond with Shylock. Bassanio attempts to dissuade Antonio from agreeing to the loan, to which Shylock responds:

Pray you tell me this:
If he should break his day, what should I gain
By the exaction of the forfeiture?
A pound of man's flesh taken from a man

> Is not so estimable, profitable neither,
> As flesh of muttons, beefs, or goats. I say,
> To buy his favor, I extend this friendship. (I.iii.163–170)

His kindness is demonstrated by his unwillingness to profit from Antonio's default on the loan—a kindness that is as fair as Antonio's assertion that he neither lends nor borrows "upon advantage." Indeed, even after hearing the terms of the loan Antonio asserts: "The Hebrew will turn Christian, he grows kind" (I.iii.178), with nothing in the exchange between the two men to suggest otherwise. Or, as Shylock asserts, "To buy his favor, I extend this friendship./ If he will take it so, if not, adieu" (I.iii.168–9).

Perhaps this repetition of "kind" and "kindness" is to offset the aforementioned use of "mercy" at the end of the play. There is a parallel structure in Balthazar's (Portia's) description of "mercy" at the end of the play and the use of "kind" in Shylock's introductory scene. As Balthazar/Portia states after the well-known "quality of mercy is not stern" line: "[…]it is twice blest;/ It blesseth him that gives and him that takes." Here we have another system of exchange: to give mercy is to receive it, much as to give "kindness" is to receive "kindness" in kind. Yet, the repetition of the word demonstrated in the last sentence—the inherence of two meanings of "kind": i.e. a system of equivalence (a group of common traits) and "kind" (to be sympathetic)—suggests that the system of exchange that marks Shylock's offer is truly without surplus value. It is a true constant system of exchange wherein the equivalent of one may stand in for the other. This is why Shylock correctly argues that his exchange is kind because there is no interest, no usury involved in his exchange.[3]

Balthazar/Portia's system is not as "kind" as she would have us believe: Critchley and McCarthy point out that mercy, in its very etymology, demands repayment. Not just any repayment, of course, but an *infinite* repayment—for how can anyone ever "repay" *God* in "kind." Portia's discussion at the end of the play alludes to this after her most famous lines: "'Tis [mercy] mightiest in the mightiest: it becomes/ The throned monarch better than his crown." Much like the word "kind," the word "becomes" here must be read in a multivalent way: "becomes" can either mean becoming—i.e. fetching, flattering, etc. (that is to say, mercy suits the monarch better than the crown; i.e. his power[4])—or it could mean that mercy, the supreme value that Portia places above all else ("mercy is above this sceptred sway"), has itself become sovereign.

Within the intellectual history of the twentieth century, no theorist has offered a more succinct definition of sovereignty than the German legal theorist Carl Schmitt. Schmitt, in his book *Political Theology*, defines the sovereign as "he who decides on the exception" (5). According to Schmitt, the exceptional situation is a "borderline case," wherein a "constitution needs to be suspended in its entirety" (7). If it seems that the mercy Portia describes in her closing speech would exist outside of juridical considerations, remember that it is she (disguised as Balthazar) who makes the initial analogy between mercy and sovereignty. Moreover, that sovereignty might exist as something alien to the theological register Portia invokes at the end of the play, is addressed by Schmitt in *Political Theology*: "Whether God alone is sovereign, that is, the one who acts as his acknowledged representative on earth, or the emperor, or prince, or the people [...] the question is always aimed at the subject of sovereignty, at the application of the concept to a concrete situation" (10). Moreover, that this discussion in *The Merchant of Venice* takes place during a *legal* proceeding should not be lost on the possibility that what we are really dealing with here is a question of sovereignty and the designation of the state of exception. To put it in more concrete terms within the context of the play: the discourse of "mercy" is the sovereign measure necessary to halt the "extreme peril" (Schmitt 6) presented by Shylock to "the state, public safety and order" (Schmitt 6). Or, not coincidentally, to put it in terms that (deplorably) Schmitt himself would have surely and readily embraced, the Jew represents a "danger" to the existence of the state and therefore, quoting Critchley and McCarthy, "then (as now) some Jew is going to have to pay" (41).

What does the confluence between mercy and sovereignty have to do with love? The answer may perhaps be found in Shakespeare's Sonnet 105, where the second quatrain reads: "Kind is my love today, tomorrow kind,/Still constant in a wondrous excellence;/Therefore my verse, to constancy confin'd;/ One thing expressing, leaves out difference" (321). "Kindness" is constant in its valuation and in that sense cannot sidestep the need for a system of exchange. Therefore, when we talk about the metamorphosis from the language of courtly love to the language of money this is not necessarily a new development. Indeed, the dowry, represented by the story of Lorenzo and Jessica in *The Merchant of Venice*, is always already inscribed in the marriage contract. What is new, what marks this transformation, is not "kindness" but "mercy." As previously mentioned, Critchley and McCarthy remind us that mercy is love as love without repayment—a debt that can never be shaken off. Moreover, what marks this new confluence between love and money is the sovereign nature of its ontological status: if kindness as love requires constancy to institute its economic regime, then mercy institutes the state of exception in creating its value. This is borne out in the logic of the play: whereas Shylock's kindness requires a contract between two autonomous subjects, Portia's mercy can only be instituted through judicial means (i.e. have mercy: be merciful or else!).

The sovereign state is antithetical to constancy, since it is always looking for a new emergency in which to install its legitimacy. If indeed mercy transforms the language of love into the language of commerce, then it is a transformative register wherein the subject, rather than giving a pound of its flesh in exchange for love and friendship, would give up its soul in exchange for deferred payment.

Of Constancy and Money; or, from a Restricted to a General Economy in Sonnet 105

Just as with the *Merchant of Venice*, Shakespeare's sonnets offer a fertile source for exploring the manner in which the ideological and linguistic economies of love both produce and are produced by the language of commerce. The formal (linguistic) and thematic (political-ideological) trope of constancy immediately tethers *Merchant* to the sonnets. Constancy, as well as kind/kindness, supply initial transformative tissue in the interpenetrating movement charted here between the language of courtly love and the discourse of money.

Perhaps nowhere does Shakespeare more overtly develop the theme of constancy than in his Sonnet 105. The poem pronounces unwavering love to an unnamed (male) friend; however, in equal measure the poem generates panegyric eloquence about the very act of delivering dedicated praise to another. In Sonnet 105 Shakespeare offers a meta-discursive love poem about the very production of love poetry—a paean to lyrical romance itself. A simple, cursory reading of the sonnet unveils a lyric voice intent on defending and justifying its (the voice's) love; hence, the poem reads as a kind of apologia for this passionate, constant love, and only obliquely does the poem actually directly praise the love object. Instead, the constancy of the lover's love takes pride of place, dethroning the traditional love sonnet motif of praising the love object's characteristics in a verse that declares adoration for those particular traits.

Sonnet 105 appears to praise the lover as much if not more than the loved. Does that suggest that perhaps constancy involves a more significant self-referentiality buried behind the veneer of inter-subjective dedication? Does constancy suggest that the structure of loving hides a kind of subjective closed- or short-circuit? Who (or what) is truly being valued here in this relationship of love? These questions demand a closer analysis of the poem:

> Let not my love be call'd idolatry,
> Nor my belovèd as an idol show,
> Since all alike my songs and praises be
> To one, of one, still such, and ever so.
>
> Kind is my love today, tomorrow kind,
> Still constant in a wondrous excellence;
> Therefore my verse, to constancy confin'd;
> One thing expressing, leaves out difference.
>
> Fair, kind, and true is all my argument—
> Fair, kind, and true varying to other words;
> And in this change is my invention spent—
> Three themes in one, which wondrous scope affords.

> Fair, kind, and true have often liv'd alone,
> Which three till now never kept seat in one. (321)

Whether the "I" of this poem has suffered the accusation of being an idolater of love or whether perhaps even a guilty conscience has motivated the speaker to convince him/her/itself of the truth of love's faithfulness, the poem's opening couplet reveals the stakes to which the voice's claim of constancy remains bound. Lest idolatry be invoked, let me (the voice of the poem) set the record straight: I was and always am steadfast in my love; no matter what the song or praise may be, or what shape it may take, the object of my focus remains my belovèd; because my love is loyal and focused, so too are my verses focused on the one object of my love. Even the directly listed characteristics of the loved one—"fair, kind, and true"—the voice does not direct toward the belovèd as addressee. Rather, this repeated inventory, held out each time as if in quotation marks[5] so as to suggest that a foreign and merely representative element of some sort has been sterilely catalogued, seems to be directed diffusedly outward toward potential accusers, or, perhaps even more profoundly, directed inwards in a sort of mono-dialogue that suggests the presence of anxiety and uncertainty that the emphasized lexical tone of security in constancy would seem to belie. True to the very end, to that very last word "one," the sonnet's object and addressee remains ambiguously determined. The three registered characteristics of the belovèd are apparently rather rarely, if ever found united in the same body and personality...until now. Now, says the constant lyricist, they rest together, co-existing, amalgamated in the common factor of this "one." But who or what is this one: the belovèd or the poet-lover? Or, still more tellingly, does this "one" in fact refer to the poet's verse itself—perhaps even to *this poem*?

While the fact of the ambiguity of the poem's final word bears with it the possibility of referring to the belovèd, the tension of the simultaneous presence of these other pronominal references suggests that the constancy thematized in this sonnet may be borne out of a crisis of sorts—a crisis of value(s), of who or what is really being valued in this constant, consistent act of love. Or would it be better phrased as a loving act of constancy, if these two acts are in fact distinguishable? Our initial reading of sonnet 105 suggests that constancy may exceed the mere signification of steadfastness that it purports solely to provide and stand for. Even from this brief reading we note that, though the poet's love poetry may be "to constancy confin'd," this poem does indeed express more than one thing. Difference—that which structuralism has taught us to understand as the very foundational condition of the creation of any value whatsoever, whether culturally, linguistically, philosophically, or otherwise—has hardly been left out here. Difference in fact makes possible the very identity in constancy that the poet-lover embraces. Paradoxically, it seems in this poem that constancy invites difference, in the form of a tension between on the one hand the equivalence and reduction of all the poet's words to the three-in-one list of loved traits, and on the other hand the ultimately unequivocal, irreducibly singular "one" which no synonym could ever faithfully, let alone constantly, replace, because it shelters the existing person (whether self or other, poet or beloved) beyond representation.

In the (Lacanian) psychoanalytic idiom this value beyond equivalence is called the real, and its motivating (absent) presence is marked by precisely the representational constancy that the poet suggests: namely, an attempt to capture that which is in the loved object, but which, by the very nature of symbolic representation, always falls beyond the field of representation. This may help explain why "fair, kind, and true" find themselves as if within the clutches of quotation mark boundaries. "Fair, kind, and true" are here hardly just three values that add up to one expression; rather, as a singular expression and force of signification, they represent value itself. Difference is constantly refused precisely because in the constancy to which this verse is confined, the poem always returns to the same place, namely, where the ambiguous subject of the poem cannot find itself. To wit: in praise of the belovèd, the poem meditates on itself; for every signifier the poet utters, its individual quality is effaced by a universal signified; but yet this "universal" signified that supposedly sponsors the constancy signals a referent both absolutely singular—"one"—and yet utterly ambiguous because prominal usage is deictic, that is, referential. And referentiality in language, no matter how seemingly clear and cogent, must utilize the operation of abstraction, which in this context pulls the rug out from under the very constancy-in-reference the poem's voice claims for itself. Roman Jakobson (and the Russian formalists more generally) argued that all predicate usage is essentially metaphor, because it ultimately boils down to indicating resemblance.[6] Paul de Man would surely call this trope of referentiality: allegory.[7]

However, this operation of constancy that depends upon the motor of referentiality for its continual movement of renewal may be equally and productively translated with still different labels. The signifiers that the poet expends as perpetual encomium to the beloved (and, as we have already demonstrated, therefore to his/her/its own love as lyric) exist in perennial exchange with one another, in so far as they stand subordinated to the "one," value itself, the referent behind the roll call of "fair, kind, and true." The poet's words have no life of their own, but are pure (dead) commodities in perpetual circulation: the poet's desire, as discourse, is also equally the discourse (and desire) of money.[8]

This "one," which exists uniquely by virtue of and in the service of the (surplus) value itself, namely, "fair, kind, and true," owes its beloved existence to the manifold that effaces itself in the production of that value. The poem (and the poet) bear the tension between, on the one hand, the subordination of the law of value to surplus value, which involves an exploitation in which use value is transformed into a form capable of exchange—here, desire as love transformed into words—and, on the other hand, value itself (or, alternately, use value), which always eludes and exceeds the categories of exchange inflicted upon it and yet provides the basis for all value—here, addressed in the force of the quotation marks around the concatenated value-cluster, as well as the insistent (perhaps we might better say constant) surplus of signification expressed in the paradoxical singular-plural pronoun "one."

Lest accusations (perhaps not dissimilar to those fictional addresses from the opening of the poem) fly that we have debased the poem in some manner by instrumentally and willfully welding an interpretation of financial analogy to it, let us look again at Sonnet 105, this time reading less rhetorically and more with an eye to the lexical patterns and indices of the poem.

> Let not my love be call'd idolatry,
> Nor my belovèd as an idol show,
> Since all alike my songs and praises be
> To one, of one, still such, and ever so.
>
> *Kind* is my love today, tomorrow *kind*,
> Still constant in a wondrous excellence;
> Therefore my verse, to constancy confin'd;
> One thing expressing, leaves out difference.
>
> "Fair, *kind*, and true" is all my argument—
> "Fair, *kind*, and true" varying to other words;
> And in this *change* is my invention *spent*—
> Three themes in one, which wondrous scope *affords*.
>
> "Fair, *kind*, and true" have often liv'd alone,
> Which three till now never kept seat in one.[9] (321)

This sonnet boasts only one other word repeated as frequently as that ever important "one": *kind*. Kind certainly offers a lexical surplus. In its usage as adjective alone, its overdetermined valences produce interesting tensions. For instance, when understood as a synonym for benevolence or benevolent behavior, kind emphasizes a particularly human quality—namely, the morally inflected intention to do good to/for others. Yet when that meaning shifts just slightly under the burden of its exchangeability, it suggests qualities of being mild, or gentle. While certainly potentially human characteristics, these terms are also notably less human, such as, for example, when they describe nature, in particular the weather. As a noun the word "kind" even more appropriately justifies its frequency within the poem, for it contains within it the same conflict with which the greater thematic material of the poem struggles (yet precisely that friction which the voice of the poem denies), namely, the strain between difference and identity, between the many and the one. The nominal usage of "kind" suggests a class or group (of individual objects) having characteristics in common. Yet that collective procedure of classification based upon commonalities stands in the service of precisely the reduction of that difference at the hand of an identificatory and essentializing move. In this usage "kind" indicates an essential nature or character—something singular—such as when we say that "the difference is one of kind rather than degree.'

But "kind" also resonates rather directly with echoes of an economic context. One speaks of payment "in kind," referring to goods, services, or commodities given as payment instead of money. It is telling that a similar idiom is used in situations in which a reply, retort, or response is given, in order to indicate that what has been given corresponds (as something of the same sort/ kind) to the action being replied to, as for instance when one repays an insult with an insult. Kind here suggests the context of an exchange, of exactly the situation in which money fundamentally develops as necessary, that is, as a means of exchange meant to help make two things otherwise incommensurable now exchangeable. To pay "in kind" therefore refers to a form other than money, but to a "kind" of money that is not money: i.e. an unconverted form, but equivalent in value. "Kind is my love today, tomorrow kind." Whereas the typical reading of this line emphasizes adjectival usage, nothing stops us from also and equally reading this as a nominal usage. In this latter interpretive gesture, the love that the implied "I" of the poem possesses is *kind*, is *a* kind. Love here is both an essential nature, a singular expression (value itself, or intrinsic value), and also an empty, abstracted category that may subsume whatever multitude shares in that common characteristic, despite any other existent, even salient difference(s) (exchange value, or market value). The act of love here is not money, though certainly love is (unfortunately; cynically) sometimes payment. Love here is the labor stored up in money, the latter modeled by the final three instances of "kind" in the sonnet, where "kind" is just another exchangeable signifying form of linguistic money among the many other "kinds' in the restricted economy of expressing love linguistically: "'Fair, *kind*, and true' is all my argument— / 'Fair, *kind*, and true' varying to other words;". At its most hermeneutically elastic, perhaps the poem even submits to a reading in which money is the belovèd of the sonnet's voice. "Fair, kind, and true" each list an ideal characteristic, or promise, of money. Ideally, money shall be aesthetically pleasing (fair); it shall be perfectly equivalent in its ability to enact exchange, i.e. so perfect that no leap of faith is necessary despite its role as a mediator and therefore empty form[10]; and, it shall guarantee its own value, such as the way in which a gold coin was supposed to be worth its own actual, "real" value. In other words, to love as this poet loves demands the discourse of modernity, that is, the discourse of money, because it demands constancy above all else, "One thing expressing, leaves out difference"—but at what cost?

Money becomes a crucial figural interstice of the sonnet, because it foregrounds the stakes of value and its creation. In that service, the terminology of cost-benefit analysis enters the sonnet's financial metaphorology in the third quatrain. This "change" in the poet-lover's pocket, the jangling sounds of which are made by the seemingly endless exchangeability of the signifiers-of-love as coins, begs to be spent; thus, the poet-lover informs us, he has "spent" this "change" on endless poetic invention, swapping this word for that, trading this term for that one. Thanks to value itself—i.e. the three-themes-in-one: "fair, kind, and true"—the poet-lover-consumer-spender can "afford" a wondrous and bountiful proliferation of individual exchange(able) values. In fact, he spends all he has, all his poetic labor, all his creative force in an attempt to halt the system of circulation by laying claim to value itself—all time, living labor, and generated value spent in the name of "one" who shall not be named—the one value beyond all equivalence. In so far as this "one" belongs to the restricted economy of language, of signifiers and exchangeability, i.e. insofar as it is belongs to the realm of representation as "fair, kind, and true," the poet's love is idolatry, and his is the craft of chrematistics. However, despite never leaving the realm of exchange and accumulation, the "one" equally points to something incommensurable, some surplus or general economy of value beyond equivalence—a love beyond the law of value, in which only value itself dwells, unrepresented and unrepresentable.

In Conclusion; or, Sealing the Bond

Both Portia's mercy and the constancy of Sonnet 105's poet-lover rely on the language of economy and exchange, and in particular the tropological dimensions of money, to render their respective messages. What remains "constant" between these Shakespearean examples shadows what Critchley and McCarthy called the "moneying of desire" (40). The social structures uniting Shakespearean (i.e. post-Renaissance European) subjects arise through the (flesh) bond of love-as-passion and yet just as equally through the (social) bond of money-as-exchange. These examples from Shakespeare's *The Merchant of Venice* and sonnet 105 demonstrate the mutual and interrelated nature of the two bond forms by ironically inverting them, and, therefore, exposing their ideological and political skeletons. In *The Merchant of Venice* an economic social bond becomes a literal flesh bond, only so as to reference the political and religious dimensions of those economic relations all the more clearly. In sonnet 105, the corporal and emotional social bond of love is voiced in the manner of economic transaction, only so as in the end to reference all the more clearly the political nature of a courtly love bond, with its essential self-referentiality, grounded materiality, and lack of actual (supposed) exchange. Both examples demonstrate ways in which economies of value—whether of justice or of love—depend on the language of money and exchange to install and maintain themselves. The question, for Shakespeare as for ourselves, is whether we simply mistake love for money and money for love; or, whether these social bonds are not, at their very ontological and linguistic roots, precisely the same thing.

Notes

1. For a more intensive, in-depth reading of this topic by Critchley and McCarthy, see their 2004 article "Universal Shylockery: Money and Morality in *The Merchant of Venice.*"
2. We follow this connection in detail in a later section of this essay ("Of Constancy and Money; or, from a Restricted to a General Economy in Sonnet 105").
3. Critics have pointed out that Portia out "Jews" the Jew at the end of the play by using Shylock's adherence to the law to undermine the very contract he defends. However, it could also be argued that Portia demonstrates precisely where the perfect system of equivalences (kind for kind) is no longer "kind" because it contains a surplus: i.e. blood—that which Shylock is not allowed to take.
4. Although even here there are echoes of the sovereign's "right" to show mercy in deciding whether or not the subject could live. See, most famously, Michel Foucault's *A History of Sexuality, Vol. 1: An Introduction.*
5. Some published versions of this sonnet in fact include "fair, kind, and true" in quotation marks, in each of the three instances of its iteration in the poem.
6. For an entertaining, though hardly light-hearted or silly explanation of this predicate use as metaphor, which is the paradox of identity (as expressed in the tension between property and existence) through quotes from Marx Brothers films, see Slavoj Žižek's *Tarrying with the Negative*, pp. 259–260, n. 36.
7. For example, see Paul de Man's "Sign and Symbol in Hegel's *Aesthetics*," in *Aesthetic Ideology*, pp. 91–104. Or, see de Man's "The Rhetoric of Temporality," in *Blindness and Insight*, pp. 187–228. Or, see also Andrzej Warminski's excellent introduction to de Man's *Aesthetic Ideology*, "Introduction: Allegories of Reference," pp. 1–33.
8. This is an excellent example of what is meant in psychoanalysis by the death drive. Though he calls it "the desire not to be" as opposed to taking recourse, as we have here, to the psychoanalytic lexicon, in his recent essay "Surplus Common" Cesare Casarino explains the mechanism marvelously: "the desire not to be is not to be confused with the desire to die. On the contrary, the desire not to be is the desire to foreclose and transcend death altogether: it is the desire to live forever as always already dead. This is the desire to live as pure dead labor in perennial exchange, as pure commodity in perpetual circulation: under capital, *the desire not to be is the desire to be money.*" Cesare Casarino, "Surplus Common: a Preface," in Cesare Casarino and Antonio Negri, *In Praise of the Common*, Minneapolis: University of Minnesota Press 2008, pp. 17–18.
9. All italicized emphases are our own.
10. This perfection of "kind" as money is even more appropriate when the etymological root of "money" is considered: from the Latin, *moneo*—I inform, I affirm. Money should be so "kind," so equivalent as to erase the very grounds of equivalence, offering value itself, indicated here in the terminological shift from "money" to "kind," or an uncoverted form of payment other than money.

Works Cited

Casarino, Cesare, and Negri, Antonio, *In Praise of the Common*, Minneapolis: University of Minnesota Press 2008.

Critchley, Simon, and McCarthy, Tom, "Interim Report on Recessional Aesthetics," *Harper's Magazine*, June 2009: 40–42.

—. "Universal Shylockery: Money and Morality in *The Merchant of Venice*" *Diacritics*, Volume 34, Number 1, Spring 2004, pp. 3–17.

Foucault, Michel, *The History of Sexuality, Volume 1: An Introduction*, New York: Vintage Books, 1990.

de Man, Paul, *Aesthetic Ideology*, Minneapolis: University of Minnesota Press 1996.

—. *Blindness and Insight*, 2nd ed., revised, Minneapolis: University of Minnesota Press 1983.

The Merchant of Venice. The Riverside Shakespeare. 2nd ed. Boston: Houghton Mifflin Co., 1997, 284–319.

Schmitt, Carl, *Political Theology: Four Chapters on the Concept of Sovereignty*, trans. George Schwab, Chicago: University of Chicago Press 2005.

Shakespeare's Sonnets, ed. Katherine Duncan-Jones, *The Arden Shakespeare*, Thomas Nelson and Sons Ltd 1997.

Warminski, Andrzej, "Introduction: Allegories of Reference," in de Man, Paul, *Aesthetic Ideology*, pp. 1–33.

Žižek, Slavoj, *Tarrying with the Negative*, Durham: Duke University Press 1993.

Part Three

GOVERNANCE, LAW, PUBLIC POLITICS

IMAGES OF THE CROWN: DEPERSONIFIED GOVERNMENTALITIES, A NEW MULTITUDE, AND PRIMITIVE THINKING

Tomas Berkmanas

We could start from the question: what are the possible images of a crown? *What* is crown and, at the same time, what is *a crown*, from, for example, a historical, theoretical or metaphorical perspective? The typical, straightforward image of the crown is of its attachment to a body. One of its functions is, as simple as it is, to be on the body—body and crown form an inseparable singular entity. This is the right image, the right placement—if there would be no bodies (in an ideal situation), what would *a crown* be? To be sure, it is *also* part of the apparel; it is like a bracelet which, without a body, would be just a round piece of metal. But the function of a crown is not only to make a body beautiful; this is not what makes a crown a Crown. There is another crown—Crown, as the symbol, the fiction,[1] or even the ghost of the body. It is the symbol of and fiction about the second "body" of/besides the natural/physical body on which it is placed.

This image is a grandiose one. We typically recognize it as that of the *sovereign*. But, in this context, we can already ask: what is the existential status of this symbolized "one"—the sovereign? Our common sense tells us that this second "body," *if/as separated*, does not exist, or at least it is not a body in any regular sense; it is a meta-physical "body." Therefore, the conclusion would be that in order for that second "body" to have an existential status or foundation, it must remain—as a Crown—on the physical body. It has to be inseparable from that body, thus making a unity of them both, and thus, in some sense, "injecting" some existence into this "body."

In this context Shakespeare's *Richard II* urges us to pose a further question: how is the complete separation of what is natural and what is fictional, what is body-physical and what is "body"-meta-physical possible? This also leads to the question as to how the sovereign/sovereignty might be abstract, purely ideal, and unrelated to the concrete body, and, thus, purely transferable? How is a Crown as such, a Crown without a body, even possible? No one doubts that there is a stage of humanity that is nature.[2] However, in *Richard II* it becomes plainly (and, in that particular case, painfully) possible that not only is there or could there be this other stage of humanity that is not nature, but, perhaps more importantly, those two stages/bodies could be separated and distinguished as two. The vision (or the dream) of this possibility is the engine for the development of modernity in its explicit form, especially as related to the ideas of the state and the rule of law. Nevertheless, as it remains a dream, or something "existing" in a dream, and in that sense a veritable impossibility "outside" the dream, the initial image of the *embodied* Crown still remains viable and survives throughout modernity. Only a real post-modernity (more precisely, an a-modernity) should open up the wholly-other image—an image of the absolute non-existence of a Crown, an image of which Shakespeare did not dream, precisely because it would require the absence of any dreaming whatsoever—including a dream in which one dares to question existence.

1. A Crown Alone: Depersonified Governmentalities

We, the people (at the same time always being the *modern* people), live with the dream of a state distinct from us. This dream is the mode of the life of our mind. It is common to think and speak of a state as "something" existing separately. We are accustomed to requiring something from the state—the state must ensure, secure, foresee, allow, give, etc. The causes of this dreaming, at least in part, may be found in medieval history. It all started, or at least was programmed, long before Shakespeare penned *Richard II*. The symbolic historical starting point might be the *Magna Carta* of 1215, which "in the recognition that acts of the king have an official character that must be exercised through certain forms [is] ... a milestone in the emergence of English governing arrangements."[3] And it should not be conceived only in this way, i.e. very regionally confined. The whole idea of the state—as the *new* and *modern* idea, the idea that was not thought prior to modernity, the idea that "emerged in recognition of the differentiation that was capable of being drawn between the personality of the ruler and the impersonal character of the arrangements through which his rule was exercised"[4]—rests on a certain medieval and apparently juristic cliché, which is represented in the *Magna Carta*. Here "our starting point must be that of the office of the crown. The origins of the distinction between king and crown lie buried in the medieval juristic thought of the twelfth century, when a distinction needed to be drawn between the personality of the king and the office he occupied."[5] But being developed in the distant past of juristic thought, this distinction (or the idea of this distinction) required a greater length of time to be sufficiently articulated in order to become *popular* in a real sense and, thus, to begin modernity in the stereotypical understanding of its beginning.[6] We could say that the transformation was essentially completed by the beginning of the nineteenth century, when this idea became a commonality—a common dream and, at the same time, the dominant mode of the life of mind or, we could even say, the dominant form of life (i.e. we think that we live in a state, and much of our life is organized/formed/guided by this thought or the related thoughts).

The original significance of the medieval theologico-politico-juridical thought on the formation of modernity (otherwise called *the West* or *the mod-*

ern West[7]) and its legal-political frameworks has been noted by many scholars. For instance, Harold J. Berman states that the Western legal tradition originates from events related to the formation of the *jus novum* of the Roman Catholic Church.[8] Ernst H. Kantorowicz elaborately explains how the theories and practices of the Middle Ages "decisively influenced the general pattern of Western social and political thought in its formative period."[9] Finally, Carl Schmitt famously declared that "all significant concepts of the modern theory of the state are secularized theological concepts."[10] However, we should also bear in mind that "the idea of a state existing only for its own sake was foreign to that [i.e. Middle] age. The very belief in a divine Law of Nature as opposed to Positive Law, a belief then shared by every thinker, almost necessitated the ruler's position both above and below the Law."[11] From this thesis we should extract not only the Schmittean necessity for the secularization of concepts at the start of modernity, but also, in some sense, their *de-naturalization*, thus leading metaphysics into its political perfection. Secularization did not lead to an anti-metaphysical approach in the political field, but, on the contrary, metaphysics in political theory as well as legal theory flourished; for example, in the form of legal positivism and normativism. Postmodern criticism of modern legal theories was very much targeted at exactly this kind of metaphysics (as, for example, in Scandinavian legal realism), which generally can be called the modern metaphysics of the state and its entire ideological framework.

One of the main elements of this metaphysical framework—the supporting pillar, we might say—is the idea/ideal of the rule of law, the ideal of putting law above humans and in this way finding the *correct* form of government. Already from the very start that was understood as the problem, comparable to the squaring of a circle in geometry.[12] It is essentially the mission impossible, or "possible" exactly in the form of a dream; it is the Foucaultian-theorized *raison d'Etat* as utopia from the very beginning, fundamentally utopia-based rationalization of the practice of government: the state should be that of the rule of law, although it is not and will never be.[13] It is the forever-guiding and never-reached light of modernity; en-lightenment dreamt and never really lived.

But this dream is definitely not practically functionless, as it is directly related to the modern practice of government. More exactly, there are two functions involved here, and they are diametrically opposed. On the one hand, the [rule of] law frees the activity of government entirely; on the other hand, it is the part of what Foucault would call the compensating mechanism, "trying to establish a boundary or frontier to the unlimited objective prescribed to the police state by *raison d'Etat*."[14] But, once again, it is (and never ceased to be) exactly "the *problem* ... how to set juridical limits to the exercise of power by a public authority."[15]

Foucault separates two approaches to [re]solving this problem: the Rousseaun (or, generally, the French) and the English approach.[16] Both of them already have a paradoxical quality—those mechanisms that compensate and restrain simultaneously have a fundamentally un-limiting power, they limit and un-limit at the same time.[17] In the first—French—case it functions as a human rights based *exclusionary-inclusion*[18] mechanism, thus forming the originary foundation of biopolitics (this facet will be analyzed more elaborately in the next part). In the second—English—case it functions as a mechanism for *enabling constraints*.[19]

The enabling constraints mechanism, of course, first presents itself as exactly that, a mechanism of *constraint*, which, in historical perspective, developed in an evolutionary way in late seventeenth-century England into a complex system of checks and balances, or a so-called balanced constitution.[20] Checks and balances first appear as a constraining mechanism, with a clear general mission to disempower and limit: to establish "a properly equilibrated political system in which power was checked by power in such a way that neither the violent urges of kings, not the arbitrariness of legislatures could impinge directly upon the individual…"[21] Carl Schmitt would see in this the very practical, although theoretically completely impossible union between liberalism and democracy— the "checks and balances" democratic element, together with the people's sovereignty, functions as liberalism's weapon in its fight against absolutism.[22] But Schmitt's insight only strengthens the notion that, starting from the very constitutional top of the pyramid (which is reflected in the institutional hierarchy), the constraints to the government also politically enable and empower the government. These constraints even empower it unlimitedly, i.e. in the Foucaultian sense, thus programming the development of the state into a police state.

The *(self-)constraining* activity of government initially functions as the tool for the de-crowning (or securing the de-crowning) of those who wore the crowns prior to our traditionally conceived modernity. As the de-personification of the crown, this constraining process turns into the practice of unlimitedly *empowering* the government,[23] followed by the fragmentation of government into depersonified governmentalities. The modern state (or the new idea/ fiction, called *the state*) consists of depersonified governmentalities, just as our physical body consists of cells. The state is the net of offices, institutions, competencies, discretions, branches, abstract powers, and the clashes and interactions of these elements are theoretically and legally defined and programmed and, thus, exist as a matter of law in a direct sense. It is a "set of elaborate and bureaucratic governing arrangements," "a variety of impersonal forms."[24] This entire varied net "is" only in law, i.e. exists as regularized or legislated; we see no body, no flesh, no concrete, "real," corporeally present ruler mixed-up in this net. We dream of a net that rules as such—a ruling metaphysical "body," otherwise called the state.

In this state we have, we might say, many crowns; but, apparently, no actual bodies beneath them. It is well confirmed by a typical phenomenon related to the modern activity of government—the phenomenon of the "evaporation" of responsibility—the responsibility, related to the concept of justice, which "always addresses itself to singularity."[25] At the very least, the net of impersonal forms of governmentalities provides the perfect means to escape responsibility or to impose responsibility as necessary. By the general law, no-body is re-sponsible, as there is no body beneath the crown[s]. However, every-body could become responsible, as the throne is empty and completely exchangeable.

This entire process of the unlimited diversification and fracturing and, thus, the spreading of fictional governmentalities happens *at the expense* of our life—our initially private, subjective, individual life. Every new "constrained" fragment of government emerges through the "conquering" of one more por-tion of a zone of individual autonomy, and the consequence of this process is that the so-called sphere of pure privacy today has dissolved to a virtual zero point.[26] To place it in a more Foucaultian context, the objectives of those who govern in the police state, those who implement policy at the internal level, "could be described as unlimited, since for [them] ... it is not only a matter of taking into account and taking charge of the activity of groups and orders, that is to say, of different types of individuals with their particular status, but also of taking charge of activity at the most detailed, individual level"; the internal policy and the police state is characterized by "the absence of a limit in the ex-ercise of government," while "government [has to regulate the life of] its sub-jects."[27] Here we are confronted with an aporetical process of subjectivization, i.e. the objectivization of what is (or should remain) purely subjective, bringing the "individual to objectify his own self, constituting himself as a subject and, at the same time, binding himself to a power of external control."[28] It is not so much that our private, subjective life turns into a completely public life, but that private life—in some sense still remaining a private, subjective life—is totally politicized, leading to the total hybridization of the private and public spheres of life.[29] This is one of the essential elements of the form of modern life as life in a state—a mutated private/public life.

In this context we can already pose the following question: has the other image of the crown, the personified (or *embodied*) crown, the crown with a tan-gible human body beneath, completely disappeared in modernity? It has not, it seems, at least because the image of the depersonified crown is the image of its total mutation; the crown cannot be depersonified conceptually, otherwise the concept is changed in the Orwellian sense. It is exactly the fiction of the crown, the crown as it is not, that pervades modernity; even though this fiction in itself (autonomously) has clear functions. Then, the other key question is: who is the modern *person* wearing the crown or, alternately, who is the *body* wearing the crown? The separation of *person* and *body* here is not accidental. The modern wearer of the crown (i.e. the modern sovereign) appears to have a twofold ap-pearance, like the moon. One "en-lightened" perspective of the person politic wearing the crown reveals the person as *the people*, being in the social state; the reciprocal perspective discloses the "shadowed" body[ies] of *the multitude*, existing (supposedly) in the state of nature. Nevertheless, despite offering two reciprocal perspectives, there is still just *one* person/body wearing the crown, *one* sovereign, and it rules biopolitically, effectively camouflaging its rule by the fiction of the rule of law.

2. The Crown On A Person/Body: A New Multitude

Here we start from an interpretation of the rather contradictory[30] or, at the very least ambiguous ending of the third chapter of Carl Schmitt's *Political Theology*. There, in the last five paragraphs, Schmitt contemplates the tension between two modes of political thinking which should appear as absolutely contradictory. One of these modes is so-called *decisionist thinking*, initially understood from the work of Catholic philosopher of the state Donoso Cortés, but then also presented as being characteristic of Hobbes' thought.[31] Beginning in the nineteenth century, according to Schmitt this thinking is disappearing, together with the epoch of royalism, which "is no longer because there are no kings." Together with the disappearance of this thinking, suggests Schmitt, the conceptions of transcendence are also disappearing from the political ideological field, taken over by the conceptions of immanence, a critical one of which is "the democratic thesis of the identity of the ruler and the ruled."[32] In this context, Schmitt's prediction for further development is as follows:

Conceptions of transcendence will no longer be credible to most educated people, who will settle for either a more or less clear immanence-pantheism or a positivist indifference toward any metaphysics. Insofar as it retains the concept of God, the immanence philosophy, which found its greatest systematic architect in Hegel, draws God into the world and permits law and the state to emanate from the immanence of the objective.[33]

This modern conception of immanence in itself shows that in modernity the medieval political conception of immanence is definitely not lost. We could even understand that the modern schema of immanence in the form of the aporetic identity of the ruler and the ruled is the consequence of the same secularization of theological concepts about which Schmitt speaks[34]. This conception (its form), through secularization, is inherited from the epoch of royalism, or, at least, the Middle Ages, which is confirmed by Kantorowicz.[35] The medieval king is both the ruler and the ruled at the same time, and, analogously, the people/multitude[36] is the ruler and ruled at the same time. In other words, the king has been replaced by the people/multitude, but the entire formal-aporetic schema of immanence persists. However, the conception of modern immanence presented by Schmitt, if we de-secularize it "back" to the medieval schema, reveals some complications related to the articulation of the planes of immanence and transcendence. The divine powers of the medieval king make him the sovereign. Those powers were considered to be of an essential transcendental quality, and perhaps even generative or originary. Therefore, in this image of the king we are confronted with a very ambiguous zone—a zone which at the same time is transcendental and immanent. In some respects the king is transcendent, although drawn into the immanent world. Therefore, the conception of immanence inherited from the medieval period as the part of the conception of people/multitude is not that of pure immanence, but that of the immanence blemished with transcendence.

But we will return to this aspect in the next section. For now it is crucial to remember from the first section that there is a sphere of pure and uncontroversial transcendence which is not lost in modernity and inherited by way of secularization. The medieval king is also strictly, undoubtedly transcendental, and in this way presupposing the existence of a pure transcendental plane, namely, God's kingdom.[37] In modernity, by way of secularization, God's kingdom turns into the state. In the previous section we attempted to show that in modernity this transcendence functions as the transcendence of the *state vis-à-vis sovereign*, if the sovereign is the people/multitude. The modern "transcendental" fiction is that the state governs in modernity through depersonified governmentalities; otherwise this is expressed through the cliché of the *rule of law* (or we could (re-)say *rule of state*). The medieval transcendental zone of God's kingdom is replaced in modernity by the fictional zone of state.

However, Schmitt conceives the modern scheme of transcendence rather differently, thus supporting his decisionist thinking. For Schmitt the secularized (i.e. 17th- and 18th-century) schema of transcendence, as applied to the political field, is condensed in "the notion of the transcendence of the *sovereign vis-à-vis the state*."[38] Also, in this context, Schmitt considers Hobbes as supporting his decisionist thinking.[39] But the question is whether he is *really* supportive? How we can conceive of him as supportive, if we can? Who is this *sovereign*, as apparently different from the state/Leviathan/commonwealth? Did Hobbes really differentiate sovereign and the state, and, especially, did he make this sovereign the ruler (i.e. vis-à-vis) of the state? Or maybe we are here *in both cases* confronted with the vague plane where transcendence and immanence converge, where transcendence blemishes immanence?

For Hobbes, and up till today, "the first and crucial question is this: what actually is a *Crowd* (*Multitudo*) of Men (who unite by their own decision in a single commonwealth)?"[40] Answering this question, Hobbes differentiates between two crowds (or two conceptions of crowds), and in this way repeats the scheme of immanence as presented by Schmitt. He recognizes that a "crowd of citizens both exercises power and is subject to power," but then hurries to add "but in different senses" [of a crowd],[41] thus paving the way for the strategy of the *transcendental* contamination of the plane of immanence. There are two senses of crowd or just two fundamentally different crowds and the concepts/words of crowd (one—collective, the other—singular). One crowd is simply *many (i.e. the number of) men*, every one being individual, concrete, natural/physical, "blood and flesh," "each of whom has his own will and his own judgment."[42] Some would say that this is exactly a/the multitude. The other crowd is "more often called a people than a number"[43], and it "is not a natural person"[44], but an artificial person; it is the *one person* made from the number (or the number turned into a person), and this one person, even though artificial/fictional, "is endowed with a will, and can therefore perform voluntary actions, such as command, make laws, acquire and transfer a right, etc."[45] The latter characteristic of this leader who commands only appears to be Schmittean.

Although to some degree it coheres with Schmitt's theories, nevertheless this "commander" is very different from the Schmittean concrete/personal (keeping in mind a natural/physical person) decision-maker/sovereign. As Loughlin puts it about the Hobbesian characterization of sovereign power, "he [Hobbes] maintained that this power is in no sense personal: the power belongs entirely to the status of 'the office of the sovereign representative'."[46] In some sense, the Hobbesian sovereign as endowed with the will of the single people is a coherent part of the same fiction/dream in which the state, consisting of depersonified governmentalities, is dreamt; the "people" is *also* fiction (or, there are no people) and the part of the modern crown alone. In this sense, for Hobbes there is no sovereign vis-à-vis the state, since the sovereign is the state and, at the same time, the people. He is both of these, united in a fictional coherency.

But only up until this moment in the sequence of ideas the conceptions of both authors are different. It appears that Hobbes' idea of sovereignty—the people—is intrinsically related to that other idea of the crowd—the multitude. The *People* are impossible without this original, ultimate multitude—possible neither theoretically nor historically. From a historical perspective, the function of the fiction of the people is not to eliminate the multitude, but to fundamentally change it, make it different—a *human* multitude. In fact, the whole second "body" of the modern crown wearer—the first body—functions as the machine of anthropogenesis. And all the alleged "post"-modernity is very much concerned with unveiling this real modern wearer of the crown: namely, the multitude. What this digging out brings to the surface, on a wider plane, is the field of biopolitics, in which the human multitude is always emergent and any multitude (or multitude at any stage of transformation) is always the ultimate sovereign. Here we will turn to the ideas of Giorgio Agamben, without entirely leaving those of Hobbes and Schmitt.

For Hobbes, initially multitude is only multitude; there is nothing of the people in it. Hobbes explicitly rejects, as he writes, the Greek superficial view of human nature—of a human as "an animal born fit for Society" (*zωon πολιτικον*).[47] For Hobbes, "all men ... are born unfit for society" and "man is made fit for Society not by nature but by training."[48] *Initially* man is just *zoē* without a social and political condition, and in the latter (or, maybe, by the latter) the former is *trained*; or, we might better say: transformed, made different and brought to a new life—*bios*. But, on the other hand, *zoē* always remains the foundation, the fundamental value—that for whom (or for the preservation of whom) the whole other "body" is instituted and serves. As Hobbes states, "the Natural law therefore (to define it) is the Dictate of right reason about what should be done or not done for the longest preservation of life and limb."[49] The conceptions of natural law and dictate of right reason could be left aside for a moment here; what is really valuable here, what remains the focus as an ultimate value is *life and limb*, which is in no way different from *zoē*. *Life and limb* is made a real, existential foundation and value upon which all modern fictional construction builds.[50]

The machine of anthropogenesis thus formed functions as a mechanism of exclusionary-inclusion (Agamben) or as a certain and specific (some might say, secret) configuration of liberalism and democracy (Schmitt-Agamben). The document placed by Agamben at the symbolic foundation of modern democracy is the 1679 writ of *habeas corpus*, at the center of which "is neither the old subject of feudal relations and liberties nor the future *citoyen*, but rather a pure and simple *corpus*."[51] Agamben very quickly endows *corpus*—what he interchangeably calls *bare life*—with the immanent (in a Schmittean sense) qualities of the medieval king and, through that, relates it to the exclusionary-inclusion mechanism (while maintaining a historical/temporal perspective) and the biopolitical secrets of democracy:

> The root of modern democracy's secret biopolitical calling lies here: he who will appear later as the bearer of rights and, according to curious oxymoron, as the new sovereign subject (*subiectus superaneus*, in other words, what is below and, at the same time, most elevated) can only be constituted as such through the repetition of the sovereign exception and the isolation of *corpus*, bare life, in himself. ... *Corpus is a two-faced being, the bearer both of subjection to sovereign power and of individual liberties.*[52]

First of all, from this extract we should take the notion that from the initial moment and through all modernity *corpus*/*zoē*/life-and-limb/bare-life is, in some sense, excluded and isolated from the plane of the state. This exclusion functions as liberation and is the core of liberalism—human rights and individual liberties protect the individual (which here is just a *corpus*) from the state. They are essentially *a-state-al* (isolating the individual from the whole domain of the state); *corpus* is, in some sense, put outside [the reach] of the state. However, it is included in the state in the form of the subjection to sovereign power, and the mechanism of human rights protection also functions as the mechanism of this subjection.[53]

But something more important than this exclusionary-inclusion procedure takes place "in him-self." It is as though the self, which initially is just *corpus*, is here fractured inside, made two-faced, although it is one and the same being. The first face represents *corpus* left free of the state—it always remains *zoē*. The second face represents *corpus* subjected to the state (or pushed into a state, as it were)—it is *zoē* transformed into *bios*, although not leading to the elimination of *zoē*, but, in some sense, to its *political* perfection as *bios*.

But we should clearly conceive what all this means. First of all, in and through bio-politics, the dream[ing] is made a correlate of *zoē*, or some other substitute, where both *zoē* and *bios* coexist through existential coincidence. For Agamben this substitute is bare life, as produced by the sovereign; as he states, "the fundamental activity of sovereign power is the production of bare life as originary political element and as threshold of articulation between nature and culture, *zoē* and *bios*."[54] To reiterate and condense: bare life is (produce as) as a threshold of articulation between *zoē* and *bios*. We could say that the modern project of sovereignty is the project to make us dream; not to make culture (as something outside us as *zoē*), but to make us cultural (to make *zoē* equally the *bios*). And we could also say that it is the dream of *another life*—a secure and happier life (otherwise called the project of *salus populi*) than the initial *life and limb* from the Hobbesian scenario. Biopolitics is the dream[ing] and, by that, the change[ing] of life into *bios*. Biopolitics is anthropogenesis in the form of a dream, which always takes place in and never leaves *zoē*.

Nevertheless, what could be revealed after "waking-up" to a new life, a new *zoē* clothed as *bios*, might appear shocking. To continue the metaphor: allegedly *zoē* once fell asleep in order therefore to be transformed upon later waking up in other clothing and another condition. It is like putting an operated patient to sleep—all this is done in order to save his life. Notably: sometimes patients do not wake up from this sleep. This is the path of the essentially liberal(ist) project to what could be called political anarchy—a reality to which nobody would like to wake up, *if in this particular situation there is any reality at all to wake up to*, and if it is not simply the continuation of a dream, which appears to be much longer in both historical directions. To conceive this, the configurations of liberalism and democracy[55] and the state of nature and the social state have to be rearticulated in a theoretical and historical perspective in order to clear out the beginnings and ends (i.e. margins) of modernity.

Here we could start from the idea addressed in section one, related to Foucault's work, that the modern system of government implements power-limiting mechanisms that at the same time have the fundamentally power of un-limiting—i.e. it limits and un-limits at the same time or, by limiting, it un-limits. The most important un-limiting happens by turning the multitude into the sovereign through the form and fiction of the people. From a Hobbesian perspective, the sovereign is the one who subsumes in himself the state of nature; or, as Schmitt suggests, the sovereign is the one "who decides on the exception"[56]. So, the democratic people's sovereignty project, if realized, should in some sense lead "back" to the state of nature or the state of exception. In this context, the start and the end positions of the development of modernity are essentially the same. But does modernity really unfold between the states of nature/exception in this Hobbesian/Schmittean sense? Is this state of nature/ exception not already modern?

From a Hobbesian perspective the state of nature is the liberal ideal, although, at the same time, it might be understood as an anarchistic end.[57] But, for Hobbes, it is not some state of total chaos or, in a Schmittean sense, a normative vacuum. It is even vice-versa—for Hobbes "there is too much normativity"[58]. It might be understood as the state of the totality of rights—each individual has a right to anything; in this context, anarchy should be understood as the state of total and uncontrolled normativity. The mechanism of a state (i.e. transference into a so-called social state) is meant to put some limits on this situation of a "totality of rights." That is exactly why state and human rights are always opposed to each other—rights, as Loughlin states, define and protect some sphere of individual autonomy from the state/government.[59] But the ultimate end of liberalism, i.e. liberation from the state, after the apparently secret deal between incommensurable liberalism and democracy, might appear dreadful. Multitude, in the form of a people (the sovereign in which state of nature is subsumed), might acquire rights to anything, including Nazism. From a Schmittean perspective, it is not only that there is no norm applied to chaos—the more important is that the sovereign decides *whether* normativity exists.[60] In some sense it may be that all normativity—its existence and/or nonexistence—is at the sovereign's discretion. At the same time, this sovereign remains the multitude in the form of (or, more exactly, forming into the) people and the last thing that this sovereign has to do is eliminate a limiting state, thus ending the transformation and revealing the new multitude (making *zoē* as/into *bios*) in anarchy/liberty.

The dreadfulness of that is also contained in the fact that the sole example of the modern crown-wearer—a human as hybrid of *zoē* and *bios*—allows and demands differentiation between human beings: there are ones that already contain *bios*; and there are others that have not and which, in this case, are in no way different from other living-beings, they are only *zoē*.[61] Finally, this anarchistic vision of the end of the modern state remains fundamentally anthropocentric, and, perhaps in the last instance it is *purely* anthropocentric, with no fictions *other than* humans, without no specters following them: all is focused in one center, the human. The human is politically purified and instituted as a crown-wearer, thus completely and definitely turning politics into biopolitics.

In this historical perspective, throughout modernity biopolitics grows from immaturity to its perfection. The secularized and separated second "body" of the modern sovereign, the modern meta-physis, is at the same time an anthropological machine—a convenient growing substratum for *anthropos*. The first, natural body of a future human as the central object/value of modern politics is born and grown in the cradle and convenient surrounding of the initially separated second, juridical "body." The modern state—the juridical body—grows a natural body in order to make it free of itself and to start living its new life (*bios*) one day, which should be the day of revolution. This revolution could be considered total liberation, leading to the completely, even existentially[62] different era of the former multitude grown up into people (*bios*), different from all other living-beings (*zoē*). The seminal fiction that should be finally eliminated (or, more exactly, consumed) one day is the state itself; in the state the human is born (as we might glean from Hobbes) in order to one day eliminate it.[63]

However—all this is the dream, the dream of *bios* to gain freedom from *zoē*, which, *in reality*, produces the *bios*-form mutant of *zoē*.[64] It is like liberation by means of consumption, producing the one new multitude, called *the People*.

Agamben's conception of biopolitics signals that the final point of this process of evolution and/or maturation of the multitude is the perfection of political theology—it is the bringing-to-light of the finally perfected, secularized modern picture of the sovereign. It is the production of bare life that subsumes *zoē* and *bios* in one, thus making, once again in history, two bodies [of a king/sovereign] inseparable. It is as though we would start not to imagine ourselves, i.e. our lives, without all the fictions ascribed to us (citizenships, personal codes, rights, obligations, etc.), exactly as Richard II could not imagine himself being other than a king, being left as a bare body (*zoē*) without the body-intrinsic divine powers. It is the final production of bare life as body-citizen, or, as sometimes is stated, citizen (and sovereign) of the world—the final coronation of a human in an original theological sense, thus making the human un-decrownable. The de-crowning of the human in the era after the revolution would be equal to complete madness, just as Richard II suffers madness in his de-crownment. In this context, the revolution is not so much *the revolution*, as a mind operation—the beginning of the perfect dream, in which it is impossible to separate fiction from reality, where all is in one, one [centralized] human/life.

Of course, it has nothing to do with pure de-crownment. In the end it is *perfectly* secularized political theology that is thus turned into biopolitics. The ultimate end of this development is the era of total hostilities as ideological wars, when ideas are conceived precisely as *embodied* ideas (as in the conception of *Volkgeist*). In these wars it is impossible to remain neutral, where all are either friends (bare lives as *correct* commonalities of *zoē* and *bios*), or enemies (bare lives, which, from the friends perspective, are only *zoē*), with no possibility to choose the camp. We already witnessed the first seeds of this new era and the search for the ways out of this doomed development path. It appears that the way out, the different path, necessitates "the step beyond the political"[65], the path against which Schmitt warned not once, and which was declared by him as utterly closed. This path is, in fact, (1) complicated for the mind, and (2) almost entirely abandoned or forgotten in the West.

In the next part we will first linger on the second aspect and then turn to the first, but before that we should focus on what is signified by the phrase "beyond the political." In some sense, it means the state of nature. But this state is probably the most complicated and vague conception in all of modern political philosophy. Dyzenhaus notes that there is "a fundamental difference between [Schmitt's] and Hobbes's understanding of the state of nature."[66] As already mentioned, for Hobbes "the problem is that there is too much normativity."[67] On the other hand, Schmitt "regarded the appropriate description of the state of nature as a state of normative nothingness"[68] or a normative vacuum, but this vacuum is left aside by Schmitt as "there exists no norm that is applicable to chaos."[69] From a Schmittean perspective it is more probable that the entrance of the sovereign into some environment, by the sole fact of this entering, transforms it into the normative/political environment. A sovereign has nothing to do and can accomplish nothing in chaos, which may never be put under his rule. Additionally, normativity, or a normal situation without a sovereign is just a theoretical concept, very quickly dismissed. What matters for both Schmitt and Hobbes is precisely the political state, i.e. its field, in its totality. Both the Hobbesian state of nature and the Schmittean state of exception are political states and, in this sense, a-natural states; although, specifically they are related to the peculiar political nature of the human.

In this context both Hobbesian states—the state of nature and the social state—are interdependent and form *one political field* of an originary nature. What originates in this field is the dreamer—a mutant comprised of *bios* and *zoē*. The origination is caused by some paradoxically *un-natural* situation in the state of nature. We all know the centrality of the instinct of self-preservation (or just the right to life) in Hobbes's idea of the origins of modernity; however, we have to carefully read how all this is phrased: "as long as this naturall Right of every man to every thing endureth, there can be no security to any man ... of living out the time, which Nature ordinarily alloweth men to live."[70] What we see here is nature (natural right) in opposition to Nature.[71] Then, what is this human nature which is against Nature? It is the human political (although, not societal) condition in the Schmittean sense which Hobbes never lost sight of:[72] by nature men "are not looking for friends but for honour and advantage from them. This is what we are primarily after; friends are secondary."[73] It is humans' natural enmity which is against Nature.

Now the correlation between Hobbes' ideology of "the state of nature + the social state" and Schmitt's ideology of the "one state of exception" can be articulated as follows: it is as though one (Hobbes) says that the mutant is comprised of two separate parts—*bios* and *zoē* (and, therefore, remains individual)—and the other (Schmitt) adds that *bios* and *zoē* are indistinguishable to the extent that his individuality is "lost" in the people/sovereign. Hobbes' saying is incomplete, with the consequent ideological difficulties; Schmitt just completes the saying and, by that, neutralizes Hobbes' difficulties. The main ideological difficulty for Hobbes is to reconcile his conceptions of individualism and the sovereign (i.e. the state).[74] He conceived that a "naturally a-Natural" individual mutates in the state; the state is against his hostile nature—but all this for the sake of Nature. The state is human path back to the state of Nature,[75] but by that mutating/changing his nature (by the way of, so to say, state-al education) and, once again, making/ producing something un-natural in itself. These alleged ideological difficulties cause Schmitt's corrective, critical reaction. It is as though he adds that this "path back" must be the path not to nature, but to some perfect or pure political condition that is also a natural state, if we remain within the framework of human nature. It leads to the restoration of politics to center stage[76] and the return to (or remaining in) the state of human nature. In some sense, we could say that for Schmitt the human is a natural mutant. It is impossible for a human not to dream—the human is a dreamer by nature, the perfect one. It is also never possible to separate *zoē* from *bios* in this perfect human dreamer. *Bios* is what is natural to him, and this *bios* is fundamentally related to enmity, forming citizenships, states, nations, sovereigns, administrators, history and other elements of a dream-world. This way Schmitt circles Hobbesian linear (and thus contradictory) development, which presupposes the transformation from one to another *different* state. Schmitt shows that all is one and the same total political field.

But is there a possibility of a state completely wiped of the Schmittean sovereign/decision-maker? Is there some path outside this circle of human nature, or path of, if not return, then to the stage prior to the Hobbesian state of nature and even Schmittean state of exception? In some sense, all this is related to the Hobbes' tacit and unelaborated differentiation between (1) Nature and (2) [human] nature / natural rights of man, which Schmitt apparently missed. How exactly is all this differentiated? Our stereotypical linear and uni-vectoral understanding of the whole Hobbesian process of development from one stage to another here should be changed with another "topological" configuration, which could allow for a clearer perspective. At the threshold between the two Hobbesian states we find the human instinct of self-preservation. From this point developments into two directions (or two vectors of development) are possible. One is the way to the state of nature; the other is the way to the state of Nature as a *different* state, and it is the way of human de-mutation. The first path is Schmittean—a path to combat and war, to the preservation of life at the expense of the negation of life; it is the path to enmity (where co-preservers of life are friends and those, whose life is to be negated—enemies), the path to the proliferation of "special places" and their hostile outsides; and, for Schmitt, the development into the other direction—through the state/sovereign—also leads to the *same* end. The other path is marked by the common intellect proliferating common places—it is guided by "a dictate of right reason, i.e. law of Nature"[77]. Also it is the way to a pre-historical stage, which, at the same time, is post-historical (therefore, the most precise term is not *post-modernity*, but *a-modernity*, in which modernity and history are "surrounded"). And, conversely to Schmitt (although, with some reservation), this is not the way to the stage of some pure chaos or normative nothingness, which should take place outside the state of exception; the world outside the state of exception is also normative, although this normativity is not at the sovereign's discretion. A metaphorical vision of this situation might be as follows: it is as though we step into the field of normativity *just before* the sovereign steps therein and decides whether normativity exists—it is the field of normativity without this sovereign decision.[78] "This is the quiet and "peaceful" field of the first battle one day before, the field in which it is still not possible to know what the peace is."

There is a slight, yet crucial difference between the decision of the sovereign and the "decision" or, more correctly, *thought* of a primitive thinker, in determining whether a normal situation exists. It differentiates between two completely different lives of the mind: one mind dreams, while the other— thinks in a waking state.

3. Pure De-Crownment: Primitive Thinking

Another image of the de-crownment of Richard II is possible—an idea which Shakespeare surely did not consider and in truth could have conceived of. In the Shakespearian version, Richard II is de-crowned because the crown, as his second "body," passes to Henry Bolingbroke (King Henry IV); but the crown remains and finally (in the uttermost historical sense) becomes inseparable from the first, natural body. The other scenario (perhaps post-modern, or we might even say *a-modern*) could be as follows: the king is de-crowned because the crown as *the Crown* completely ceases to exist. We could call it *pure* de-crowning. The pure de-crowning should not only coincide with all modes of metaphysics ending in politics, with its becoming purely immanent—more important is that the political theology should also be completely dissolved.

Political theology is fundamentally related to *[human] decision making*—it is a decision, which starts this modern and history-creating undertaking. But a human is very different as a *decision maker* versus as a *thinker*[79]; and there is a *thought* which is not (or which in no way contains or presupposes) a *decision*. This thought is, at the same time, a confrontation with what *is*, with the truth, which is impossible to usurp, and which in some sense protects the human from the unforeseen. Decision, on the other hand, is at the same time confrontation with what *should be*. Decision (being the "blow of random chance") is preceded by the situation of undecidability, uncertainty, and, therefore, anxiety—the dominant mode and the driving force of modernity.[80] Thinking about this *thought*, in no way related to *decision* (therefore, modernity, positivism or political theology), throws light on natural[81] law, primitive thinking and non-Popperian/Humean science, en-lightening the path for "the step beyond the political"[82].

It should be first noted that this path was still rather well known before the Hobbessian era, even in the Middle Ages. As noted in one general book on law:

> In the early stages of English law, the power of Parliament to intervene and change the accrued customs of time was cloaked in ambiguity. It was commonplace in medieval statutes to begin with apologetic preamble stating that because the *common law* was controverted, it was necessary for Parliament to intervene. Today we just assume that legislatures can change Law at will. It is as though the community of citizens as well as professional community of lawyers simply agreed to defer to elected officials as oracles of the Law.[83]

The conception of this *common law*, which is the same as natural law, is *allegedly* inconceivable as of today. All attempts to revive it are considered failures. The most notable—that of Finnis—is considered to be "natural law without nature."[84] As Agamben explains while focusing in on Hobbes's ideas, we live with the idea that the state of nature with natural law is not a real historical epoch.[85] We conceive natural law as some historical fiction; and, when by saying that "law must rule over men, and not men over law" it is affirmed "not law's sovereignty over nature but, on the contrary, its "natural" ... character,"[86] we conceive of classical natural law as contradictory or even impossible. In modernity sovereignty "presents itself as ... a state of indistinction between nature and culture,[87] between violence and law"[88], and, as sovereignty belongs to people, [natural] law is essentially human law, and precisely not natural law. We tend to conceive of natural law as human law in the sense that the nature here is human nature, not nature in general. In Lithuanian *natural law* is therefore translated as *prigimtinė teisė*—literally, the law that is *birthed-in*—and directly associated with [human] rights. This confirms that the "declaration of rights represent the originary figure of the inscription of natural life in the juridico-political order of the nation state"[89], and the beginning of bio-politics together with the era of the rights of man. The Lithuanian phrasing tellingly demonstrates that "it is precisely bare natural life—which is to say, the pure fact of birth—that appears here as the source and bearer of rights."[90]

Nevertheless, there is this other natural law—natural law not as *prigimtinė teisė*. In some respects, even though as a kind of threshold mode and as some sort of inertia, it survives in such conceptions as *common sense, common law, situation sense* (Llewellyn), *situation law* (Schmitt), or *common places*, offering "some sort of refuge from the direction in which the world is going" (Virno)[91]. These are not only artificial consonances. Their last instance indicates that there are still other possibilities of development in the contemporary multitude, different from the doomed one—development not into the status of a *multitude of decision-makers*, but to the, as Paulo Virno calls it, a *multitude of thinkers*, who are "without home" and place their trust in the "common places."[92] These "common places" are at the same time the fundamental core of the "life of the mind," which becomes, in itself, *public*—i.e. the life of mind of this other multitude is very different from the one developing in the anarchistic direction.[93] But how is this publicly living mind, which otherwise appears as *general intellect*, possible? Precisely this intellect "becomes the *concrete* compass whenever the *substantial* communities fail, and we are always exposed to the world in its *totality*."[94] What is this vision of the failing end of the project/ dream of a substantial homogeneity (i.e. democracy) without entering into total war, but instead entering and living-in the immanence of the total world?

Here we will turn to the second aspect, related to the forgotten path: it is a path complicated to mind. It is complicated to the uttermost level as it entails a change of mind, a change of ways of saying and thinking something(s) and, in this way, a change of world—moving from "special places" to "common places," although, as Virno points out, that might be already happening as a parallel development.[95] It is this other anthropogenesis included in the modes of production and indicated therein by the "distinguishing traits of the human animal, above all the possession of a language."[96] For Virno, the post-Fordist "political" condition is or at least might be also the one where "we no longer face the well-known processes of rationalization of the State; on the contrary, we must acknowledge the achieved *statization* ... of the Intellect which has occurred."[97] This statization which is achieved as an end to the process provides us with this landscape as a result—we see *the multitude* and *general/public intellect*, intellect scattered among the plurality of individuals; in this landscape "the many are a *singularity*"[98]. This singularity is formed by a *pre-individual reality*[99] consisting of three unifying elements: a biological basis[100], language, and the relation of production.[101]

However, there is also something cyclical in this development: it is not so much a genesis as a *change*. It is more like a *return*—a recovery or a wake-up call after the politico-theological dream, although this dream will never be forgotten. It is a return to primitive thinking, and at the same time primal, non-theological natural law.

Modern conceptions of law are usually founded on the radical and critical opposition to *primitivity*.[102] This could be understood as primitive mind, primitive thinking, primitive/early man, primitive mentality or primitive society. This opposition is essentially built on the well-known fundamental issue of jurisprudence—the originally Humean issue of the relation/non-relation between *is* and *ought*. The critical opposition, essentially in all cases, presupposes the thesis that the origination of *ought* from *is* is impossible and inconceivable. But, that was indeed possible and conceivable for the primitive mind,[103] although the modern cautious mind is always inclined to add here *probably* [possible/conceivable].[104] And, *probably*, not in vain, as it is very easy to err here; misunderstandings flourish here.

For example, Hans Kelsen lingers here on the idea that for primitive, or early man, nature was part of society; this man "interpreted facts perceived by his senses according to the same principles which regulated relationships to his fellow men, namely according to the social norms," it being "a normative interpretation of nature."[105] But as Kelsen points out, all this leads to a paradoxical formulation: "at the beginning of evolution, during the animistic period of mankind, there existed only society (as a normative order); nature as a causal order was created by science only after the latter liberated itself from animism."[106] We should not fail to see here how this formulation completely inverts the fundamental Hobbesian idea: at the beginning we have only the society (it is the total societal state), and only after that does nature *appear*, as the consequence of the aforementioned process of liberation. But by his normativism Kelsen proves that that which happens precisely after the beginning, after what is *prima*, is the "schism" of law. It is the division of law, lying at the foundations of modernity, division in the form of the secession of social/humanitarian/human-created law from the initially *one* natural law, then the latter remains in the political exile of the former as science[107]. The Kelsenian *liberal* creation of nature, paradoxically, might appear as its (more exactly, its law's) exile, arranged by the new born sovereign.

Friedrich Hayek also differentiates between two modes of thinking—primitive thinking and modern anthropocentric thinking,[108] and in some respects he repeats Kelsen's conception of the thinking of the primitive man,[109] although without the Kelsenian paradox revealed as a consequence. In some respects, his allegedly liberal conception of the spontaneous order[110] is about the return/wake-up that we are dealing with here. Nevertheless, it fails to articulate the mind-change related processes that are necessary to go through in order to overcome the modern biopolitical paradigm.

As Hayek points out, laws of nature (and also of human behavior) for the primitive thinker were those laws that might be discovered by a human, although a human may not change them.[111] And at the same time it is right that this thinking is fundamentally societal or, to make an allusion to Virno's conception, *public*. Law, in this view, is *public*, or, to use the other equally appropriate word, *common*. In the same way the common law courts in the more originary sense were conceived not as creating law, not as changing it, but only as pronouncing it, founding it already existent. Here we are talking about the pre-modern common law, the common law before the positivistic doctrine of *stare decisis* started being dominating characteristic of this legal tradition.[112] It is essentially the conception of natural law which makes the *stare decisis* doctrine and tool completely unnecessary. It as well renders futile the *writing* of the constitution,[113] and thus, by the bare fact of its writtenness, expresses the distrust in common morality.[114] This is because, as simple as it is, the distrust in natural law would be equal to madness, the complete change of mind.

Nevertheless, how is a conception of law possible that is not created, but founded as already existing, and, at the same time, how are we to conceive a vision of a judge (or the parliament, or the king of the early stages) as only the *mouth of law*? The primitive man conceived neither kings, nor parliaments, nor courts as the sources/creators of law in themselves, and this is the essence of this entirely different mentality—a completely other life of mind before the dream of modernity. In this context we should remember not only that the image of the *mouth of law* originally is the image of the Messiah, but also that the opposite image is that of Christ, not as Messiah, but as God-Man, as the image of the possibility of the hybridization of *zoē* and *bios*. Therefore biopolitics in its originary essence is Christian. The Schmittean secularization of theology in the direction of the formation of modern politics is the secularization (and inheritance in the secularized form) of Christian theology.[115]

The image of the Messiah presents different perspectives, including the perspective of the configuration of the planes of immanence and transcendence—the perspective of their pure separation and, by that, their creation/de-termination. From the Christian perspective we encounter the tendencies towards the absolutization/totalization of either one or the other plane, and, by that precisely their elimination. From a more mundane perspective, the Middle Ages, guided by the principle of *memento mori*, was oriented towards the totalization of the transcendental plane. All that is here and now, in this life, is unimportant—the important plane is there, after life. Our contemporary age, guided by the principle of *carpe diem*, is oriented towards the totalization of the immanent plane—only here and now is important. In both cases these are logically paradoxical and, therefore, doomed perspectives. Neither total transcendence nor total immanence appears to be possible; e.g. if all is here, then there is no here.[116] On the one hand both planes must exist to make each other possible; on the other hand, both of them should be pure and removed of each other, because the totality of one plane is possible only at the expense of the elimination of another by the way of the inclusion of the latter into the former—i.e. the hybridization of the planes. Immanence has to be generated *without* transcendence in order to properly be, and to be properly pure. In the same way, transcendence has to be generated without immanence. Only in this way could the image of pure immanence appear, and, at the same time, the image of the nature without transcendence, the latter being left completely outside the plane of immanence.[117] In this context purity and totality are completely different categories: purity is related to the Messiah[118], totality is related to Christ; the Messiah makes both planes pure, while Christ destroys one by totally destroying another.

In the same line, there are two modes of thinking: primitive (pre/post-modern; a-modern) and modern. The latter is totality oriented, necessitating the creation of a hostile environment, the environment that should be eliminated in the existential sense. This is the Schmittean thinking, inherited in modernity through the secularization of theology. In this context the real *post*-modernity has to be fundamentally post-Schmittean as concerns his concept of political.[119] The a-political condition means that there should be neither enemies, nor *friends*, neither wars, nor *peace*. In this context the images of absolute revolution, leading to absolute friendship, or absolute peace, are self-contradictory and self-eliminating. If all of us were friends, there would be no friends; there has to be an enemy for a friend to exist—"these two concepts co-determine one another"[120]. Similarly, what is the sense of peace, if there is no possibility of war? And in the same way, "the very concept of neutrality ... is swept away by its own possibility; it contradicts itself and is destroyed in itself."[121] All this allows us to understand why all the banners from the Soviet era with the words "Peace," "Friendship," etc. were little more than blunt lies. They could have just as well have been re-written as "War" or "Enmity." There is no politics of friendship without, at the same time, a politics of enmity, and no politics of peace or neutrality without, at the same time, a politics of war.

As discussed previously, the modern mode of thinking is "thinking" as *deciding*—deciding not only "who the enemy is"[122], but more essentially (or, firstly) "who is who"[123]. Political discourse in this sense is identity discourse in the broadest sense.[124] It starts from naming[125] this and that person, in this way producing the citizen, and ends up by naming and producing the concrete communities[126]. Nevertheless, from a Schmittean perspective this identity discourse only proliferates potential enemies: it is in its very essence friend/enemy, inclusionary/exclusionary discourse.[127] However, it might also be called the process of the *forming of cultures*[128]—thus affirming its bio-political nature.[129]

We should also consider that this differentiating decision, this including and at the same time excluding decision, is also a decision (but not thought) on law. In this case we mean the law of community in the sense that a community (represented by sovereign) decides what law is and by that creates both law and itself. In a sense, through the production of law community is produced and differentiated—these are reciprocal processes. As H.L.A. Hart notes, what differentiates primitive societies or communities from the later ones (allegedly modern ones) is that all that they (i.e. primitive societies) have *ex hypothesi* is only the so-called primary rules, i.e. those which impose obligation and duty.[130] Those rules are uncertain in the same sense as the rules of classical natural law—their authorship (or, simply, legal authority) is unclear. Non-primitive societies already have the secondary rules (rules of legislation, adjudication, and rule of recognition), the sole purpose of which is the establishment of the legal authority of a social group and the social group's very existence at the same time.[131] The secondary rules are meant not only to establish the already discussed mechanism of depersonified governmentalities (i.e. the modern state), but also at the same time to provide the conditions to externalize conflict,[132] which also means to totalize it.[133] All this demonstrates the tendency towards the absolute, world-consuming hostility and even a so-called *world* war, of which we have already experienced twice. In a world war nobody may remain neutral—all the world is divided into enemies and friends; theoretically, all here are enemies (because my friends, together with me, are enemies of my enemies). Some communities during these wars required the *whole world* to answer the question—are you with us, or are you, by virtue of not being with us, therefore against us?

Nevertheless, following Virno's ideas, this modern mode of thinking might also be at its furthest margin and, at the same time, at the end of the dream. But the turning to the other mode of thinking requires abandoning the whole conceptual field, changing the life of the mind. How can we *think* in this other mode of thinking, a mode which for Schmitt is impossible and for others forgotten and lost? Perhaps this life of the mind has survived, even if in some niche of exile?

First of all, we should bear in mind the fundamental logical structure of this mentality—it is the mentality about laws that could only be found, but not changed or created.[134] In some sense, this mentality survives[135] in natural science, despite all the Humean, Kantian and Popperian attempts to transform it or, more exactly, show it to be already transformed—i.e. logocentric and deductive. But it is not so much (or not necessarily) the mentality of the profound scientist (and, especially, the one holding the respectable administrative position), but more the mentality of a naïve, even childish scientist-thinker, the thinker who may "have only an elementary school education and never read a book, not even under torture"[136]. This mentality has much more to do with reality (what *is*) then the other one. This mentality requires *Einfühlung*[137] into what *is*, not dreaming of what *ought* to be. The other one lingers on the ideology of *raison d'Etat*—it seeks not to find, but to change, to bring into being what should be constructed and built, but not what is given or could be found as given.[138]

However, this life of the mind of the thinker in modernity was made into a *private* undertaking—moved into *political* exile in relationship to the public sphere. This event even might have accelerated the *dreaming* modernity. As Virno notes, "if the publicness of the intellect does not yield to the realm of a public sphere, of a political space ... then it produces terrifying effects," the central one of which is "an *unchecked proliferation of hierarchies*."[139] In this context we should keep in mind that the primitive and the modern intellect are one and the same intellect, only alternately dreaming or awake. We should also keep in mind that for the primitive mind, as Kelsen depicts its, all is social, all is public. For this thinking there is no sphere which is not public—it is in no way dreaming of privacy/individuality, as something separated from publicness. For this thinking all is public, all is abstract, all is general. In it there are no dreams of nations, homes, parties, religious communities, sport fan clubs, etc.

But, once again, the proliferation of hierarchies and "special places" is not a product of one or *another* intellect; as we have already determined, the intellect is one. For Virno, the "publicness of the intellect, when it does not take place in a public sphere, *translates*..."[140]; we could add that although it transforms (and, by that, starts dreaming), it remains the same intellect. In other words, this intellect should remain public, but, unfortunately, it is not. And then *the same* intellect, by falling into the aforementioned dream and, by that, starting modernity, starts proliferating hierarchies. In this context we should revisit Loughlin's text:

> As a general phenomenon, the activity of governing exists whenever people are drawn into association with one another, whether in families, firms, schools, or clubs. In order to maintain themselves, and certainly to be able to develop and flourish, such groups must establish some set of governing arrangements, however rudimentary. The formation of governing arrangements is a ubiquitous feature of group life. ... Since it simply is not possible for associations of any significant scale and degree of permanence to be capable of governing themselves, the business of governing invariably requires the drawing of a distinction that has become fundamental to the activity: the division between rulers and ruled, between a governing authority and its subjects.[141]

This is the *dreamer's* vision of the public sphere—a lost public sphere, lost for the public/primitive intellect, which, by consequence of this loss, transforms and translates into the modern intellect, and starts dreaming—i.e. proliferating "special places" and hierarchies, being nationalistic and Schmittean, requiring sovereign[ty]'s subjects (lieges, nationals, citizens) and enemies. "Special places" are families[142], firms, schools, clubs; and it may be continued: parties, religious communities; continuing still further: nations, states, organizations, administrations, bureaucracies, axes, andantes, unions, and so forth... On the other side of the chain, at the micro-level, "special places" are citizens, nationals, even names and surnames, personal codes—precisely all that we are not.[143]

Virno notes that "in today's world, the 'special places' of discourse and of argumentation are perishing and dissolving" and "the 'common places' ... are moving to the forefront."[144] This is the dream that Schmitt could not have dreamt, because it is un-dreamable. This path is completely closed to the dream or as a dream. The return to the political arena of a thinker *instead* of a decision-maker completely transforms, translates, and dissolves it. And the extremity of this process should not be forgotten or misplaced—the abstract, general intellect is a de-individuating intellect in the extreme. It requires *political de-naming*, and, by that, turning communities, people, and citizens into one multitude. "This concrete" should remain un-named. The practice of naming, if it remains, might be perhaps only that of the Native Americans (keeping in mind their non-sacred names). Their names were not John, Paul, or Adam, but eagle feather, owl eyes, etc.; thus, by this naturalistic metaphoro-logical apparatus, entrenching the human into the commonality of the world. The abstract, general intellect only accepts generalities and universalities, and by that leaves what is concrete in absolute "peace," and does not provide the mind an appropriate environment for Schmittean politics, with enemies being always concrete. In other words, it is the mind and discourse not of artificial names, but of words-of-things—names in Walter Benjamin's sense.[145]

Finally, it is only the metaphor of *waking up* which is really correct and proper here, not the other, much more frequently used in this context, i.e. that of *revolution*. Any image of the revolution should be abandoned, since to date too many revolutions have been followed by further coronations, thus discrediting the image of the revolution in the same way as the Nazis discredited the swastika. Pure de-crownment is to be viewed as an awakening from the deadly dream of *the Crown*. In the a-modern drama (if such a thing is possible at all), those who were in the modern one called *Richard II* and *Bolingbroke* would awaken and the cause that in the dream had made them enemies would disappear.

Notes

1. Ernst H. Kantorowicz, *The King's Two Bodies: A Study in Medieval Political Theology* (Princeton University Press, 1957), p. 336 *et al.*
2. Walter Benjamin, "Theologico-Political Fragment": 313; in: *Reflections*, trans. Edmund Jephcott (New York: Schocken Books, 1986).
3. Martin Loughlin, *The Idea of Public Law* (Oxford University Press, 2005), p. 21.
4. *Ibid.*, p. 6.
5. *Ibid.*, p. 20 (relying on George Garnett's essay "The Origins of the Crown").
6. *Ibid.*, p. 6 ("It was not until the beginning of the modern period that the idea of the state as an entity distinct both from its members and from its officers was articulated").
7. Michel Foucault, *The Birth of the Biopolitics: Lectures at the Collège de France, 1978–1979* (Palgrave Macmillan, 2010), p. 34.
8. Harold J. Berman, *Law and Revolution. The Formation of the Western Legal Tradition* (Harvard University Press, 1990), p. 2.

9. Ernst H. Kantorowicz, *supra* note 1, p. 273.

10. Carl Schmitt, *Political Theology: Four Chapters on the Concept of Sovereignty* (Chicago and London: The University of Chicago Press, 2005), p. 36.

11. Ernst H. Kantorowicz, *supra* note 1, p. 144.

12. Martin Loughlin, *supra* note 3, p. 115 (relying on Rousseau).

13. Generally, see Michel Foucault, *supra* note 7, p. 4.

14. *Ibid.*, p. 7.

15. *Ibid.*, p. 39 (italics—TB).

16. Generally, see *ibid.*, p. 39–41.

17. This is related to the underlying task/problem, which is mentioned by Foucault: "how can be the necessary self-limitation of government be formulated in law without government being paralyzed" (ibid., p. 38).

18. This term and, at the same time, the corresponding approach is offered by Giorgio Agamben (generally, see Giorgio Agamben, *Homo Sacer: Sovereign Power and Bare Life* (Stanford: Stanford University Press, 1998).

19. This term and, at the same time, the approach is taken from the work of Martin Loughlin *The idea of Public Law* (for example, see Martin Loughlin, *supra* note 3, p. 51).

20. *Ibid.*, p. 23.

21. *Ibid.*, p. 43 (relying on Montesquieu).

22. Carl Schmitt "took liberalism and democracy to be antithetical, and the reliance of liberalism on democracy is but a conjunction of its general need for a principle of political form in order to organize itself as a public force and of the particular circumstances of liberalism's political struggle against absolutism in the nineteenth century" (David Dyzenhaus, *Legality and Legitimacy: Carl Schmitt, Hans Kelsen and Hermann Heller in Weimar* (Oxford University Press, 2003), p. 79).

23. As Loughlin states in the other place, "authority (competence) is directly linked to power (capacity)" (Martin Loughlin, *supra* note 3, p. 85). In other words, setting of competence/discretion in law, being the apparently constraining process (and that this process is understood as constraining one is proved by the phenomenon of judicial review of administrative actions, where the main issue to be reviewed is the possible acting *ultra vires*), at the same time empowers, provides with the capacity.

24. *Ibid.*, p. 6.

25. Jacques Derrida, "Force of Law: the "Mystical Foundation of Authority" (trans. Mary Quaintance), *Cardozo Law Review* No. 11, 1990: 955.

26. *Ibid.*, p. 11 ("At the beginning of the nineteenth century, government was mainly concerned with law and order, external affairs and defence, and raising revenue to finance these activities. By the end of the twentieth century, there were few areas not only of public but also of personal life in which government performed no role").

27. Michel Foucault, *supra* note 7, p. 7 (brackets—original).

28. Giorgio Agamben, *supra* note 18, p. 119 (commenting on the ideas of Foucault).

29. As Agamben points, relying on Karl Löwith, here we are confronted with "total politicization ... of everything, even seemingly neutral domains of life" (*ibid.*, p. 121).

30. This is not the only place filled with contradictions in Schmitt's ideology. For example, the last paragraphs of *Legality and Legitimacy* might also appear "rife with contradiction," if put into the wider context of Schmitt's ideology (David Dyzenhaus, *supra* note 22, 71 p.).

31. Carl Schmitt, *supra* note 10, p. 51–52.
32. *Ibid.*, p. 49.
33. *Ibid.*, p. 50.
34. I.e., "all the significant concepts of the modern theory of the state are secularized theological concepts" (Ibid., p. 36).
35. To repeat the citation: "the idea of a state existing only for its own sake was foreign to that [i.e. Middle] age. The very belief in a divine Law of Nature as opposed to Positive Law, a belief then shared by every thinker, almost necessitated the ruler's position both above and below the Law" (Ernst H. Kantorowicz, *supra* note 1, p. 144).
36. Initially we will take those concepts together.
37. In some sense, king is the liege only of God (thus, he is ruled; the only kingdom which is above king's kingdom is God's kingdom), and, because of that origination of his power, all below, in immanent world, are his lieges (thus, he is ruler). But the king thus is lingering in the vague zone of indistinction of what is transcendental and immanent. The conception of the identity of the ruler and the ruled here appears definitely as not that of only/pure immanence.
38. Carl Schmitt, *supra* note 10, p. 49 (italics—TB).
39. *Ibid.*, p. 52.
40. Thomas Hobbes, *On the Citizen* (Cambridge University Press, 2007), p. 75.
41. *Ibid.*, p. 76.
42. *Ibid.*, p. 75.
43. *Ibid.*, p. 77.
44. *Ibid.*, p. 76.
45. *Ibid.*, 76–77.
46. Martin Loughlin, *supra* note 3, p. 55. *In this context*, we could say that the decisionism of Schmitt and the decisionism of Hobbes, and the conceptions of *sovereign* of both, are fundamentally different. Hobbesian sovereign is the fictional/artificial one, more akin to the juridical person/body and identified with state/commonwealth/ people. Schmittean sovereign is the concrete sovereign—it is the concrete dictator or president, the extraordinary lawmaker, akin to the concrete medieval king. Here the allusions to the Chapter 5 of Schmitt's book *Legality and Legitimacy* could be made, where the extraordinary lawmaker, who interchangeably is called dictator or President, is he, who in one person combines legislative and executive powers, or he, who can always immediately and directly issue an individual order (Carl Schmitt, *Legality and Legitimacy* (Duke University Press, 2004), p. 70–71.
47. Thomas Hobbes, *supra* note 40, p. 22.
48. *Ibid.*, p. 25.
49. *Ibid.*, p. 33.
50. This is evidenced by a certain development in modernity: essentially only one right of all human rights—the right to life –rather conversely to other rights, becomes more and more absolute, the right without exceptions.
51. Giorgio Agamben, *supra* note 18, p. 123. Strangely enough, Agamben clearly differentiates between this writ and the Magna Carta; in our perspective, those two documents should appear as the elements of one and the same coherent historical chain.
52. *Ibid.*, p. 124–125.
53. See *ibid.*, p. 121 ("It is almost as if, starting from a certain point, every decisive political event were double-sided: the spaces, liberties, and the rights won by indi-

viduals in their conflicts with central powers always simultaneously prepared a tacit but increasing inscription of individuals' lives within the state order, thus offering a new and more dreadful foundation for the very sovereign power from which they wanted to liberate themselves").

54. *Ibid.*, p. 181.
55. See also *supra* note 22.
56. Carl Schmitt, *supra* note 10, p. 5.
57. The oscillation in the so-called postmodern discourse between the concepts of chaos and liberation (David R. Dickens and Andrea Fontana, "Postmodernism in the Social Sciences": 9; in: David R. Dickens and Andrea Fontana, eds., *Postmodernism and Social Inquiry* (New York, London: The Guilford Press, 1994)), shows the proximity between anarchism and liberalism.
58. David Dyzenhaus, *supra* note 22, p. 88.
59. Martin Loughlin, *supra* note 3, p. 127.
60. Carl Schmitt, *supra* note 10, p. 13.
61. This idea was supported by Nazis.
62. Revolution is often equated with apocalypse.
63. This is not unlike the embryo-womb/placenta relation. The placenta is detached after the baby is born, but before that it is existentially necessary, essential for growth.
64. In this context, people/*bios*, as the form of multitude, might be rendered metaphorically as the form/mold of a cake, which has to be put aside after the new cake is baked.
65. Jacques Derrida, *Politics of Friendship* (London, New York: Verso, 1997), p. 123.
66. David Dyzenhaus, *supra* note 22, p. 88.
67. *Ibid.*
68. *Ibid.*, p. 89.
69. Carl Schmitt, *supra* note 10, p. 13.
70. Extract from Hobbes's *Leviathan*; in: *Lloyd's Introduction to Jurisprudence*, 6th edition, edited by M. Freeman, D. Lloyd (London: Sweet & Maxwell Ltd., 1994), p. 137.
71. This picture resembles *human* fall from heaven to earth. Human perverts Nature by his nature.
72. On this aspect they definitely agree; see also David Dyzenhaus, *supra* note 22, p. 94.
73. Thomas Hobbes, *supra* note 40, p. 22.
74. David Dyzenhaus, *supra* note 22, p. 95.
75. And it might coincide with the doing away with politics (see *ibid.*, p. 94).
76. *Ibid.*
77. Thomas Hobbes, *supra* note 40, p. 31.
78. Compare Carl Schmitt, *supra* note 10, p. 13.
79. This concept, as used in this paper, has very much in common with the one used in Paolo Virno's book *A Grammar of the Multitude* (for example, see Paolo Virno, *A Grammar of the Multitude*, trans. Isabella Bertoletti, James Cascaito, Andrea Casson (Cambridge, London: The MIT Press, 2004), p. 38–39, etc.).
80. Compare, *ibid.*, p. 38: "Those 'without a home' have no choice but to behave like thinkers: not in order for them to learn something about biology or advanced mathematics, but because they turn to the most essential categories of the abstract intellect in order to protect themselves from the blows of random chance, in order to take refuge from contingency and from the unforeseen."

81. If law is natural, in the exact sense (i.e. as nature's law), there is no sovereign over it. Natural law is outside of anything related to sovereignty.
82. Jacques Derrida, *supra* note 65, p. 123.
83. George Fletcher, *Basic Concepts of Legal Thought* (New York, Oxford: Oxford University Press, 1996), p. 66 (my emphasis).
84. *Lloyd's Introduction to Jurisprudence*, *supra* note 70, p. 122.
85. Giorgio Agamben, *supra* note 18, p. 36.
86. *Ibid.*, p. 35.
87. The same wording is used in the conception of the bare life (see *ibid.*, p. 181).
88. *Ibid.*, p. 35.
89. *Ibid.*, p. 127.
90. *Ibid.*
91. Paolo Virno, *supra* note 79, p. 37.
92. *Ibid.*, p. 39.
93. *Ibid.*, p. 37.
94. *Ibid.*, p. 37 (italics—TB); the conceptual consonances with Schmitt's ideas and their context here are striking.
95. *Ibid.*, p. 36.
96. *Ibid.*, p. 63.
97. Ibid., p. 67.
98. *Ibid.*, p. 76.
99. Relating all this to liberalistic idea of human equality—here it might appear only as a substantial one. This is also the counterargument to the idea of Schmitt that liberalistic idea of equality is only abstract, and only the democratic one (as an ideal/aim) is substantial. The difference also is that liberalistic idea/thought, in this context, is about what *is*—it is not aim.
100. This biological basis is in no way related to the Savigny's style *Volkgeist*; it is *general, a-national* biological basis.
101. *Ibid.*, p. 76–77.
102. It is a discussed question, when modernity starts and when it ends, if it has ended at all. But what is rather certain is that primitive thinking/mind/man belongs to the pre-modern era. Authors are rather certain that opposition with primitivity is opposition with pre-modernity, which could be used to make/show modernity different and, by that, even to define modernity. We could even say that modernity is built on the opposition to the primitivity. Modernity is what is *secundo* to the *primo* of primitivity, what goes, maybe, directly after.
On the other hand, the development of modernity or the processes related to that are rather often parallelized with what is called *anthropogenesis* (for example, see Virno, 63, Agamben/Open, 79); consideration of the threshold between primitivity and modernity definitely might involve consideration of the margins of ontology, metaphysics, language, and—politics. It might be the problem of only-*physis*, *zωon* without πολιτεια, *homo alalus* (man without language) but still not *homo sapiens*.
103. In this context modernity could be understood as a non-primitive age, and all that is after this primitive age—including Middle Ages and maybe even some earlier times—is the age of modernity.
104. For example, see Hans Kelsen, *Pure Theory of Law*, trans. Max Knight (New Jersey: The Lawbook Exchange, Ltd.: 2009), p. 82, 84.
105. *Ibid.*, p. 82–84.

106. Ibid., p. 84.
107. What we have in mind here, essentially, are so-called natural sciences, but not social sciences.
108. Friedrich A. von Hayek, *Teisė, įstatymų leidyba ir laisvė, 1 t.: taisyklės ir tvarka*
(Law, Legislation and Liberty, vol. I: Rules and Order), vertė Algirdas Degutis (Vilnius: Eugrimas, 1998), p. 114–115.
109. *Ibid.*, p. 122; there he reiterates that for the primitive thinking the rules of causality
and the rules of societal behavior essentially are the same/coincide.
110. This order has something in common with the Schmittean normal situation, *before*
the sovereign steps in and decides that this situation exists (Carl Schmitt, *supra*
note 10, p. 13). This situation in itself is not (or, at least, not necessarily) chaos. The
sovereign's decision *that* this situation exists, as a matter of logic, does not preclude
the existence of such a situation before this decision. In some sense in this situation
the sovereign could be understood as *an inspector*—he steps into some environment, makes a check, and decides that the normal situation actually exists there.
But by that we should also accept that this is one of the mysteries of all of Schmitt's
ideology, i.e. whether such a situation—one without the sovereign and his decision,
just the *spontaneous order* in the exact sense—was possible for him at all.
111. *Ibid.*, p. 114.
112. George Fletcher, *supra* note 83, p. 69–70: "In the last two hundred years there has
been a movement in Anglo-American law to make case law more like statutory law.
In the mid-eighteen century, in the writings of Blackstone, judicial decisions are
treated as evidence of the law, not as the law itself. … The English positivist movement of the nineteenth century generated the idea that judicial decisions were not
just evidence of the law, but conclusive on the law. Thus emerged the idea of *stare
decisis*—the principle that precedents must be followed as binding law."
113. Common law, in a more original sense, is the law of unwritten constitution.
114. Sanford Levinson, "Law as Literature," *Texas Law Review* Vol. 60, No. 3 (1982):
375–376: "The very existence of written constitutions with substantive limitation
on future conduct is evidence of skepticism, if not outright pessimism, about moral
caliber of future citizens; else why not simply enjoin them to "be good" and "do
what you think best"?"; this in itself proves the ideological structure of biopolitical
project as the one of *salus populi*: i.e. this project must presuppose that something
is wrong with society/human, that society/human is sick, thus making the whole
project possible and the state resembling the association of invalids (see Martin
Loughlin, *supra* note 3, p. 19).
115. In this context it is rather obvious that modernity starts with Christianity.
116. In the same way as if we were all friends, there would be no friends; to this aspect
we will return shortly.
117. In this view the transcendental plane might be left, so-to-say, completely alone/
unchallenged; this view allows piety-in-immanence.
118. An important function of the Messiah is just to remain the Messiah while facing
God's presence and not to turn into God. By that the Messiah consummates history,
if history is that of the divinity in this world, history of the blemishing of the plane
of immanence with what is transcendental.
119. Although, as we know, this *post-* is impossible for Schmitt.
120. Jacques Derrida, *supra* note 65, p. 122.
121. *Ibid.*, p. 126.

122. *Ibid.*, p. 125.
123. Ibid., p. 127.
124. This discourse also might be considered as fundamentally philosophical, if philosophy is, at its core, the creation of concepts; we are faced here with philosophizing politicians—real/practical *political* philosophy.
125. This should be conceived in a broader sense; it includes, for example, the giving of a personal code.
126. It includes not only the nations/states; these might be also the communities of classes, women, sexual minorities, races, certain professions, as policemen, factory workers, peasants, craftsmen, etc. But it is exactly important here their understanding/thinking of them. For Marx, workers are like a nation—they should be ready for a combat and revolution. Other thinking presents very different visions of workers.
127. Martin Loughlin, *supra* note 3, p. 35.
128. *Ibid.*
129. As we have seen, Agamben uses the concepts *bios* and *culture* in parallel.
130. H.L.A. Hart, *The Concept of Law*, 2nd edition (Oxford: Clarendon Press, 1997), p. 92.
131. *Ibid.*, p. 100.
132. Martin Loughlin, *supra* note 3, p. 36.
133. Externalization, at the same time, is expansion and totalization.
134. Friedrich A. von Hayek, *supra* note 108, p. 114.
135. From Virno's perspective, it might be considered to be *reviving*—reviving the public sphere. Nevertheless, the more adequate conception of the contemporary situation as that of a clash of the two lives of the mind, which is externalized into the clash between dreamers and thinkers; this is more adequate, as simple as it is, because "special places"—nations, communities, fan clubs, etc.—are still very viable. Of course, more and more wake-up-ers appear, although, they still very much find themselves completely surrounded by dreamers.
136. Paolo Virno, *supra* note 79, p. 39; the very well known story of Einstein at school is in conformity here.
137. See Karl Raimund Popper, *The Logic of Scientific Discovery* (New York, 1965), p. 32.
138. Michel Foucault, *supra* note 7, p. 4.
139. Paolo Virno, *supra* note 79, p. 40–41 (my emphasis).
140. *Ibid.*, p. 41 (italics—TB).
141. Martin Loughlin, *supra* note 3, p. 5.
142. In Virno's work, this concept is contained in the concept *being at home*.
143. It is not so much that I am not my name, but that my name says nothing about me—it only has the political function in a Schmittean sense.
144. Paolo Virno, *supra* note 79, p. 36. See also note 135.
145. Although Benjamin attributes abstraction to the Fall of language/mind (see Walter Benjamin, "On Language as Such and on the Language of Man": 326–330; in: *Reflections: Essays, Aphorisms, Autobiographical Writings*, trans. Edmund Jephcott (New York: Schocken Books, 1986)), we should keep in mind that the abstraction that we have here in mind has nothing in common with Benjamin's mentioned abstraction. The abstraction of primitive thinking is about what *is*—and every-thing for this mind *is* (society and nature *are* one), there is nothing that *ought to be* without relation to/origination from *is*; this mind is absolutely fiction-less. It is related to

another type of discourse –one which Benjamin would call the/a language of things. Exactly the names that we are used to are abstract in the Benjaminian sense—they are "empty words"; for example, what does the name "John" says about John? Or what does "England" says about England? These names are empty and artificial—we can give them completely arbitrary, at-will, by our arbitrary judgment.

The image of *judgment*, which is important to Benjamin in this context, could be related to Schmitt's conception of *decision*. It is precisely up to the sovereign to decide/judge *whether* normality exists (Carl Schmitt, *supra* note 10, p. 13); normality as what *is*—all that might be left aside; the decision of the sovereign might not correspond to that. In Benjamin's words, it presupposes the possibility of the betrayal of the thing. In this context, the judgment to give a name as an empty word, as a/the feature of modernity, might have only one function: the bio-political function. Our names say nothing about us, they only have a simple function: to purely individuate/specialize, create the subject of [bio]politics. This approach also allows what Benjamin calls "over-naming"; if names may be given at will, arbitrary, without any relation to what *is*—there is nothing that could stop naming.

The opposite is with the non-sacred names of Native Americans. In this other type of naming, names are not empty words. They say something about the named one. An abstraction is also involved here—but an abstraction in the form of metaphor, which is always turned to what *is*. Native Americans abstract one feature of what is (as, for example, some feature of animal), and make it a "name" of what also is (human). Only in this way can a name be made something other than an empty word. Here there are no intentions to impose the name arbitrarily, *just to name* the human-body, with the always following suspicion that this kind of naming has a bio-political function. Also, in this case over-naming is impossible—what *is* delimits it. It is never possible to name/re-name the *eagle's eye* into the *mole's eye*.

However, the discussed artificial naming *originally* had only sacred meaning almost universally, including in the Christian tradition, where the tradition of baptismal names survives. In modernity this facet, which was once related exclusively to what is sacred, started to have a [bio]political function. But the ideological configurations that could be revealed by the analysis of the secularization (or, maybe, secularization of what is in-secularizable without the complete transformation; i.e. if these names are really sacred, their secularization transforms them beyond recognition) of this facet of theology here are left aside.

Eight

KATYN DOES NOT HAPPEN TWICE

Tomas Kavaliauskas and Rūta Bagdanavičiūtė

British poet Desmond Graham wrote a poem in 2007, prior to the tragedy of Katyn in Smolensk airport; however, the poem can be read as if it were written for the occasion. Although the airport of the poem is not of Smolensk, coincidentally it is also set in springtime:

> *Spring, Lech Wałęsa Airport, 2007*
>
> *The pilot announces*
> *„Spring has come*
> *All over Europe"*
>
> *The giant beside me*
> *Still prays*
> *For safe landing*
>
> *The weight-lifter*
> *Who put down his case*
> *Like a glass of champagne*
> *Dares not look out*
>
> *There's a bundle of wrestlers*
> *Clamped to their seats*
> *In the back dreading*
> *The slightest of shocks*
>
> *The priest up and down*
> *Like a steward assures us*
> *If anything happens*
> *His route is up*
>
> *The rest of us*
> *Make it to land*
> *If at all*
> *In deep shock[1]*

The recorded voices recovered from the black boxes revealed that, just before the tragedy at the Smolensk airport, passengers realized that they were doomed to catastrophe. In the words of Desmond Graham, they landed in deep shock—forever. The Polish President Kaczynski seems to be Kat(cz)ynski, as the Katyn ghost of seventy years prior had been a part of his identity. On the one hand, this death of the Polish elite was meaningless, unexpected, unprecedented. They died in a catastrophe because of thick fog and low visibility. Lacking a conspiracy theory the tragedy loses its drama, meaning and purpose. From this perspective it has nothing to do with patriotism or martyrdom. Not coincidentally a Belgium cartoon pictured the Polish eagle landing on its head with a mocking comment: "The eagle has landed."[2] Knowing the ostentatious posture of President Kaczynski and his frequently pretentious attitude, such a crash en route to such an event brought a genuine smile to his opponents' faces. President Kaczynski was apparently notorious for his willingness to make impressive landings in spite of warnings of low visibility—for instance, in one case he threatened to give a pilot the sack for not landing in Tbilisi. But the witnesses who cite the opposite might be equally in the right: this Polish President would also close the plane's window blinders due to his discomfort of flying.

From the mystical perspective we may easily suspect destiny—an unavoidable death in the land of the 1940 massacre of Katyn. In this sense the Polish elite united with the victims existentially and commemorated them by losing own lives. It is as if the seventy year old ghost(s) of the Katyn massacre had taken down the plane and crashed it. Just as the characters die in Shakespeare's *Hamlet* because the ghost of Hamlet's father haunts the castle of Kronborg at Elsinore, similarly the ghost of the past of Katyn brought death to the passengers of the presidential plane. That plane was traveling for the anniversary commemoration of this tragic event. But in *Hamlet* characters die because of revenge and a battle for power. In the case of Katyn 2010, the victims die merely in their nationalist attempt to commemorate Katyn of 1940. Political insinuation of Russian conspiracy was apparent while watching the exclusive and almost royal funeral of the President in Krakow—the solemnity created out of respect for the President and the First Lady implied a martyr status for the glory of Poland.

Symbolically appropriate, during the time of the funeral Europe's sky was covered with the ash smoke steaming from Iceland's volcano. Russian President Dmitrij Medvedev ignored it and took the risk of flying in to attend the funeral, whereas Barack Obama, Nicolas Sarkozy, and Angela Merkel all used the ashy air as an excuse for their absence. It seems like Medvedev had no choice but to arrive, regardless of the circumstances, in order to avoid conspiracy theory. Did his flight imply a personal risk of his life? What was the degree of likelihood that he would crash? Would he have taken the risk if there was a high degree of likelihood? Thus, did Obama, Sarkozy and Merkel use the possible risk only as an excuse to avoid attendance at the funeral ceremony or was the risk indeed quite high? In this case the President of Russia, Dmitrij

Medvedev, is a hero. But the ash smoke was not coming from the Russian side. Most likely we may leave open the question of what of the value was to him of attending the funeral "under any circumstances" as for him the flight zone conditions were acceptable.

At any rate, in the official image-making rhetoric Medvedev made his purely humane effort in solidarity with the grief-stricken Polish nation. We may never know the true answer, despite the potential simplicity of that answer: Medvedev followed the rule of a diplomatic "ought" for international relations. When the President of another country dies in the territory of Russia, attendance at the funeral ceremony for the Russian President is not a matter of choice. Then not much merit is left even for coming "under any circumstances."

Nevertheless, a strange contingency lurks behind both the purely pragmatic and the purely humane motive to attend the funeral ceremony in Krakow—after the tragedy and after the follow-up of Bronislaw Komorowski's election as the new President, Poland became a strategic partner of Russia, whereas before Poland was a geopolitical hurdle. Poland of Lech Kaczynski had its independent stance sandwiched between the interests of mighty Germany in the West and of mighty Russia in the East. That independent stance evaporated like the smoke of Katyn. After the crash, Poland is no longer the Central European preclusion for Russia's strategic geopolitical partnership with Germany (suffice it to recall the geopolitical meaning of the gas North Stream project in the Baltic Sea) and with France (suffice it to recall French/Russian deal for the amphibious warship Mistral for the protection of the same North Stream zone). In other words, the consequences of the plane crash at Smolensk airport are not limited to human casualties as we are witnessing a geopolitical shift as the result of it.

For Radoslaw Sikorski, the Polish Defense Minister, the North Stream is a new Molotov-Ribbentrop pact: by joining NATO and the EU in 2004 the Baltic States suddenly felt psychologically secure fortifying their border with Russia in the East, but the gas pipe line of the North Stream brought the border back to the West. By the same token, Poland, which was a loud voice in Europe criticizing the North Stream as the German/Russian geopolitical affair, was supported by the Baltic States. These countries also had anti-Russian influence in the *Orange revolution* in Ukraine and later in Georgia in its 2008 military conflict with Russia.

Needless to say, after the Smolensk airport tragedy and its resultant shift in Polish politics from anti-Russian to pro-Russian, Poland's former geopolitical ego has vanished. Bronislaw Komorowski emphasized during his Presidential campaign his willingness and interest in listening to his European neighbors. And this is really what is happening. Conveniently for that "listening," on the 29th October, 2010, Russia signed a contract with Poland gaining permission for gas transit further West via Poland. The estimated annual value of the contract is 3 billion; the contract is for a decade.[3]

The economic benefits for Poland are visible in the same way as the dominance of the economic paradigm over the spirit of what Dostoevsky pointed out in *The Brothers Karamazov*: the masses want bread, the masses are weak. The Grand Inquisitor accused Jesus of having standards that were too high for the few, not for the masses. For Dostoevsky, industrial and material-oriented 19th- century Europe was obviously devoid of spirit and deeper meanings. In the 21st century the hope was that at least post-communist Europe, with Catholic Poland at the fore, will know more about freedom than materialistic realpolitik. That hope is evaporating. And the smoke of the second Katyn has lifted. Post-communist Poland and Central Europe fuses its goals with pragmatic Western European ones. The Iron Curtain falls into the past of 1989 as something no longer related to the present geopolitical shifts in the region(s) of the Warsaw Pact formerly dominated by the Soviet Union. Politicians of today forget the initial premises of freedom and independence as economic needs dictate choices.

Needless to say, the contingency of the tragedy and of economic contracts does not have to imply a conspiracy plot for the tragedy at Smolensk for the 70th anniversary of Katyn. However, the contingency itself is strange. It lurks behind the new unfolding events of billions, which Gasprom has been interested in for a long time. The contingency lurks ominously considering how easily Poland became a transit country for Russia's interests in Western Europe. It does not lurk ominously for anyone who interprets the new positive Polish-Russian economic relations as an outcome of existential solidarity in the face of the tragedy at Smolensk's airport. But can spiritual solidarity deliver an economic paradigm that quickly?

Russia commiserated with Poland and unified with it to a degree, strengthening mutual affection and changing the model of diplomacy. The Prime Minister Donald Tuska got a personal chance to grieve in Smolensk in the tight embrace of Vladimir Putin. That appeared as solidarity and in that embrace the tragedy got its final image of an air space catastrophe, which, supposedly, could happen to anyone anywhere, including all anniversary contingency factors. That tight embrace of Tuska in the caring arms of Putin indeed consoled the Polish Prime Minister both politically and economically. This instantly famous photo, which circulated the web globally, recalls Hamlet's words to Horatio: "the play's the thing wherein I'll catch the conscience of the King." The thing is that in this context the play seems to be set up by the Russian side, not the Polish. This is especially peculiar in retrospect—at that time of seeing the photo of the "embrace" we did not know that some months later the Poles will obtain evidence from a sound record at the office of Smolensk ground controller/dispatcher that the command "horizon" was given at 70 and not 100 meters, as it should have been. Moreover, the record provided further evidence that "the landing zone commander reports all the time that everything is OK.[…] No information is given to the crew that they are not on the right approach path," Polish investigator Colonel Robert Benedict told the press conference.[4]

We are left to wonder if that Russian condolence and mutual grief was honest and genuine, just like we are doomed to question honesty *per se* in the domain of Realpolitik and international diplomatic relations. We are doomed to question it especially if we are influenced by Machiavelli's understanding of Realpolitik—i.e. moral behavior that is expressed by a politician does not have to coincide with his personal beliefs. Machiavelli is quite clear making this point: virtues sometimes become vices and vices become virtues. When he accused Soderini for not "taking care" of De Medici when he had power, Machiavelli accuses him of being moral and virtuous, which in political reality was a virtue turned into a vice as Soderini lost power and Machiavelli was persecuted.[5]

The Kremlin's Machiavellian type of condolence to Poland is more believable in the milieu of the 2008 conflict between Russia and Georgia, when Poland supported Tbilisi together with the Baltics. Then Vladimir Putin announced quite passionately that these countries will regret lending such support. Shall one dare to recall those threatening words at the moment of a staged consolatory embrace at the scene of the smashed aircraft in 2010? Are those threatening words two years before the crash just a contingency that has no rational validity? Shall one dare to imagine Machiavellian upside down morals at the moment of Putin holding Donald Tuska and grieving together? Is it possible to master Machiavellian technique and apply it to perfection in practice?

Not without good reason do scholars of Niccolo Machiavelli cite Shakespeare and seek links between the cold-blooded hypocrisy of politicians and their moral image in public. Leonidas Donskis, when analyzing the reasons for Niccolo Machiavelli's demonization,[6] quotes Shakespeare's historical drama *Henry VI*, where Richard, Duke of Glouster, believes in his ability to surpass Machiavelli in his dubious moral behavior:

Why, I can smile and murder whiles I smile,
And cry Content to that which grieves my heart,
And wet my cheeks with artificial tears,
And frame my face to all occasions.
I'll drown more sailors than the mermaid shall;
I'll slay more gazers that the basilisk;
I'll play the orator as well as Nestor,
Deceive more slily than Ulysses could;
And, like a Sinon, take another Troy.
I can add colours to the chameleon,
Change shapes with Proteus for advantages,
And set the murderous Machiavel to school.
(Part 3, Act 3, Scene 2)

The level of Shakespeare's infatuation with Machiavelli's school of thought is also evident in *Hamlet*. The re-playing of Hamlet's father's murder by comedians is supposed to test Claudius' reaction, asking: could Claudius wet his cheeks with artificial tears? Could Claudius set the murderous Machiavel to school? Surely he could not.

Hamlet, ever suspicious after falling privy to the whisperings of his father's ghost about the true murderer, seeks revenge; however, not having rational evidence, he embarks on a trip into quasi-madness and an artistic and affected form of behavior, in short assuming a kind of role of a fool jester. Hamlet turns to the strategy of artistic "argumentation." He hires performers to play a story that follows his father's murder plot, both according to his imagination and based on his father's ghost narrative. The play has to be performed in the presence of the suspect. The play has a symbolic title—*The Mousetrap*. Only Horatio learns from Hamlet the true purpose of the Mousetrap play:

> Hamlet:
> There is a play to-night before the king;
> One scene of it comes near the circumstance
> Which I have told thee of my father's death:
> I prithee, when thou seest that act afoot,
> Even with the very comment of thy soul
> Observe mine uncle: if his occulted guilt
> Do not itself unkennel in one speech,
> It is a damned ghost that we have seen,
> And my imaginations are as foul
> As Vulcan's stithy. Give him heedful note;
> For I mine eyes will rivet to his face,
> And after we will both our judgments join
> In censure of his seeming.
>
> Horatio:
> Well, my lord:
> If he steal aught the whilst this play is playing,
> And 'scape detecting, I will pay the theft[7]

The king betrays himself when, as the scene of deadly poisoning unfolds, he abruptly stands up, demands light, and then isolates himself in his chambers in shock, fury, fear, and—to be sure—guilt. Now having his suspicions duly confirmed, Hamlet is even more obsessed with the spirit of revenge:

> *Tis now the very witching time of night,*
> *When churchyards yawn and hell itself breathes out*
> *Contagion to this world: now could I drink hot blood,*
> *And do such bitter business as the day*
> *Would quake to look on. Soft! now to my mother.*
> *O heart, lose not thy nature; let not ever*
> *The soul of Nero enter this firm bosom:*
> *Let me be cruel, not unnatural:*
> *I will speak daggers to her, but use none;*

My tongue and soul in this be hypocrites;
How in my words soever she be shent,
To give them seals never, my soul, consent![8]

In the case of the Polish tragedy a semi-secret play also took place, at the St Mary's Basilica in Krakow—all eyes were riveted to the Russian President Dmitri Medvedev. His face did not reveal for the TV cameras anything unusual or suspicious, but at that time one could recall the words of Hamlet explaining the ruse of the Mousetrap to Horatio: "the play's the thing wherein I'll catch the conscience of the King." Perhaps this is because the truth says that his sympathy was honest and wholehearted; or, perhaps he is a better actor than Claudius, and it is perhaps Medvedev who could "set the murderous Machiavel to school."

Interestingly even Russo-phobic Lithuanian Europarlamentarian Vytautas Landsbergis, who is keenly attuned to KGB methods and Kremlin's geopolitical games, did not rush to accuse Russia of quietly abetting or even causing the catastrophe. It was clearly understood that without evidence such charges would mean a new cold war between Russia and Poland, albeit not necessarily between the liberal and democratic West and Russia, as Lech Kaczynsky's self-confident foreign politics agitated Paris and Berlin in their political and economic flirtations with Moscow. However, EP Vytautas Landsbergis after some time said: "No country—neither Poland, nor the EU, nor the United States—dares to demand an independent investigation in order to make sure that the investigation is not done by potential criminals. Therefore, this disaster is still over the heads of all of us and it is a disaster of the entire shocked world."[9]

Even if the thickness of the fog is the only factor to blame for the lethal landing (after how many attempts? After the first attempt or after the fourth attempt? The question, which was disputed as the Russians initially claimed "four attempts," implying incompetence on the part of the pilots, then, suddenly agreed that there was only one lethal "attempt"), the scope of the consequences of the crash reaches the domain of geopolitical dominance/submissiveness. Russian dissident Andrey Piontkovsky in his public lecture in Lithuania at Vytautas Magnus University in 2009, prior to the tragedy at Smolensk airport, said that if Russia was left one on one with Europe without the might of the U.S., Russia would win quite easily. He did not refer to a military victory, but to geopolitical dominance, using economic means as better and more effective ammunition for re-occupation than tanks. A considerable lack of vigilance of the process of shifting and overlapping political tectonic plates in Central/Eastern Europe is to the benefit of today's imperialistically minded Kremlin.

The tragedy at Smolensk airport for the day of the commemoration of the Polish soldier massacre overlaps with the death of the Polish elite at the same place seventy years ago. That is inseparable from the complexity of Central/Eastern European history. The history of this part of Europe apparently is not just a matter of the past, but rather it surfaces—and haunts. The horror of the past easily becomes the horror of the present. Evil in this part of Europe seems to proliferate as the fog here is sometimes thicker, more lethal, and more mystical than elsewhere. The complexity of historical-political narratives testifies to the fact that that post-communist European drama experience is a never-ending process, in spite of the illusion of Poland's belonging to the EU, NATO and peaceful coexistence with their "neighbor" to the East.[10]

Freedom for Poland today includes the smoke over Katyn. Central and Eastern Europe cannot talk about freedom without that smoke. Before the catastrophe it seemed obvious that Katyn is just an object to be commemorated, but the plane crash added a freshly caked layer of smoke and blood. The "dead" Katyn of 1940—supposedly good for commemoration only—came alive in 2010 almost like a zombie presence—truly a day (and night) of the living dead—for those who dared to commemorate it. If that is a contingency of no rational validity, then what a mystical, ghost-like contingency that is!

What superstitions will the Polish President have in 2020 (whoever he or she will be) while boarding the Presidential plane before leaving Warsaw for Smolensk to commemorate what by then will be the 80th anniversary of the Katyn massacre and by then the 10th anniversary of those top countrymen who died for the occasion of commemoration of 1940 in 2010? What "irrational" superstitions and ghosts will have to be chased away by rational arguments in the minds of those who will board a new Presidential plane in the spring of 2020? Will the Polish President of that day close the plane's window blinder? Will he or she board the plane or will he or she send the Prime Minister instead? How many Polish elite people will join the President or the Prime Minister? Will they travel to Smolensk by car or by train instead? And what will they be dreaming on the night before the new anniversary of the dead Polish patriots? Will they say good-bye to their families in a light-hearted way or will there be a moment of silence before closing the door after themselves? Will their farewell kiss to their Polish daughters and sons linger a bit longer than it normally would?

> *And then they'll be on/in a f(l)right*
> *"Clamped to their seats*
> *In the back dreading*
> *The slightest of shocks"*
> *The shocks of Katyn of 2020*
> *For the 80th and 10th jubilees*
> *And then their farewell kisses*
> *To Polish daughters and sons*
> *Will linger on their lips ablaze[11]*

Hence, it is just like in Henrik Ibsen's *Ghosts* — one cannot escape from the past as it is inherited: dead thoughts, dead beliefs, and dead events haunt us in the present. The past lies as an unfathomable collective unconscious under a veil of current, conscious action and it reemerges in a ghost-like manner — unexpectedly, shockingly. We are haunted, not left lonely, by what we inherited from our parents; we are haunted by various old beliefs and events as they are permanently carved in us. If Ibsen is right, we cannot get rid of them. The past awakens our memory, immerses us inside ourselves, and plunges us into an abyss of our own irresolvable existential drama. In that drama we find as many ghosts as sand through which we struggle. Sand storms (perhaps not unlike fog) sometimes overwhelms our vision.

In Shakespeare's *Hamlet* the ghost of the past turns the present upside down, and finally it even succeeds in destroying the present, submerging the present in a smoke of confusion, passion, madness with a method, and violence, which could be compared to the acrid, confusion-causing, pain-inducing smoke of a burning nation. The post-communist Polish present—submerged in the haunting smoke where we find the stench of the more than 20,000 rotted bodies from 1940 Katyn—bespeaks of the unique location of Central Europe. In this part of the world freedom of the present should not (cannot!) be separated from the horrors of the past. In this context the economic paradigm should never be able to take over the spiritual one, but it does, as the past is left to rot, as a past supposedly unrelated to the present.

The stench of the reeking bodies of the Polish officers made Jósef Mackiewicz cover his mouth and nose when he went to Katyn from Vilnius in 1943 for exhumation excavations.[12] He witnessed the layers of elite officers, the corona of the Polish army. They were not naked. These thousands of officers were shot into the back of their skull and pushed into a pile, but three years later the Germans laid them in rows, hundreds of rows for thousands of bodies in military outfits wearing orders, signs of accomplishment, special officer buttons, and the Polish blazon of the eagle. Thus, the logic of contingency is incomplete when we say that the place and time coincided in 2010 at Smolensk airport. The logic of contingency includes the fact that after the plane crash there were no survivors, just like seventy years ago.

But unlike seventy years ago, the relatives of the victims received exclusively humane comfort and all possible help in Moscow. For this reason Jaroslaw Kaczynski did not dare to announce that his brother and the Polish elite had been murdered. But his personal effort to bury President Lech Kaczynski in Wavel Palace as a national hero bespeaks of his belief and inner feelings. Caught in a Hamlet-like situation, not having evidence at hand, Jaroslaw Kaczynski could not act, could not take his longed for revenge. If it is true that Hamlet's hesitation to take revenge for his father's murder is due to a lack of evidence, and not only a bout of moral conscience, then the question whether "to be or not to be" is question animating Jaroslaw Kaczynski and the entire Polish nation as well. Hamlet relied on the whispered revelations of his father's ghost; on whose whispered accusations and confessions can Jaroslaw Kaczynski rely? Interestingly, the director of the film *Katyn*, Andrzej Wajda, expressed disbelief in the Katyn 2 conspiracy plot, and his voice is significant.

Yet there is still another contingency between the first Katyn and the second—the lack of certainty! Jósef Mackiewicz, in an essay which in Poland is considered classical, he reveals how the Soviets were interested in convincing the Poles that their officers in Katyn were murdered by the Nazi Germans. However, the Nazis did investigation in Katyn in 1943 in the presence of international journalists in order to prove that it was a Soviet job. The bullets were German-made. Among the Polish officers were dozens of Jewish names like Gutman Izaok, Niremberg Abram, Rozen Samuel, etc. But the Jewish names found in the list of victims contradicted the text of the popular brochure in Poland published by the Germans that Bolshevik Jewish was responsible for the execution.[13]

Thus, what did the Polish people believe in 1940? What was the truth in their minds when they stared in awe at posters that read: "Jewish and Bolshevik executioners in Katyn"? Is it possible that the truth of Katyn 2 that is available today will change tomorrow? After all, the truth of the first Katyn is still under investigation, as the Russians opened the archives to the Polish historians after the second Katyn. Thus the past of a now doubled Katyn still haunts the Polish nation as well as post-communist Europe.

The ghost of Katyn sends us hidden premises that are existentially dented in our historic memory. An attempt to get rid of hiddenness and mystery would be equal to the Enlightenment illusion of handling memory rationally: supposedly, once we understand the past, once the cause and effect have been mutually clarified, the past can be discarded as of myth.

Such rational thinking condemns historical myths to ghosts, and haunts those who believed in a closed chapter. In the case of the second Katyn this truth of a haunting myth came alive in the most painful way. What does the true number of landing attempts change? It cannot change the fact of the tragedy; it can only raise further questions for investigation. What does it change if it is true that the pilots did have a miscommunication in English with the Russians at Smolensk airport? This truth can lead to further investigation, strengthen suspicions, or leave us agape in awe at the quality of coordination when visibility is low in that country.

Can the haunting myth of the first Katyn disappear if it is true that the airport lacked additional illumination for the fog conditions, although they were available? What if it is true that only after the catastrophe that illumination was switched on and the landing lane was lit up for the urgent arrival of Vladimir Putin? None of the facts, whether true or false, can chase away the all-embracing myth of Katyn. The facts for investigation—the smoke, as it were—are not magical, burning incense whose sweet, thick scents cloud the clarity of thinking. Rather it is time to face the past as lively and transient, without the historic borders of WWII and the supposedly peaceful borders of the 21st century EU.

If one does not want to debase the meaning of freedom by reducing it to consumption, human rights (including sexual gay rights), election democracy and freedom of speech, then the freedom of Poland and post-communist Europe is to be sought in the smoke of Katyn.

If the tragedy of Katyn in 2010 is a contingency, a great misfortune, then Lithuanian writer Herkus Kunčius has a list of such political contingencies:

- The inter-war President of Lithuania, Antanas Smetona, later in his life in the U.S. died because of a fire in his house and supposedly only because he was greedy enough to attempt to save his Persian carpet;
- Two brothers, whose same last name was spelled differently in Poland and Lithuania—Stanislavas Narutavičius and Gabrielius Narutowiczius—were killed. The Lithuanian Narutavičius was a lawyer and a signatory of the first Lithuania's independence in 1918, who worked as a politician. Then, supposedly, he killed himself on December 31st, 1932. The Polish version of Narutowiczius was the first President of the second Polish independence and was shot dead on December 16th, 1922 on the stairs of Warsaw National Gallery Zacheta on his fifth presidential working day. He was shot by a Polish nationalist artist, Eulegiusz Niewiadomski.[14]

What does Herkus Kunčius, whoes novels are translated into Polish, have to say about the second Katyn in this essay of his?

A few days before the loss of [his] life Lech Kaczynski visited Vilnius. On April 8th he went to the Lithuanian Presidential house on Simonas Dau-kantas square through the same streets as I wander, seeing out his car window the same people walking towards the University, just like I see them every day. Suddenly by paradox the tragedy of Katyn was repeated. That was suspiciously similar to a ritual homicide of 96 people (not just of military command, but also political, and church elite). [...] Thus, standing in front of Poland's embassy on Smėlio ["smėlio" means sand—*author's note*] street, inevitably I was thinking both of stage-managed death of Władisław Sikorski—the Head of Polish Government—in Gibraltar's air space catastrophe on July the 4th, 1943, and of the "first" and even more so of the "second" Katyn massacre.[15]

On the day of the second Katyn we may also recall the death of Anna Politkovskaya, "coincidentally" murdered on Vladimir Putin's birthday, October 7th. As Chechen journalist Manat Abdullajewa commented, "Putin will never have another birthday. It will always be the day on which Anna Politkovskaya was murdered, a woman who could neither be bought nor intimidated."

According to Kunčius, Poland in 2010 was stabbed in its back just like it was in 1940. Interestingly and/or coincidentally, in Gdansk Lech Kaczynski "reminded Mr. Putin that the Soviet Union had "stabbed Poland in the back" with its own invasion on September 17th, 1939. He compared the wartime Katyn massacre of 20,000 captured Polish officers by Stalin's secret police to the Holocaust.[16] As we know, such reminders are not among Putin's favorite topics, to say the least.

The best indicator of who is a conspiracy adherent of Katyn and who is not is the national split of the Polish people themselves. The controversy (to put it mildly) over the royal type of burial of Kaczynski in Krakow tells us that part of the Polish people did not see his death as worthy of such respect. Polish citizens even boycotted such a plan. It provoked anger and disappointment. This is more important in terms of sudden change of mood—from grief and national mourning for a week to outrage over the body of the deceased President and his wife. Suddenly Poland had two Polands.

The new Polish presidential election that resulted in Komorowski's win over the brother of the deceased president confirmed it. The slogan that Jaroslaw Kaczynski used during his presidential campaign—*Polska Najiewazneisha!*—did not help, although it almost helped. But the outcome is that the second Katyn became a means for the Presidential campaign's final goal, whereas such a tragedy should not be a means for anything. But was it treated as a means? Perhaps the event of the second Katyn obligated Jaroslaw Kaczynski to speak up about his motivation to become the President? We may wonder to what extent the Presidential campaign's rhetoric abused the sacred status of the tragedy. But it did not appear to be so in the eyes of his voters, who sympathized with Jaroslaw Kaczynski and felt sorry for him after the loss of his brother.

But de-sacralization seems to be only partial, limited to the controversy of Lech Kaczynski and his wife's burial in Wavel Palace. Other passengers of the fatal flight are considered martyrs and had public support. For instance, Anna Walentynowicz's name was exclusively mentioned, implying her individuality. As the right hand of Lech Walęsa in the *Solidarnośc* movement since 1980, she could be an equal contestant for the Wavel Palace burial next to Polish heroes and poets. A historian of the Holocaust, Timothy Snyder, wrote in memoriam not to Lech and Maria Kaczynski, but to the other famous passenger of the fatal flight—Tomasz Merta. The text by Timothy Snyder is called *Ghosts: could the plane crash bury Stalinism forever? In memory of Tomasz Merta.*[17]

The Polish nation was not divided over the burial and sacredness of the passengers, except perhaps in the case of the President and the first lady. But then there is also the wooden cross controversy.

At last the ghost reappears anyway—the very catastrophe of the presidential plane will continue to haunt as in a nightmare. The mysterious contingency of the 70th anniversary commemoration does not allow for a stripping off of the veil of fatalism. Although in the established and institutionalized discourse of the second Katyn is almost guilt- and accusation-free—the Polish crashed themselves—and for that reason there is no room for Hamlet-like metaphysical revenge, which should stem out of the darkness of the past; still the tragedy at the Smolensk airport (a military port!) raises passionate judgments. These judgments proliferate; sometimes they proliferate rather dangerously, losing the weight of the original meaning of the tragic event.

The follow-up was unexpected: a new discourse of the "wooden cross defenders" developed. People in Warsaw, who liked to have a wooden cross in front of the Presidential Palace in commemoration to the second Katyn, protested its removal against the official demands of the Polish Catholic Church. The protestors defended the wooden cross day and night. This story reveals an even larger gap between the divided sides of Poland. Usually tragedies unite nations, but in this case it is a paradox: instead of famous Polish solidarity we bear witness to a national split. Moreover, the split is double, as the Polish Catholics themselves in the heated debate could not agree where the cross shall be.

Suddenly the haunting ghost of Katyn 2 transformed into a sequence of protests of its own, like the postmodern theory of a signifier that becomes unrelated to its originally assigned signified. In just a few months (not even years) the signified tragedy of the second Katyn turned into a streaming multi-voiced discourse of heteroglossia. Initially the tragic event took away the tongue of the Polish nation; for a moment it seemed Poland was united. When the national mourning in Poland started everyone understood what he or she was mourning: the death of the Polish elite at the mystically fatal place. The traumatizing truth seemed to be here and now. But soon that singular meaning transformed and evolved into a proliferation of other meanings on the basis of self-contradictory national discourses over the burial place and over the location of the wooden cross.

Consequently, in one *Augenblick* the tragic "truth" of the second Katyn lost its luminosity. With the clearing of the fog and smoke over the airport of Smolensk, the tragic "truth" was sucked into a new, independent multi-voiced discourse. The tragic event itself and its mournful discourse were dwarfed by proliferating discourses. That inevitably plunges us into poststructuralist theory, where we find ourselves surrounded by a constant flow of signifiers. The signified lies under that flow like an empty, but active black hole that usurps the truth. In this domain the very truth appears as a construct. We exist within the domain of signifiers, in the domain of intertextual discourse and interpretation.

These signifiers—like dispersed traces—extend to new horizons away from their origin. New directions appear that distract us from the attraction of initial motivation of the sign. To what extent is this indeterminate discourse, in which no answer achieves finality, applicable to our present case of two Katyns? Is it possible to manage this kind of dispersed discourse when emotions and national pride is involved? For now we have kept divided the self contradictory Polish discourses that refuse to merge into one *grand narrative* (Lyotard).

Thus, even in this Polish catastrophe case we have witnessed how the multi-voice and multi-perspective Polish discourse distanced itself from the existential basis of the second Katyn. We have witnessed how pre-discursive reality and trauma turned out to be intertextual interpretative reality and trauma.

In Foucaultian terms, we might say that *the will to Truth* of the cross defenders (i.e. keeping the cross in place preserves justice for the memory of the crash) was contested by the other *will to Truth* of the Church and State (i.e. removing the cross appeals to justice because it does not violate the memory of the crash). Just before it, the *will to Truth* of Jaroslaw Kaczynski to bury his brother Lech Kaczynski in Wavel Palace was contested by the other *will to Truth* of those who did not see Lech Kaczynski as a martyr worth such a royal honor. Here the will to Truth becomes equal to a Nietzschean *Wille zur Macht* as the truth—or, perhaps better rendered in the plural as "truths"—constructed discursively by using the logic of power. The result is a battle field of various truths. Behind each truth stand believers who compete over their singular truth. But they overlook how their competitiveness helps proliferate new meanings of what was initially sacred.

The polyphonic discourse of Katyn makes Poland look like a Dostoevsky novel. According to Mikhail Bakhtin, Dostoevsky's novels are dialogical, as when characters have separate and contradictory consciousnesses. Moreover, there is no room for an autonomous consciousness which would in a mono-logue-like style embrace that polyphonic dialogue. On the contrary, the textual dialogues are doomed to impasse. The third person view does not correspond to any one particular element. In this way Dostoevsky achieved a new author's position, which is hierarchically higher than the position of a third person's monologue.[18]

Poland is the case where the polyphonic discourse is contradictory, but pas-sionate and without a superior "third person" who would consolidate the dia-logue of impasse. John Paul II was such an authority for Poland as well as for post-communist Catholic Europe. In the case of the discourse over the second Katyn there was no moral authority on the level and dignity of John Paul II.

In Shakespeare's *Hamlet* we do not find that "third" voice that would in a monologue complete the story. In the play there are monologues, both in the play and in the play-within-the-play, but the overall text of *Hamlet* leaves us with a feeling of total destruction. Everyone involved in the matrix of hatred and revenge is murdered (except Hamlet's mother, whose life has nevertheless been destroyed, despite not physically dying within the course of the dramatic time. It is a festivity of revenge and death, but after the macabre dance is over there is no winner. The winner is the one who will have to take the throne, but he is not a true winner; the ghost of the bloody throne will haunt him too. In this sense it is also a situational impasse. But before this impasse we have a multi-voice conspiracy discourse, the whispers of which wait around each cor-ner. Polonius even dies behind a rug, like a rat, for eavesdropping. There is no dignity in his death. No dignity is found in the scene of the King's poisoning and Hamlet's duel resulting in his death either. Rather it is a one dimensional discourse of revenge, hatred and will to power in spite of its complexity, since ultimately the polyphonic discourse is self-annihilating on the basis of mutual conspiracy that is inexorably saturated with corrupt Elsinore politics.

The castle of Kronborg at Elsinore is located at a place where the strait of Öresund (Swedish) or Øresund (Danish) is only 4 kilometers wide. In the 15th century it was the gateway from the Baltic to the North Sea and the Atlantic Ocean.[19] The toll for the ships and their cargo financed the ambitious plan of the castle of Kronborg—the castle permeated with lies, distrust, hatred, re-venge, deceit, and greed. In essence Kronborg castle's culture is the culture of sins that haunt and the culture of making creating sins anew in response to the now recrudescent ones. At least this kind of picture we get reading Hamlet's story.

The play is not about resurrection or spiritual development. It is not about a humane effort to become forgiving, or praying for one's enemies. Shakespeare's *Hamlet* is not in the spirit of Christianity, despite its Reformation setting. Altruism and sacrifice for the Other is not in the narrative of *Hamlet*, just as it is not in Machiavelli's oeuvre. The ghost of Hamlet's father haunts in order to ignite revenge, possible Machiavellian justice, which we fail to see since there is no survivor to enjoy the achieved "justice." Machiavelli's case is similar: after completing a falsified history book of Florence in hypocritical praise of the De Medici family, he no longer had the good health to enjoy his privileged presence in Florence's political life, and died several years later.

Hamlet as a play is an abyss of destructiveness. The famous question of Hamlet—"to be or not to be" may also be interpreted as a choice between acceptance of what the Kronborg culture embodies and its rejection. In this respect "to be or not to be" means more than mere survival in Machiavellian Kronborg *a la* De Medici Florence, but victory over the abyss of destructiveness (which is not achieved). The political culture of the castle swallows the what goodness may rest in Hamlet's heart. The story ends up in stunningly debased terminus, in which Hamlet, "sweet prince" though he may be, gains revenge what at an extraordinary cost. The moral of this tale could have been written ironically on the last page of the play—*this is the end of good intentions.*

Shakespeare, willingly or not, showed us Hamlet's inability to rise above the discourse and culture of ill-will that haunted Kronborg castle in spite of his supposed status of a "righteous" personality. The lines that show his moral superiority do not save his character—he ends up dying in the bloody context of Elsinore politics and its ghostly matrix.

Some Shakespeare experts may believe that Hamlet is too contemplative, too moral, too sensitive to act immediately. Supposedly, he misses his opportunity of grasping and acting in the here-and-now. Alfonsas Nyka-Niliūnas, the translator of *Hamlet* into Lithuanian, argues that Hamlet is a victim of a non-traditional fate of inevitability: he dies within himself by submitting to the law of self-awareness of his humane condition.[20] But what would be left of the tragedy's quality if Hamlet acted immediately? There would be no point in creating the scene of comedians to test Claudius' reaction and Hamlet would not have to play the role of a mad, yet witty jester.

But Hamlet as a character at least shows both mental and physical activity. It is quite astonishing that the 20,000 Polish elite military officers caught in the even more dishonored and dreadful WWII context did not show Hamlet-like activity. If we are to believe in the accuracy of Wajda's film *Katyn*, the execution scene of the 20,000 top Polish men does not even remotely resemble the tragedy of Hamlet—the latter does something, the former nothing. Even if our imagination is contaminated by Hollywood's superheroes like Rambo or Rocky, still the level of submissiveness to the Soviet executioner is beyond comprehension—at least the way Wajda portrayed it. But his film is accepted by the Polish people and historians, and is considered to be classic. Thus, was it the result of the deep disbelief of those 20,000 men that made the first Katyn so cruel? Can 20,000 wise military men even have, let alone sustain such disbelief? At the beginning of the film *Katyn* we see another scene of submissiveness at the university, when Nazis arrest professors disrupting their academic discussion. The Polish academic elite refuse to believe the savage Nazi power till they are physically forced to.

Earlier we provided a list of similarities between the first and the second Katyn. But at this point yet another similarity creeps forward: double submissiveness at Smolensk airport. Firstly, the passengers of the Presidential plane died unable to show any resistance, just like in the first Katyn (we do not dare to consider if some had perhaps survived the crash, at least until the rescue came...). Secondly, the Polish authorities were unable to conduct the investigation themselves as the head of investigation was Vladimir Putin and, consequently, the Polish submitted to the Russian demand to perform dissections of the bodies of the victims in Moscow, not in Warsaw. But was it according to international standards?

Submissiveness and helplessness mark the first and the second Katyn. We may counter-argue that the passengers were not passive, but extremely active before the catastrophe. Some were *Solidarnosc* people. But an underestimation of possible Russian negligence at Smolensk airport becomes the result of a final submission to the circumstances of the catastrophe. And if we are to admit that there was negligence on the Polish side as well (e.g. ignorance of the fog conditions; using same air craft for all political elite), then it indicates an overestimated confidence in the Polish–Russian geopolitical flight zone. The question is where that confidence comes from? Our hypothesis is that it is because of psychological relaxation and political belief that "Katyn does not happen twice."[21]

Hamlet was ready to die for his truth. He did not overestimate his might and was aware of death lurking just around the corner. His path to the final scene of death was paved by his readiness to die. The passengers of the Polish Presidential plane were not ready for it nor even considered it as a possibility. It came as a surprise.

When political circumstances and the cruelty level are underestimated, then one could expect almos anything, except the evil perpetrated at Katyn. If it is a mystery why 20,000 officers were so helpless at the first Katyn massacre, then is it equally a mystery as to why almost a hundred passengers comprised of Polish intellectual and political elite took the same plane at the same time? Isn't it because we all knew—we *thought* we knew—that Katyn does not happen twice? Especially in civilized Europe, where:

- in general Presidential plane pilots simply do not encounter English language barriers or communication hassles from the ground commanders/ dispatchers at hosts' airports, not to mention in this case receiving incorrect "horizon" updates of 70 meters when it is in fact 100 meters;

- after catastrophes credit cards of the victims are not used for shopping by the security guards;
- witnesses are not murdered just for placing video material on the internet taken by mobile phone recording shooting sounds at the catastrophe scene, which was done by a Ukranian bypasser;
- the eye color description from an autopsy coincides with the memory of the victim's family, bafflingly in contrast to the Russian documents, which raises the additional question about the identity of the corpse buried in Wavel Palace under the name of Lech Kaczynski.

The disturbing autopsy data mismatch may also mean that the signified Kaczynski might be false or void. Considering that the truth about the real reasons for the catastrophe may remain officially undisclosed, it is quite symbolic that previously discussed Polish multi-voice discourse remains scattered into bits and pieces of signifiers that do not match. Very postmodern—and corresponding all too conveniently with the postmodern foggy circumstances of the fatal crash.

Nevertheless, what seems to be postmodern might be simply the Russian way of handling the catastrophe both before and after. If the list above means negligence or just a "cultural" way of Russian behavior, then—contrary to the lack of foresight of Lech Kaczynski—Hamlet never underestimated the morally corrupt culture of his Kronborg castle. How could he? But how could Lech Kaczynski? Was not it his ultimate mistake? Russian dissident Valeria Novodvorskaja wonders why anti-Soviet Lech Kazcynski would not be killed by those who poisoned with polonium candies Litvinenko in a London cafe without punishment? According to Novodvorskaja, Kaczynski was the Polish Ronald Reagan, the follower of Kosciuszko and Pilsudski. Kaczynski made only one mistake when he took a Russian-made aircraft into Soviet territory trusting Soviet authorities. The wording of the previous sentence is not an instance of carelessness: Novodvorskaja purposefully calls current Russian territory "Soviet." And she concludes that the West will not accuse the Kremlin because everything would be covered by gas, oil and smoke.[22]

If the words of Novodvorskaja are too strong or too mad for her audience, perhaps not unlike Hamlet's method-laced madness strikes the ears of thos in the castle and in his audience, then suffice it to bear in mind what *has happened*, when *it happened*, where *it happened*, and how it was handled. That combination in itself is a political narrative worthy of the Shakespearean imagination.

The second Katyn is the price paid for the Polish existential relaxation, lost vigilance, and lack of geopolitical acuity while living on the edge of the geopolitical abyss of Central/Eastern Europe. Hamlet never lost his vigilance and was in the state of ambiguous madness, wondering as to the proper action, but despite not forgetting his charge of revenge, he and many others (many innocents?) paid a cruel price. The second Katyn is a an extraordinary and haunting price to pay for a ghostly lapse in memory, which in the freedom of post-communist Central/Eastern Europe is veiled by a mysterious smoke.

Notes

1. Graham, Desmond. (2009) *A Gdansk Sketchbook. Polish Poems 1984—2008.* Gdansk: European Center for Solidarnosc, p. 50.
2. Gazet van Antwerpen, Belgium newspaper, April 15, 2010.
3. http://www.rferl.org/content/Poland_Russia_Ink_LongTerm_Gas_Supply_ Deal/2205074.html
4. Polish—Russian errors and negligence to contributed to Smolensk disaster. Polskie radio, the news.pl. Available at: http://www.thenews.pl/international/artykul147580_ poland---russia-errors-and-negligence-helped-lead-to-smolensk-disaster.html
5. Niccolo Machiavelli, *Discourses of the First Decade of Titus Livius.* A Penn State Electronic Classics Series Publication.
6. Donskis, Leonidas. (2008) *Power and Imagination: Studies in Politics and Literature.* New York: Peter Lang, pp. 8–9.
7. Shakespeare, *Hamlet*, Act 3. Scene II
8. Ibid.
9. Landsbergis, Vytautas (2010) *Smolensko nelaimė tebekybo visiems mums virš galvos* [The disaster of Smolensk is over our heads.] Available at: http://www.alfa.lt/ straipsnis/10434388/?Landsbergis..Smolensko.nelaime.tebekybo.visiems.virs.galvos=2010-12-31_12-37
10. The story comes to mind of how in November 2009, a few months prior to the catastrophe, a Russian participant at an international conference in Warsaw, seeing how relaxed the organizers were while being half an hour behind schedule, said: "If the Polish continue to be so relaxed, they will oversleep the third war."
11. This poem was written by the authors for the occasion of this article.
12. Mackiewicz, Jósef (2010) *The Smoke over Katyn.* In: Fredriksson, Carl Henrik & Samalavičius, Almantas (eds.) Europos istorijos: Rytų ir Vakarų patirtis [European Histories: the Experience of East and West]. Eurozine&Kultūros barai, pp. 240–268.
13. Ibid.
14. Kunčius, Herkus. (2010) *Apie atsitiktinumo logiką ir teisę gyventi* [About the Logic of Contingency and Right to Live]. Kultūros barai, [The Domains of Culture], Vol 5, pp. 2–7.
15. Ibid, pp. 4–5.
16. http://edwardlucas.blogspot.com/2009/09/putin-in-gdansk_04.html
17. Snyder, Timothy. (2010) *Ghosts: could the plane crash bury Stalinism forever? In memory of Tomasz Merta.* http://www.tnr.com/article/world/ghosts
18. For more see chapter 1 of Mikhail Bakhtin, *Problems of Dostoevsky's Poetics.* ed. and trans. Caryl Emerson. Minneapolis: University of Minnesota Press, 1984.
19. North, Michael. *The Sea as Lieu de mémoire.* The paper read at Baltic Studies conference at Vytautas Magnus Univeristy, Kaunas, Lithuania, 11th June, 2009.
20. Nyka-Niliūnas. (1999) *Vertėjo post scriptum* [The Translator's Post Scriptum]. In: William Shakespeare, *Hamletas.* Vilnius: Baltos lankos, pp. 191–192.
21. Who expected the first 9/11 in New York? American embassies in Germany were warned about the suspects, but they got visas in spite of it, since such things do not happen. However, after the first 9/11 Americans are vigilant about protecting the country from a second 9/11, as they have realized that such things do happen.
22. Novodvorskaja, Valerija (2010) Tough landing. Available in Russian at: http://grani. ru/Events/Disaster/m.176940.html

Works Cited

Bakhtin, Mikhail. (1984) *Problems of Dostoevsky's Poetics*. Ed. and Trans. Caryl Emerson. Minneapolis: University of Minnesota Press.

Donskis, Leonidas. (2008) *Power and Imagination: Studies in Politics and Literature*. New York: Peter Lang, pp. 8–9.

Graham, Desmond. (2009) *A Gdansk Sketchbook. Polish Poems 1984—2008*. Gdansk: European Center for Solidarnosc, p. 50.

Kunčius, Herkus. (2010) *Apie atsitiktinumo logiką ir teisę gyventi* [About the Logic of Contingency and Right to Live]. Kultūros barai, [The Domains of Culture], Vol 5, pp. 2–7.

Landsbergis, Vytautas (2010) *Smolensko nelaimė tebekybo visiems mums virš galvos* [The disaster of Smolensk is over our heads.] Accessed at: http://www.alfa.lt/str aipsnis/10434388/?Landsbergis..Smolensko.nelaime.tebekybo.visiems.virs.gal-vos=2010-12-31_12-37

Machiavelli, Niccolo, *Discourses of the First Decade of Titus Livius*. A Penn State Electronic Classics Series Publication.

Mackiewicz, Jósef (2010) *The Smoke over Katyn*. In: Fredriksson, Carl Henrik & Samalavičius, Almantas (eds.) Europos istorijos: Rytų ir Vakarų patirtis [European Histories: the Experience of East and West]. Eurozine&Kultūros barai, pp. 240–268.

North, Michael. *The Sea as Lieu de mémoire*. Conference paper read at Baltic Studies conference, Vytautas Magnus Univeristy, Kaunas, Lithuania, 11th June, 2009.

Novodvorskaja, Valerija (2010) Tough landing. Accessed at: http://grani.ru/Events/Disaster/m.176940.html

Nyka-Niliūnas. (1999) *Vertėjo post scriptum* [The Translator's Post Scriptum]. In: William Shakespeare, *Hamletas*. Vilnius: Baltos lankos, pp. 191–192.

Snyder, Timothy. (2010) *Ghosts: could the plane crash bury Stalinism forever? In memory of Tomasz Merta*. Accessed at: http://www.tnr.com/article/world/ghosts

Part Four

SHAKESPEARE AND THE POLITICS OF TRANSLATION

Nine

INTERVIEW WITH TOMAS VENCLOVA

Questions from
J. D. Mininger and Justas Patkauskas

Among other results, translations always enrich the translator. Having trans-
lated Shakespeare [into Lithuanian], do you see Shakespearean influence in
your own poetry and writing as a result of your translation and appreciation
of Shakespeare's work?

The work of translation always expands the consciousness of the translator,
probably the sub-consciousness as well. Amongst other things, it forces you
to master such resources of your own language that otherwise might have remained unknown. This concerns even the ordinary translations, but especially
translations of Shakespeare. To match a poet of such magnitude is, of course,
impossible, but while working a translator must transfer such sentiments "beyond the margins"—one must contend with authors as if they were equals, all
the while realizing the audacious absurdity of such a pretense. Either way, the
exercise strengthens the muscles and the whole body. If a poet simply reads
Shakespeare, to say nothing of translating, that inevitably somehow transforms
his style of writing, but he himself does not necessarily realize that. It is similar
to how extensive training improves the heart rhythm—for you it seems absolutely natural; but only a doctor would notice that it has changed.

In my youth, what first attracted me about Shakespeare was probably his
metaphorical language, the "misshapen chaos"[1] common to his works (back
then I would mention him in the same breath as Blok and Rimbaud, poets otherwise quite unlike him). Now I am perhaps more affected by his ability to tell dramatic and complex stories, usually presented from a somewhat ironic angle. But
I repeat, it is not something I can judge myself. References to Shakespeare are
contained within a couple of my poems such as *Pasakykite Fortinbrasui* (1959)
and *Arieliui* (1997). In the first one Shakespeare is "refracted" through Zbigniew
Herbert; the poem contains an Aesopian element characteristic of those times
(Denmark is likened to Lithuania). The second, I would say the more mature one,
is perhaps a closer match to Shakespeare's timeless dimension.

What was the social and political (not to mention literary and dramatic)
significance of translating The Tempest *in the seventies? Did you (and others)*
see in it an obvious allegory of the fate of Lithuania under Soviet occupation?
Were there any special challenges in the translation that arose due specifically
to the historical-political context of your translation? Were there particular
characters, plot devices, themes, linguistic tropes, or quotations which reso-
nated with you then (and now)?

The Tempest is the only work of Shakespeare I have translated. The story of that translation I have told in the post script attached therein twenty eight years later. The text was commissioned by a famous stage director Juozas Miltinis because the previous translation did not satisfy him. Possibly that was a specific "move" by the Soviet government: at that time I had been in a stage of open conflict with them, therefore it was decided to demonstrate (to the Lithuanian intelligentsia and the international community) that I am not being persecuted and continue to do cultural work. I warned Miltinis and the others that sooner or later I will end up either as an émigré or as a prisoner, which would render my translation unusable for producing the play, though nonetheless I took the job (and not without pleasure, by the way). In the play I did not find an allegory for the fate of Lithuania: Shakespeare was concerned with wholly different problems. Maybe some did see such an allegory but for that one must surely be heavily invested in the emotions of his time. What is reminiscent in *The Tempest* of Lithuania's occupation? Prospero who had lost his homeland and rather successfully established himself „in exile"? Or perhaps his enslaved Caliban? Perchance even Ariel, also forced to do Prospero's bidding? No, that does not seem to fit.

In this drama I was and still am most attracted by the two characters of Ariel and Caliban. Shakespeare created two entities of purely mythical proportions, equal to Greek (and perhaps Biblical) protagonists. Even for Shakespeare this was no common feat, though in people's minds Hamlet or King Lear are not far from Oedipus or King David. As for specific parts of the text—while translating I found the songs of Ariel to be of greatest satisfaction, though whether I succeeded in conveying them I do not know.

What draws your sympathies to Ariel in particular? Her unusual, ambiguous identity (e.g. birdlike but not animal; many human qualities and yet not really human; ambiguous gender coding)? Her fate as Prospero's servant, sometimes a begrudging and bitter laborer and at other points a grateful, alacritous sidekick? Despite often acting as Prospero's mouthpiece, Ariel is a poet too: is there one song, or even one particular stanza or phrase that especially resonates with you?

Ariel is a mediator between the human and subhuman (and, at the same time, super-human) world, which makes him/her into a truly mythic figure—in the terms of Claude Levi-Strauss, if you want. The song „Five fathoms deep" made the strongest impression on me, mainly because of its purely phonetic qualities which I did my best to convey.

In your writings you have touched upon the importance of context for understanding politically motivated art, suggesting that the historical genesis of texts and artworks, including the intellectual influences and personal experiences of the author, should be taken into account for a comprehensive interpretation. Is this equally true for both producing and studying a (literary) translation? To what degree did historicist considerations influence your translation of The Tempest*?*

If I understood the question correctly, you mean that the context of the translator's epoch can (must?) influence the translation. Without a doubt, yes. Translated Shakespeare must be accessible to the modern reader or spectator, therefore it is appropriate to translate him using the language of one's own time, to avoid stylization (or to do so from a distance), to risk references to situations, genres, tropes characteristic of the different era. That is what I tried to do. By the way, when translating Shakespeare such was the attitude of Pasternak (not so much of Mikhail Lozinsky). This becomes especially important when you try to convey the wit of Shakespeare, which for the translator is most difficult (to use a direct translation means to lose all the fun).

If you had the time and the opportunity, would there be a specific work of Shakespeare you would like to translate or retranslate now?

Something that has not been translated into Lithuanian as yet (*Coriolanus* perhaps?).

In the postscript to your Lithuanian language translation of Shakespeare's The Tempest [Audra], *you describe the island as, among other possible readings, "the world of the dead where people reveal themselves as they really are—a sort of a purgatory" where the characters confront the bare truth about themselves and then either turn out the better for it or sink into their own vices and worst qualities. This interpretation recalls a phrase you once wrote to Czeslaw Milosz, that life in exile "is a sort of life after death." You emigrated shortly after completing your translation of* The Tempest. *Do you see a significant relationship between the abovementioned interpretation of* The Tempest *and contemporary situations of exile and dislocation (e.g. forced emigration, Diasporas and their attendant culture(s), hybrid identity(s), but also self-chosen emigration such as we now witness in massive numbers from*, inter alia, *Lithuania and its surrounding countries)?*

When I emigrated in 1977 it indeed seemed like an afterlife because I had no hopes of returning, of seeing my family and friends (unless they too would "pass the threshold of Hades," i.e. emigrate). Now it is different: both I and any other emigrant can choose to visit Lithuania at our leisure, which I do with great frequency. Thus the metaphor of emigration as the world of the dead has disappeared or at least considerably faded. But, most likely, there remains the metaphor of a purgatory of sorts. Emigration forces you to really exert your strength in order to remain an independent, ethically worthwhile being. Most fail—and not just those who hit rock bottom, but also the ones who achieve.

You draw a correlation between ethically valuable existence and the favor of homeland in living that existence. Perhaps you can share an example or two of émigrés whose success is in fact failure; or, put differently, émigrés who fail themselves ethically despite their achievements abroad?

I could mention many Russian émigrés, including Vladimir Maksimov and Aleksandr Zinovyev. There are also Lithuanian examples, but I would prefer to be silent on the topic.

Given the radical difference in the political-historical context in Lithuania between now and the time of your own translation (1975), do you think that translating Shakespeare (into Lithuanian or into any central or eastern European language and context) remains a germane, even pressing task? How does the value of encounters with Shakespeare compare with the benefit of making contemporary authors and thinkers more widely available in central and eastern European countries?

Shakespeare (just like Sophocles, Plato, Dante, Cervantes, Tolstoy and other authors of such magnitude) has to be translated everywhere and at all times, regardless of the turning of the epochs. Nevertheless, the new translations must be good, at least not worse than the previous ones, which is not always the case. These authors can be substituted neither by Joyce, nor Heidegger, nor Freud, though translating the moderns too is fine (besides, they are often heralded by or even contained within the classics). Even less can they be replaced by the likes of Stephen King, Castaneda or Coelho, who are sadly the ones who push the classics out of the bookstores and out of people's imagination.

In your published epistolary exchange with Milosz, you suggest that literature functions as a means of resisting indoctrination within a totalitarian regime; should literature (or art in general; or Shakespeare in particular) equally play a reciprocal role in supporting a free and democratic society, and if so, how? In his introduction to your Winter Dialogue, *Joseph Brodsky comments that your poetry is convincing proof that poetry, when "true," is democratic, in that it seeks a better alternative to an imperfect reality. Does Brodsky's description of "democratic" poetry faithfully capture the spirit of your artistic endeavors?*

I have often said that any literature of quality is a counter-weight against totalitarianism. Stalin committed a huge error by not prohibiting the majority of world classics—had he done that, his system would have survived longer. I do not remember whether Brodsky uses the term "democratic poetry" (after all he leaned towards aristocratism) but he is right in saying that the majority of poetry, mine included, is an alternative to objectionable reality.

In his introduction to your volume of essays Lietuva pasaulyje [Lithuania in the World], *Aleksandras tromas maps the transformation in your general view(s) towards politics, art and critical writing. He states that in the sixties "it was difficult to believe that the aesthete and poet Tomas Venclova, who acknowledged only pure art, would someday "descend" to the "lowly" genre of social and political writing"; but he goes on to note that later in your career you "agreed that politics is a normal, useful and necessary human activity." Do you agree with his assessment? If your views did shift in the way tromas suggests, what prompted or influenced your change in attitude? More generally, what role did your friendship with tromas play in these matters of inquiring into the political and social efficacy and place of art and literature in society?*

In the Soviet times I used to be reproached for being "detached from reality," in spite of even then having written a good deal of civic poetry—perhaps even more than the other Lithuanian poets of that day. Only it was not the kind of "civic-mindedness" and "reality" which the government back then demanded and which meant nothing but the simplest lie and conformism. True, I was also rather distant to the so-called national strain which too contained elements of conformism: Lithuania mattered to me then as it does now, although not its purely ethnical existence, but rather its intellectual and moral maturity. In the seventies I started to feel that a decent individual must react to purely political questions as well, even if that is more the domain of social and political writing rather than of poetry (the historic role of poetry is primarily or even exclusively the cultivation of language). My stance on this remains unchanged. The late Aleksandras tromas undoubtedly played a significant role in here.

In Pokalbiai apie atminties ateitį [Conversations About the Future of Memory], *you write that in culture the mechanisms of memory and forgetting compete, yet both are necessary. Because of that struggle some important texts get pushed to the periphery, to be discovered later by new generations. Today, you stated, the role of the guardians of memory belongs to—or at least should belong to—writers and intellectuals. In what manner should these writers create and maintain what you once called a "fearless memory"?*

It is important not to remain silent on thorny issues, to be unafraid of breaking the "social contract" which is not always clearly articulated but nevertheless maintains a sort of (mostly internal) censorship. As if bringing up this or that problem is improper, or it can only be approached so that you do not "harm the nation" or "consort with the enemy." There is only one choice to be made—not between the positions of "the nation" ("the state") and "the enemy," but between what is true and untrue. For the nation—and, besides, the state—only the untrue is harmful.

You have said in an early interview ("Svarbiausia išsaugoti blaivų žvilgsnį" [A Sober Perspective is Paramount]) that the mission of the poet is "to maintain a sober perspective and help others maintain it as well." In our contemporary world, what do you believe are the areas most in need of poetry's sober perspective? What does poetry (and art in general) offer to individuals and societies that other disciplines, discourses, and creative mediums do not or cannot?

Poetry, as I have said, cultivates the language, while art deals with language in a wider sense: for example, painting and architecture develop the language of spatial relations, music—the language of temporal relations. "Our little life is rounded with a sleep" and language is what enables us to orient ourselves within it, while at the same time—even if indirectly—ensuring a sober perspective.

Even though the totalitarian political structures that enforced censorship across Europe during so much of the twentieth century are no longer in place, do you think censorship remains? If so, in what forms (both external and internal)?

I have already said that there exists an unspoken "social contract" which leads to national and similar censorship. On the other hand, there is also the excessive "political correctness" (though actually many of its requirements are simply based on common sense and tact).

It is worth mentioning another point here. In literature the censorship of sexual matters has practically vanished. Consequently a new danger arises, that of boredom. When sexual acts are described in broad daylight, I lose interest because, like the great majority, I am rather knowledgeable in that area anyway. Without a doubt the sexual sphere plays a very important role in life, yet intercourse as such is—well, a bit monotonous. Of interest is only the complicated system of symbols and even euphemisms by which humanity has cloaked that sphere (this was well known by Shakespeare and Rabelais amongst others). In the past I, like many, rejoiced at the authors who tried to defeat external and internal sexual censorship. Now it makes me rejoice less. However, I certainly do not support such attempts at legal sexual censorship by which the Lithuanian parliament has recently been made "famous."

In "Žaidimas su cenzoriumi" [Playing with the Censor] *you suggest that "playing" with censorship in the eastern European context was a kind of mode of psychoanalysis or psychoanalytically significant behavior—it offered people a kind of self-importance or self-fulfillment that they could not otherwise have achieved. Does this mechanism still exist today, if perhaps in a different form?*

In a way it still exists. Aesopian, insinuating language is nowadays most frequently used for smearing an opponent (he will not be able to sue you but *sapienti sat*). With that in mind I would say it is rather better to engage in "censorship games" reminiscent of the past, though they scarcely impressed me either.

In the article "Apie rašymo meną Tarybų Sąjungoje" [On the Art of Writing in the Soviet Union] *you state that Solzhenitsyn inspired you to write, and that he taught a whole generation about respect for human dignity and freedom; yet you also criticized him for what can only be described as a "distorted perspective" that marked his later writings. (E.g.: You wrote that "until now Solzhenitsyn cruelly berated only the individuals who fully deserved it; but now even more poisonous tirades can be heard against liberal editors, human rights defenders, intellectual democrats.") In other words, it seems that later in his life Solzhenitsyn lost sight of the true enemies and grew embittered. It seems that such a fate might be logical for one who suffered many cruelties in his lifetime, like Solzhenitsyn did, and who spent much (if not all) of his life fighting injustice. This fate of embitterment seems to relate to the Nietzschean metaphor of staring into the abyss while the abyss stares back. Is this the potential fate of every devoted life-long writer, poet, or critic committed to combating injustice and advocating for humans rights and freedom? How does one avoid such a destiny?*

The case of Solzhenitsyn is very sad because from a herald of freedom he turned into an almost black-hundredist[2]—and, consequently, lost influence almost everywhere except in the ranks of extreme conservatives (of which, thankfully, there were few). I do not think that is what threatens to become of every freedom fighter—although that was, also in Lithuania, the fate of many. The best medicine here is rationalism, irony and self-critique, even a sense of humor. The dissidents who exhibited these qualities in times of communism usually did not turn into extremists or fanatics.

The writings of Albert Camus have clearly had a great influence on you. In the late sixties you claimed that the role of art was to oppose entropy—in the nineties, you updated this with the claim that a great need exists for "stoic, consistent and un-hysterical opposition to 'the plague'." What is the significance—in general, and for your work in particular—of Camus' politically and socially engaged literature and critical writings? Are Camus' writings still relevant today?

For me Camus is just as important as before. He teaches that evil does not wither, it only changes shape (for example, from communism it turns into nazism or para-nazism, and vice versa). We must always be prepared to adequately meet its rebirth in our closest surroundings. And this has to be our natural impulse and not just a dogma which in itself becomes an evil. Commiseration and support for humanity are called for, not utopic attempts to "uproot evil in its entirety." If we adopt this approach of Camus, defeat is probably inevitable—but not irredeemable. In the case of Solzhenitsyn, it is both inevitable and irredeemable.

Here is it worth returning to Shakespeare. I believe his dramas, portraying the infinite diversity of man and his inexhaustible potential in the spheres of evil and of good, speak the same as does Camus, only more strongly—and, by the way, four hundred years afore.

Notes

1. Venclova here alludes to Romeo's phrase from Act 1, scene 1, *Romeo and Juliet*: "Here's much to do with hate, but more with love. / Why, then, O brawling love! O loving hate! / O any thing, of nothing first create! / O heavy lightness! serious vanity! / Mis-shapen chaos of well-seeming forms! / Feather of lead, bright smoke, cold fire, / sick health! / Still-waking sleep, that is not what it is! / This love feel I, that feel no love in this."
2. The Black Hundreds was an early twentieth-century Russian counter-revolutionary movement infamous for its xenophobia and anti-Semitism.

CONTRIBUTORS

RŪTA BAGDANAVIČIŪTĖ is a doctoral student in Philosophy at Vytautas Magnus University, Kaunas, Lithuania. She has copyedited numerous scholarly books and journals on business ethics, literature and philosophy. The topic of her dissertation is: "The Problem of Interpretative Truth in Hermeneutics."

ERVIN BECK, of Goshen, Indiana, is Emeritus Professor of English at Goshen College, where he taught British literature, Shakespeare, postcolonial literature and folklore. He earned a PhD in English Literature from Indiana University in 1973. He has been a visiting professor at the University of Sheffield and the University of Warwick in England and Fulbright Professor of English at University College, Belize. In 2006–2007 and in 2008 he taught at LCC International University, Klaipeda, Lithuania.

Dr. TOMAS BERKMANAS is Associate Professor of Legal Philosophy at Vytautas Magnus University (VMU), Lithuania. He received his B.A. degree in philosophy and M.A. in Law at VMU, and in 2005 he defended his doctoral dissertation, "The Legality of Court Decision and the Limits of Language (a Postmodern Approach)", at VMU. His areas of teaching and research include: legal philosophy, political philosophy, philosophy of language, postmodern and contemporary philosophy, and problems of legal interpretation. Berkmanas has served as the Senior Editor-in-Chief of the *Baltic Journal of Law & Politics* since 2008.

D.L. (DAVID) COOMBES is Professor Emeritus of European Studies of the University of Limerick, Ireland, where he lived and worked from 1982 until 2001. He had previously taught at several universities in the UK, and has continued to undertake shorter teaching and research engagements on the mainland of Europe and elsewhere. He has published widely on subjects ranging from public administration and policy to European integration and peace studies. In 2001 Professor Coombes embarked on a period of international service, first with the United Nations Development Programme (in the Kyrgyz Republic and later in former Yugoslavia), and then as a consultant successively with the World Bank and the European Commission. He now lives in retirement in the Languedoc region of France. Professor Coombes is a native of the ancient Celtic province of Cornwall (Kernow), where he was born in 1940 and attended his local state schools, until going to Brasenose College, Oxford where he studied Philosophy, Politics and Economics, graduating with M.A. (1962) and M. Litt. (1964).

LEONIDAS DONSKIS, Ph. D., is a Member of the European Parliament. As an academic writer and editor, he has written and edited twenty seven books, twelve of them in English. An interdisciplinary scholar, he combines political theory, history of ideas, philosophy of culture, and essayistic style. Among other books, he is the author of *Modernity in Crisis: A Dialogue on the Culture of Belonging* (2011), *Troubled Identity and the Modern World* (2009)*, Power and Imagination: Studies in Politics and Literature* (2008), and *Forms of Hatred: Troubled Imagination in Modern Philosophy and Literature* (2003). He lectured and researched in the United States, Great Britain, and Europe. He also acts as a Visiting Professor of Social and Political Theory at Vytautas Magnus University in Kaunas, Lithuania. Donskis holds an Honorary Degree of Doctor of Letters from the University of Bradford, Great Britain.

TOMAS KAVALIAUSKAS is a lecturer in the Department of Social and Political Theory at Vytautas Magnus University, Kaunas, Lithuania. His reasearch interests are: post-communist transitional Europe, business ethics, and literature. For the last ten years he has been an active essay writer for Lithuanian cultural journal *Kultūros barai* [*The Domains of Culture*], which is a member of the European intellectual website *Eurozine*. He is a member of the Lithuanian PEN club and European SPES—Spirituality in Economics and Society.

J. D. MININGER, Ph. D., is Associate Professor of Social and Political Theory at Vytautas Magnus University, Kaunas, Lithuania. He works at the intersections of social and political philosophy, literature, aesthetic theory, and psychoanalysis. He has published inter alia on Immanuel Kant, Søren Kierkegaard, Theodor Adorno, Walter Benjamin, Marcel Proust, Paul Celan, William Shakespeare, Paul de Man, and Jacques Lacan, and has collaborated with Jason Peck on numerous projects, including the forthcoming *Keywords in German Aesthetics: from Baumgarten to Adorno* (Harvard University Press). He is co-editor with Leonidas Donskis of the book subseries *Philosophy, Literature, and Politics*, within the framework of the Value Inquiry Book Series (VIBS), Editions Rodopi, B.V. (Amsterdam and New York).

JUSTAS PATKAUSKAS received his MA in 2011 in Social and Political Critical Studies at Vytautas Magnus University, Kaunas, Lithuania.

JASON MICHAEL PECK is Visiting Assistant Professor in the Department of Modern Languages and Cultures at the University of Rochester in Rochester, New York, U.S.A. His current areas of research are the history of aesthetics, philosophy, poetics and Jewish Studies. He has published on such figures as the philosopher Immanuel Kant and the poet Paul Celan, and he maintains an ongoing collaborative project with J. D. Mininger on the relationship between ethics and poetics.

BARTHOLOMEW RYAN received his PhD in Philosophy from Århus University, Denmark in 2006, with a dissertation on Kierkegaard's resonance in the work of Georg Lukács, Carl Schmitt, Theodor Adorno and Walter Benjamin. He holds an MA in European Philosophy at University College Dublin, where he was awarded the Professor Magennis Prize for first place in the year. His BA is in Philosophy and Political Science from Trinity College Dublin. A Visiting Lecturer at European College of the Liberal Arts (ECLA) since 2007, he has also taught philosophy at the Universities of Oxford, Aarhus, and University College Dublin. In 2005 and 2007, he worked at the Kierkegaard Research Centre in Copenhagen. His research and teaching interests include the tension between faith and nihilism in philosophy and theology, European modernist literature, and critical theory.

CORY STOCKWELL, Ph. D., is a Teaching Fellow in the Foundation Year Programme at the University of King's College, Halifax, Canada. His current book manuscript is a comparative investigation into the nexus of secrecy, violence and community. He has published on topics such as voice and attunement in Kant, and death and secrecy in Sade and Philippe Sollers, and has translated three essays by Jean-Luc Nancy.

TOMAS VENCLOVA, Ph. D., is an eminent Lithuanian poet, translator, and literary scholar. A former Soviet dissident, he acts now as Professor of Slavic Literatures at Yale University, U.S.A.

VIBS

The **Value Inquiry Book Series** is co-sponsored by:

219.   Mary K. Bloodsworth-Lugo and Carmen R. Lugo-Lugo, *Containing (Un)American Bodies: Race, Sexuality, and Post-9/11 Constructions of Citizenship*. A volume in **Philosophy of Peace**

220.   Roland Faber, Brian G. Henning, Clinton Combs, Editors, *Beyond Metaphysics? Explorations in Alfred North Whitehead's Late Thought*. A volume in **Contemporary Whitehead Studies**

221.   John G. McGraw, *Intimacy and Isolation (Intimacy and Aloneness: A Multi-Volume Study in Philosophical Psychology, Volume One)*, A volume in **Philosophy and Psychology**

222.   Janice L. Schultz-Aldrich, Introduction and Edition, *"Truth" is a Divine Name, Hitherto Unpublished Papers of Edward A. Synan, 1918-1997*. A volume in **Gilson Studies**

223.   Larry A. Hickman, Matthew Caleb Flamm, Krzysztof Piotr Skowroński and Jennifer A. Rea, Editors, *The Continuing Relevance of John Dewey: Reflections on Aesthetics, Morality, Science, and Society*. A volume in **Central European Value Studies**

224.   Hugh P. McDonald, *Creative Actualization: A Meliorist Theory of Values*. A volume in **Studies in Pragmatism and Values**

225.   Rob Gildert and Dennis Rothermel, Editors, *Remembrance and Reconciliation*. A volume in **Philosophy of Peace**

226.   Leonidas Donskis, Editor, *Niccolò Machiavelli: History, Power, and Virtue*. A volume in **Philosophy, Literature, and Politics**

227.   Sanya Osha, *Postethnophilosophy*. A volume in **Social Philosophy**

228.   Rosa M. Calcaterra, Editor, *New Perspectives on Pragmatism and Analytic Philosophy*. A volume in **Studies in Pragmatism and Values**

229.   Danielle Poe, Editor, *Communities of Peace: Confronting Injustice and Creating Justice*. A volume in **Philosophy of Peace**

230.   Thorsten Botz-Bornstein, Editor, *The Philosophy of Viagra: Bioethical Responses to the Viagrification of the Modern World*. A volume in **Philosophy of Sex and Love**

231.   Carolyn Swanson, *Reburial of Nonexistents: Reconsidering the Meinong-Russell Debate.* A volume in **Central European Value Studies**

232.   Adrianne Leigh McEvoy, Editor, *Sex, Love, and Friendship: Studies of the Society for the Philosophy of Sex and Love: 1993–2003.* A volume in **Histories and Addresses of Philosophical Societies**

233.   Amihud Gilead, *The Privacy of the Psychical.* A volume in **Philosophy and Psychology**

234.   Paul Kriese and Randall E. Osborne, Editors, *Social Justice, Poverty and Race: Normative and Empirical Points of View.* A volume in **Studies in Jurisprudence**

235.   Hakam H. Al-Shawi, *Reconstructing Subjects: A Philosophical Critique of Psychotherapy.* A volume in **Philosophy and Psychology**

236.   Maurice Hauriou, *Tradition in Social Science.* Translation from French with an Introduction by Christopher Berry Gray. A volume in **Studies in Jurisprudence**

237.   Camila Loew, *The Memory of Pain: Women's Testimonies of the Holocaust..* A volume in **Holocaust and Genocide Studies**

238.   Stefano Franchi and Francesco Bianchini, Editors, *The Search for a Theory of Cognition: Early Mechanisms and New Ideas.* A volume in **Cognitive Science**

239.   Michael H. Mitias, *Friendship: A Central Moral Value.* A volume in **Ethical Theory and Practice**

240.   John Ryder and Radim Šíp, Editors, *Identity and Social Transformation, Central European Pragmatist Forum, Volume Five.* A volume in **Central European Value Studies**

241.   William Sweet and Hendrik Hart, *Responses to the Enlightenment: An Exchange on Foundations, Faith, and Community.* A volume in **Philosophy and Religion**

242.   Leonidas Donskis and J.D. Mininger, Editors, *Politics Otherwise: Shakespeare as Social and Political Critique.* A volume in **Philosophy, Literature, and Politics**